DEENA KATZ'S

TOOLS and TEMPLATES

FOR YOUR

PRACTICE

Also available for planners from
Bloomberg Professional Library

The Financial Planner's Guide to Moving Your Practice Online:
Creating Your Internet Presence and Growing Your Business
by Douglas H. Durrie

Deena Katz on Practice Management
for Financial Advisers, Planners, and Wealth Managers
by Deena B. Katz

Getting Started as a Financial Planner
by Jeffrey H. Rattiner

Best Practices for Financial Advisors
by Mary Rowland

Protecting Your Practice
by Katherine Vessenes in cooperation with the
International Association for Financial Planning

A complete list of our titles is available at
www.bloomberg.com/books

BLOOMBERG ®WEALTH MANAGER magazine is the premiere professional
information resource for independent financial planners
and investment advisers who are serving clients of high net worth.
See wealth.bloomberg.com or call 1-800-681-7727.

BLOOMBERG PROFESSIONAL LIBRARY

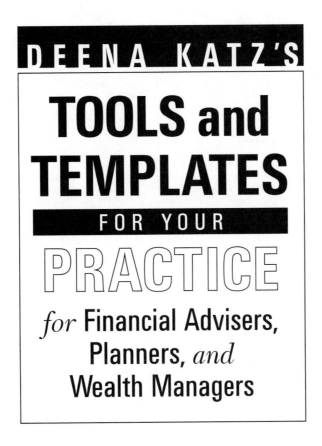

DEENA KATZ'S
TOOLS and TEMPLATES
FOR YOUR
PRACTICE
for Financial Advisers, Planners, and Wealth Managers

Deena B. Katz

BLOOMBERG PRESS

PRINCETON

Books are available for bulk purchases at special discounts. Special editions or book excerpts can also be created to specifications. For information, please write to: Special Markets Department, Bloomberg Press.

BLOOMBERG, BLOOMBERG NEWS, BLOOMBERG FINANCIAL MARKETS, OPEN BLOOMBERG, BLOOMBERG PERSONAL FINANCE, THE BLOOMBERG FORUM, COMPANY CONNECTION, COMPANY CONNEX, BLOOMBERG PRESS, BLOOMBERG PROFESSIONAL LIBRARY, BLOOMBERG PERSONAL BOOKSHELF, and BLOOMBERG SMALL BUSINESS are trademarks and service marks of Bloomberg L.P. All rights reserved.

This publication contains the author's opinions and is designed to provide accurate and authoritative information. It is sold with the understanding that the author, publisher, and Bloomberg L.P. are not engaged in rendering legal, accounting, investment-planning, or other professional advice. The reader should seek the services of a qualified professional for such advice; the author, publisher, and Bloomberg L.P. cannot be held responsible for any loss incurred as a result of specific investments or planning decisions made by the reader.

First edition published 2001
1 3 5 7 9 10 8 6 4 2

Library of Congress Cataloging-in-Publication Data

Katz, Deena B., 1950-
    Deena Katz's tools and templates for your practice : for financial advisers, planners, and wealth managers/
Deena B. Katz.
      p. cm. -- (Bloomberg professional library)
    Includes bibliographical references and index.
    ISBN 1-57660-084-X (alk. paper)
      1. Finance, Personal--Handbooks, manuals, etc. 2. Financial planners--Handbooks, manuals, etc.
3. Business enterprises--Finance--Handbooks, manuals, etc. I. Title: Tools and templates for your practice. II. Title. III. Series.

    HG179 .K376 2001
    332.6'1068'1--dc21
                                            2001025593

Edited by TRACY TAIT

Book Design by LAURIE LOHNE/DESIGN IT COMMUNICATIONS

For my Bashert, Harold

CONTENTS

SECTION 3 FIGURE 'EM OUT 116

SECTION 4 TAKE CARE OF 'EM 176

CONTENTS

ACKNOWLEDGMENTS

Writing books must be somewhat like having babies. Eventually you forget what pain they caused during birth. Which is why, I assume, that I agreed in a weak moment to write another one. Fortunately, many great advisers and other smart people I admire contributed their thoughts, ideas, and energies to making this book a useful professional tool. My profound thanks to:

The Alpha Group
— **Mark Balasa, CPA, CFP,** Balasa & Hoffman, Inc.; Schaumburg, Illinois
— **Eleanor Blayney, CFP,** Sullivan, Bruyette, Speros & Blayney, Inc.; McLean, Virginia
— **James L. Budros, CFP,** Budros & Ruhlin, Inc.; Columbus, Ohio
— **David H. Bugen, CFP,** Bugen Stuart Korn & Cordaro, Inc.; Chatham, New Jersey
— **Chris J. Dardaman Jr., CPA, CIMA, CFP,** Polstra & Dardaman LLC; Norcross, Georgia
— **Charles D. Haines, Jr., MBA, CFP,** Charles D. Haines Financial Advisors, Inc.; Birmingham, Alabama
— **Tucker Hewes,** Hewes Communications; New York, New York
— **Mark Hurley,** President and CEO, Undiscovered Managers LLC; Dallas, Texas
— **Ram Kolluri, CFP,** GlobalValue Investors, Inc.; Princeton, New Jersey
— **Ross Levin, CFP,** Accredited Investors, Inc.; Edina, Minnesota
— **Donald J. Philips,** Morningstar Inc.; Chicago, Illinois
— **Peggy M. Ruhlin, CPA/PFS, CFP,** Budros & Ruhlin, Inc.; Columbus, Ohio
— **Lou Stanasolovich, CFP,** Legend Financial Advisors, Inc.;

Pittsburgh, Pennsylvania
— **Gregory D. Sullivan, CPA/PFS, CFP,** Sullivan, Bruyette, Speros & Blayney, Inc.; McLean, Virginia
— **Mark C. Tibergien,** Moss Adams LLP; Seattle, Washington
— **John W. Ueleke, CFP,** Legacy Wealth Management; Memphis, Tennessee
— **Robert C. Winfield, CFP;** Memphis, Tennessee

Ben Baldwin, CLU, ChFC, CFP, Baldwin Financial Systems, Inc.; Northbrook, Illinois

Jack Blankinship, CFP, Blankinship & Foster; Del Mar, California

Norman Boone, CFP, Boone Financial Advisors, Inc.; San Francisco, California

John Carey, CFP, R.W. Rogé & Co, Inc.; Bohemia, New York

Damian F. Carroll, J.P. Morgan Fleming Asset Management; New York, New York

Larry Chambers; Author and Public Relations Adviser; Ojai, California

Lisbeth Whiley Chapman, Public Relations Counselor, Ink & Air; Wellfleet, Massachusetts

Tom Connelly, CFA, CFP, Keats, Connelly & Associates; Phoenix, Arizona

Christopher Cordaro, CFP, Bugen Stuart Korn & Cordaro, Inc.; Chatham, New Jersey

Roy Diliberto, CLU, ChFC, CFP, RTD Financial Advisors, Inc.; Philadelphia, Pennsylvania

David Drucker, CFP, Sunset Financial Management; Albuquerque, New Mexico

David Evensky, AXA Advisors, LLC; Miami, Florida

Fidelity Investments Institutional Brokerage Group; Boston Massachusetts
— Scott D'Alessandro, Senior Vice President
— Gary Gallagher, Senior Vice President Product Management
— Trevor Norton, Director, Business Development

Jack M. Firestone, CFP, Firestone Capital Management, Inc.; Miami, Florida

Barry Freedman, CFP, Freedman Financial Associates, Inc.; Peabody, Massachusetts

Cheryl Garrett, CFP, Garrett Financial Planning, Inc.; Overland Park, Kansas

Roger Gibson, CFP, CFA, Gibson Capital Management, Ltd.; Pittsburgh, Pennsylvania

Robert J. Glovsky, JD, LLM, CFP, Mintz Levin Financial Advisors, LLC; Boston, Massachusetts

Andrew Gluck, President, AdvisorSites; Syosset, New York

Gary Greenbaum, CPA, CFP, Greenbaum and Orecchio, Inc.; Oradell, New Jersey

Lynn Hopewell, CFP, The Monitor Group, Inc.; Fairfax, Virginia

Patricia P. Houlihan, CFP, Houlihan Financial Resource Group, Inc.; Oakton, Virginia

Kirk Hulett, Securities America, Inc.; Omaha, Nebraska

Joel Isaacson, CPA, CFP, Isaacson & Company, Inc.; New York, New York

Craig Junkins, AXA Advisors; New York, New York

William T. Knox, IV, CFP, Bugen Stuart Korn & Cordaro, Inc.; Chatham, New Jersey

Tim Kochis, CFP, Kochis Fitz Tracy Fitzhugh & Scott; San Francisco, California

Linda Lubitz, CFP, The Lubitz Financial Group; Miami, Florida

William Mattox, CPPC, Financial-Coaching; Cheshire, Oregon

Metropolitan Life Insurance Company; New York, New York

Jerry Neill, CFP, BKD Investment Advisors; Kansas City, Missouri

David S. Norton, CFP, Norton Partners; Bristol, United Kingdom

Tom Orecchio, CFP, Greenbaum & Orecchio; Oradell, New Jersey

David Polstra, CFP, Polstra & Dardaman LLC; Norcross, Georgia

Mark Ralphs, The Financial Planning Corporation; Southport, United Kingdom

Lawrence Rybka, CLU, ChFC, ValMark Securities, Inc.; Beachwood, Ohio

Charles Schwab Institutional; San Francisco, California

Spraker, Fitzgerald & Tamayo, LLC; Maitland, Florida
— Charlie Fitzgerald
— Susan Spraker, CFP
— Ron Tamayo, CFP
Ben Tobias, CPA, CFP, Tobias Financial Advisors; Plantation, Florida
Lew Wallensky, CFP, Lewis Wallensky Associates; Los Angeles, California
Dick Zalack, Founder and CEO, Focus Four, LTD; Brunswick, Ohio.
Evensky, Brown & Katz Super Team
— Mena Bielow
— Johaira Castillo
— Michelle Grillone
— Lane Jones, CFP
— Deana Kelly, CFP
— Matt McGrath, CFP
— Veronica Vilchez
— Scott Wells, CFP

Thanks to Peter Brown who offered invaluable advice on the manuscript, to Randi K. Grant for encouraging me when I needed it, and to my partner, Harold Evensky, who assisted in every way possible and lived through my mercurial personality while I completed the book.

I particularly want to thank Bob Curtis and Karla Curtis at PIE Technologies in Richmond, Virginia, who created the Monte Carlo Card Game for us, and who have worked with us over the past years to build useful tools for Evensky, Brown & Katz.

My deepest gratitude to Jennifer Arbeene who provided her ever-dependable and invaluable assistance, and to Tammi Wells who runs my business life so I can have time for writing and other good stuff.

Of course, I express my great thanks to my super editors, Tracy Tait and Jared Kieling and all the good folks at Bloomberg who make this process a pleasure.

INTRODUCTION

What is this world dot-com-ing to?

My first laptop computer weighed seventeen pounds and was referred to as a "portable." To break it in, I decided to carry it with me on a business trip to Lubbock, Texas. What a disaster! It nearly broke the airplane tray, was too bulky to use on my lap, and was such a battery-hog that after twenty minutes it died. Yet, I could console myself that I was on the cutting edge of technology. More important, the computer industry knew laptops were the future and continually strove to produce more advanced and sophisticated models.

Today when you purchase a new laptop, it's still on the verge of obsolescence. The sad truth is that mere weeks after your purchase, a smaller, cheaper, more compact, faster, double-the-storage-and-memory model appears on the shelves and you live with sheer frustration until you can pretend to justify buying a new one.

The evolution of the financial advisory business is beginning to look a bit like the development of the laptop. The original concept seems timeless, but recently it has become necessary for us to regularly improve and reinvent ourselves just to stay ahead of the competition and, frankly, just to remain in business. We need to be cost efficient, streamlined, convenient, and user-friendly. Step back with me for a minute to review what has been happening so quickly over the past few years.

The Blurring of Professions

IT USED TO BE THAT FINANCIAL PROFESSIONALS had clearly defined roles with their clients. A CPA provided tax advice and prepared tax returns,

1

an attorney provided legal advice and prepared legal documents, a broker traded securities, and an insurance agent sold policies. Over the past few years, the landscape has changed dramatically. CPAs discovered that they have really been financial planners all along and began getting their securities and insurance licenses. Brokers have been forced to accept minimal transaction fees and told they will charge fees for advice. At this writing, twenty-five state bar associations are lobbying for permission to operate multidisciplinary practices so that tax, financial-planning, and investment advice can be included in their members' law practices. Domestic securities and insurance companies that historically have registered representatives and captured agents now offer "independent" affiliations to qualified advisers. Banks are purchasing financial planning offices, selling insurance and mutual funds, and trading stocks. Discount brokers, mutual fund companies, and even independent research companies are offering advice, trading, analysis, and support—both live and on the Web. International financial firms have purchased insurance and securities companies, and their advisers are being retrained to become financial planners.

All this blurring and overlapping must be confusing to the consumer. I believe your client hasn't a clue about what to expect from his professional advisers anymore, and frankly, I'm not too sure we know what to expect from ourselves. Additionally, this abundance of professional competition will undoubtedly affect your fees and services. No matter what your professional affiliation, you'll be compelled to deliver far more services for far less cost.[1]

The Internet's Role

IN THE NOT TOO DISTANT PAST, our edge as advisers was access to information, research, and analysis. With the advent of the Internet, information and research are easily available. Our client can sign up for any stock, mutual fund, or bond site and receive instantaneous information. Analysis and advice are overwhelmingly available, as well. For example, Financial Engines (www.financialengines.com) calculates risk, designs an appropriate asset allocation, and makes recommendations for funds for 401(k) investors. MyCFO (www.mycfo.com) works with high-net-worth individuals, giving financial planning, investment, and estate planning support, using high-touch/high-tech solutions.

Our client also used to need us to provide the products and services he required. Today he can do his own analysis, then purchase competitively priced investment vehicles and insurance products through the Internet on his own time. Much of the value-added that justified our fees and commissions in the past has become a commodity. This does not mean that the Internet is replacing us. The VIP Forum reports that the majority of the value-added services that the financial adviser formerly delivered can and will be replaced by Internet providers;[2] however, knowledge, judgment, client intimacy, and emotional insight are values that remain.

I have always maintained that information is not knowledge or judgment—which is where we come in. Remember the movie *Ghost*, with Demi Moore? There is a scene in which she is sitting at a potter's wheel, throwing clay. While the wheel is turning, a lot of clay splatters onto her shirt. With the bulk of the clay remaining on the wheel, she (with some help from Patrick Swayze) forms a vase. That's how I think of the Internet. A volume of garbage spins off the Web every day; our job is to get our arms around the best of what's there and form it into something that we and our client can use. And just like working with clay, if the basic material isn't quality from the beginning, subsequent modifications are worthless.

I'm told that during the days of space exploration in the 1960s, U.S. scientists approached several pen companies, explaining that astronauts were unable to write in space because of the lack of gravity. The pen companies immediately began to work on the problem. After millions of dollars, Fisher produced the first space pen in 1965, gifting it to NASA, explaining that American astronauts could even use it in zero gravity while hanging upside down. Years later, a reporter asked the Russian scientists if they had invented a space pen for their cosmonauts. "Why?" they replied. "They had a pencil."

If you were just starting business today, felt little competition, and had loads of money, you'd probably have the luxury of taking your time thinking out every aspect of every system and problem within your practice. You might even be able to generate some creative spin-off, like a space pen. Unfortunately, I don't know anyone who has that kind of time or money. I do know some successful planners, including those in our own shop, who can give you a jump-start with practice tools that work. Don't underestimate the value of the "pencil." Read on.

Why This Book?

DURING THE PAST FEW YEARS, I have had the opportunity to meet with financial advisers from all over the world. Many expressed frustration at the growing necessity of building more systems into their practices in order to keep them efficient and competent. Many started out as sole practitioners, only to find themselves years later hiring support staff, other professionals, and taking on new partners or strategic alliances. Most wish for a quick fix for their problems, an integrated, technology-driven system that will allow them to do what they do best—support the client. Although much better software is being written every day, there is no total system that facilitates all our daily activities and keeps us in business. And, keep in mind, we may yearn for a space pen, but a good sharp pencil still gets the job done.

In talking with my planner friends, I realized that collectively we have a wealth of systems and programs we've invented out of necessity—resources that if shared might make our business lives easier while we're waiting to reach Utopia. So, what you'll find here is a collection of ideas, forms, and systems you can put to use today. I've also included a CD-ROM with user-ready Word, Excel, and PowerPoint files ready and waiting for your customization. You can thank the many planners listed at the beginning of this book for sharing their intellectual property so freely.

What Is This Book?

IT'S A WORK TOOL IN BOOK FORMAT (with a CD-ROM attached), full of charts, form letters, concise tips, and ideas from experienced practitioners from around the world. They are loosely grouped together under general themes for one purpose—to help you become a more successful practitioner.

Who Is This Book for?

IF YOU ARE ONE OF THE PROFESSIONALS I described a few paragraphs ago— accountant, insurance adviser, attorney, broker, banker, or anyone delivering financial advice to clients—then this book is for you. If you're a sole practitioner, work with a partner, or even have the luxury of a big corporate back office, you'll find something in here that will make life easier and more streamlined. In particular, if you are migrating from a practice to a business, you'll benefit from the forms and systems found here.

My husband told me that when he was a child, his mother kept Dr. Tichenor's All-Purpose Antiseptic Elixir at hand. If he had a cut or a scrape, she poured it on the wound. If he had an upset stomach, she gave him a spoonful to drink. She made him brush his teeth with it, used it as a mosquito repellent, and frequently gave him some, "just for good measure."[3]

In thinking about it, I guess you can consider this book a kind of Dr. Katz's All-Purpose Elixir.[4] There's gotta be something in here that will fix what ails you (or your business).

How Do You Use This Book?

USING AN EVENT-DRIVEN MODEL, I have divided this workbook into five sections. Section One provides components for a public relations and marketing plan, with form letters and a do-it-yourself system for gaining credibility with the media. I've also included guidelines for brochures and marketing pieces. Section Two offers ideas and forms for the initial client approach, with methods for qualifying the client, structuring the first interview, and gathering data. Section Three provides useful PowerPoint tools for educating the client, as well as introducing you to a game program you can play with clients to easily explain risk and return relationships. You will also find formats for new client communications, plans, and policies. Section Four deals with the handling of "established clients;" its subjects include reviews, client diaries, and rebalancing accounts. Section Five is divided into two parts. Chapter 10 is dedicated to client and business-related documents to manage the client process, and facilitate organized practice routines, staff maintenance, and compliance. Chapter 11 is a collection of neat things I like that don't fit anywhere else.

I am particularly pleased that Bloomberg has decided to include the CD-ROM with this book. In addition, you can log on to our Web site (www.evensky.com) to access continually updated materials and ideas, as well as links to some nifty Web sites, like www.morningstar advisor.com, www.pietech.com, www.Pro2Net.com, and www.Finance ware.com, where you can get more material that you can use immediately.

Well, that's the obligatory introduction of this book. So, what are you waiting for? Turn the page.

GET 'EM IN THE DOOR

NO MATTER HOW LONG YOU'VE been in business, if your practice is growing to include services that you have not provided before, or if you are just refining your practice, there is no better way to reposition yourself than to use the media and public relations to gain credibility.

Of course you'll want to think it through before you start. Many years ago a planner friend contacted one of his local papers, offering to serve as a local resource expert in financial affairs for the paper. My friend sent in his résumé, which happened to include a statement that he was listed in *Who's Who in American Finance*. The paper responded by printing an article blasting my friend for sending such a presumptuous letter and attacking the credibility of listings in *Who's Who*.

I chose to focus on public relations, marketing, and seminars at the beginning of this book, because if you can't get clients in the door, you don't need the remaining chapters. I believe this is the one area where all of us can use some help. Chapter 2 is a juxtaposition of "old" marketing techniques versus "new" techniques for the Internet. This section wouldn't be complete without a discussion of brochures and other marketing material in Chapter 3.

CHAPTER 1

MARKETING, PUBLIC RELATIONS, AND COURTING THE MEDIA

The fact is, we own the ink; we own the paper.

— BOB CLARK,

then editor of *Dow Jones Investment Advisor* magazine

When Mark Hurley, president of Undiscovered Managers, produced his white paper, *The Future of the Investment Advisory Business*[1] in 1999, it was met with mixed reviews. If you have not read it, do it now (www.undiscoveredmanagers.com). I'll wait.

As the last two years have unfolded, many of the things that Mark predicted have come true. Mark's premise is that the industry is changing rapidly. With consolidation and new entrants, competition will be the theme of the future. The biggest change will be that advisory firms will no longer get clients for free.

Until now, we have not had to spend money for clients; they fell in the door. Roy Diliberto of RTD Financial Advisors, Inc. in Philadelphia once described his marketing plan to me as "watching the phone ring." In recent months he complains that he is doing more watching than answering. Many advisers I've spoken with have commented that their conventional referral sources, (e.g., CPAs) are now their competition. To meet this increased competition, many advisers are hiring marketers and developing marketing teams to beat the bushes and get potential clients in the door.

Historically we've been entrepreneurs, quite comfortable wearing fifteen different hats, including marketer, planner, bean counter, analyst, and trash collector. However, in my experience, very few people are really good at everything. We usually fall into one of two camps: rainmakers or "brainmakers." You will need to decide which role is best for you and your practice. Are you better at obtaining and handling relationships or managing the practice? However you see yourself in your practice, in the future with the new competitive environment, you must have a marketing plan. You will also need to have a designated marketing person as well. That person might be you. If so, you'll need to delegate some of your other activities to someone else. See Chapter 10 for some help on this concept. Even if you have no desire to increase your practice, you'll probably need to consider a designated marketer just to stay in business.

The Marketing Plan

THERE ARE THOUSANDS OF MARKETING resources available to you, including books, Web sites, and professional consultants. I won't pretend to compete with any of these. I am not a marketing expert. Most planners I know aren't, either. And most of us do not have the time to research everything about marketing, or the resources to hire marketing consultants. If you too are on your own, here are a few tips to consider in developing your marketing plan. Even if you do ultimately hire an expert, developing a basic marketing plan ahead of time will provide a handle for these issues and make the process easier and more cost efficient. The following discussion covers the basic issues.

❶ **Know your target market.** Interview your staff and current clients to better define the market you are interested in. For example, when we wanted to expand our services to doctors we had targeted, we interviewed our current doctor clients to find out what issues were important to them and how we could get better visibility among physicians. From those chats we determined that it is important to differentiate

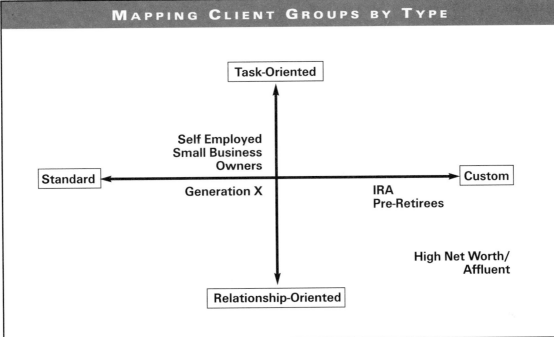

MAPPING CLIENT GROUPS BY TYPE

our marketing according to the medical specialty and practice size. Fidelity Investments Institutional Brokerage Group has allowed me to share their "Customer Profile" (see FORM 1-01 on page 30) to help you target a desirable market. It's a great format because it allows you immediately to see any client patterns. The idea is to look at your existing client base for a pattern of client types.

J. P. Morgan Fleming Asset Management has a similar approach. First, divide your client base depending on whether they are task or relationship oriented. Next, divide them according to how standardized or customized your relationship needs to be. You can plot these following the axes shown in the illustration above. You then can get a sense of whom you want to target as clients and how.

❷ **Determine your resources.** Marketing in any form takes human and financial capital. Be realistic in budgeting for a dedicated marketer; good ones don't come cheap and they will need staff support. If you elect to serve as your firm's marketing guru, remember that you will limit your ability to function elsewhere (and probably in a more valuable capacity) in your business. I've learned from the experience of successful global financial services firms that good marketers don't cost money; they make money.

❸ **Target your resources to specific activities/goals.** It's not enough to say that you have $30,000 for marketing this year. You'll need to know how you will match that money to a specific seminar, mailing, or other marketing activity. Also, just as we benchmark our managers' performance, benchmark (by careful recording of the source and quality of new business) your marketing results in order to avoid ongoing funding of nonproductive campaigns.

❹ **Get free or low-cost help.** Many practitioners have confirmed the same experience we've had. Local college or university marketing students can provide valuable and cost-efficient help in developing and implementing a marketing program. Prepare a preliminary plan, describing in some detail the target market you wish to reach. Contact the dean of the business school or chair of the marketing department to discuss the possibility of student interns and/or a class project directed toward your goal.

❺ **Look to your service providers for assistance.** The best resources for helping you design a marketing plan are likely underutilized. There is fierce competition among product and service providers for relationships with successful practitioners. The better companies have learned that they can best get your attention by helping you be successful. Take advantage of their willingness to help. For example, Fidelity's Institutional Brokerage Group (IBG) has an excellent comprehensive program accessible via the Web called "PracticeMark" that will help you develop your own marketing plan. They even have professionally designed and instantly customizable materials (such as brochures and seminar kits) to help implement your plan. If you want a look at PracticeMark, contact IBG at 800-854-4772.

❻ **Use joint marketing efforts to leverage effectiveness.** Search for opportunities to partner with others (both other planners and related professionals) in your area to reduce costs and gain higher visibility. For example, you and several advisers can get together to sponsor a special event to introduce your expertise to the public.

Successful examples include:

Women's Expo. A program with speakers, products, and services (including health and nutrition specialists) specifically for women.

Fiduciary Management. A program targeted at fiduciaries for trust and ERISA accounts. Participants include attorneys with an expertise in fiduciary law.

Financial Planning for Physicians in Independent Practice. This program includes experts in practice management, insurance, and Medicare reimbursements.

While a "joint" program means you have to share the exposure, developing a program with multiple professionals not only leverages your marketing budget, it helps position the program as a "public" event rather than simply your firm's marketing vehicle.

❼ **Include a robust public relations program in your marketing plan.** Most of the senior advisers I know have built excellent relationships with the media and have used those relationships to gain credibility and expand their businesses. Because this is so important, I am devoting a big chunk of this chapter to it.

❽ **Track your progress.** As I noted earlier, marketing is only worthwhile if it works. It's important to know what works for you and what doesn't. Monitor and benchmark, ask new clients how they heard about you, and keep the results in a database.

Put Your Plan to the S.W.O.T. Test

A GOOD MARKETING PLAN WILL MAXIMIZE strengths, compensate for weaknesses, take advantage of opportunities, and minimize threats. Take your plan through the S.W.O.T. (which stand for Strengths, Weaknesses, Opportunities, and Threats) Analysis and recognize where you might need to make changes (see illustration *S.W.O.T. Analysis* on the following page). Look at your plan from six different perspectives.

Here are examples of the issues you should address in your S.W.O.T. analysis:

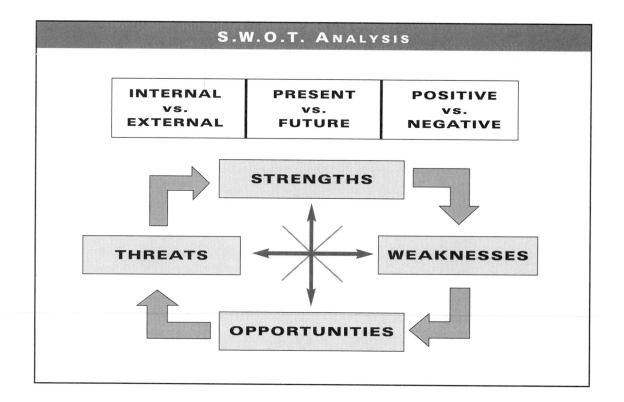

INTERNAL

➲ **Staff.** What is the number of staff, their education, experience, credentials, interests?

➲ **Technology.** What types of hardware and software do you have? Are you using these to their fullest capabilities?

➲ **Facilities.** List your location, size, layout, attributes (e.g., kitchen, conference space)

EXTERNAL

➲ **Vendors.** List vendor relationships, such as fund companies, financial services providers, technology providers

➲ **Professionals.** Do you have formal or informal relationships with accounting firms, law firms, trust companies, and banks?

➲ **Organizations.** What are your relationships with other professionals, regulatory agencies, nonprofits, or businesses?

➲ **Clients.** What are their skills and businesses? Are you making the most of your clients' knowledge and ideas? For example, one of my clients has her own advertising and public relations company in New York. We pass ideas by her creative brain every chance we get. Do you have or should you establish a client advisory panel?

PRESENT
➲ **Vendors.** What present relationships are working well?

➲ **Professionals.** What professional relationships (accountants, attorneys) are working well?

➲ **Organizations.** With what organizations do you retain memberships, such as FPA, AIMR, or Rotary?

➲ **Clients.** What clients can you rely upon as a resource? For example, we have six physician clients in established practices that we use as a focus group to create services for others like them.

FUTURE
➲ **Vendors.** How can you use these relationships into the future? For example, you might establish a relationship with an insurance vendor experienced in underwriting medical disability or extensive property/casualty coverage if you do not presently have such a relationship.

➲ **Professionals.** Should you formalize current relationships, by either outsourcing or bringing these professionals in-house? Should you add more specialized resources? For example, should you establish a relationship with a law firm specializing in representing physicians in medical malpractice cases? Another example, should you consider moving your accounting relationship to a CPA firm with a well-established physician practice (if you are targeting physicians) and add in-house expertise in medical practice management?

➲ **Organizations.** Consider more active participation. You could become chair of the local FPA public relations committee, join the chamber of commerce and become a member of the new member committee and entertainment committee, join the Planned Giving Council of the local hospital, or sit on the board of a community foundation.

POSITIVE

➲ **Vendors.** What resources do your vendors provide in support of your practice? For example, our financial services vendor provides significant target marketing education support; our primary mutual fund company developed a database to assist us in evaluating our specific market opportunities.

➲ **Professionals.** What value do you receive from your professional relationships? An example, your new accounting firm and law practice affiliates may be interested in developing new business and willing to provide gratis support in return for possible referrals.

➲ **Organizations.** Are your current membership organizations providing support for your practice or insurance arm?

➲ **Clients.** Have any clients indicated a willingness to participate in an advisory role?

NEGATIVE

➲ **Vendors.** Are your vendors becoming your competition? Many financial services firms are beginning to provide direct client advice in areas across the country.

➲ **Professionals.** Are your current accounting and legal relationships establishing their own financial planning practices?

➲ **Organizations.** What competition do you have from organizations? For example, perhaps a local hospital Planned Giving Committee has an entrenched executive committee.

➲ **Clients.** What are the negatives in your current client base? For example, if you are targeting physicians, do you have a relatively low number of physician clients in independent practice? Is your client base so widely varied that it is impossible for you to see a target market or a market trend?

The process of the S.W.O.T. analysis will help you clarify many of the issues you need to address when developing your marketing plan. Consider sharing your ideas with key staff or partners for their perspectives.

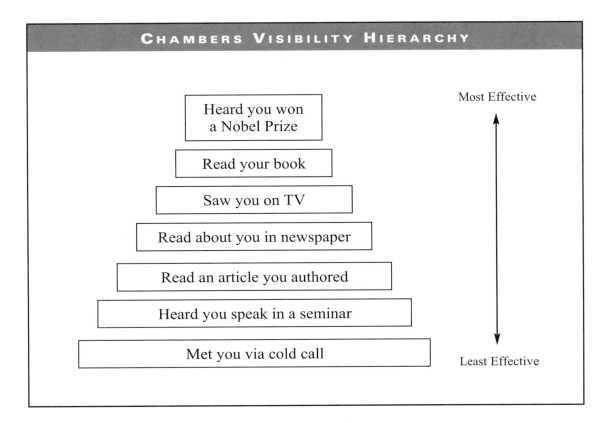

CHAMBERS VISIBILITY HIERARCHY

Heard you won a Nobel Prize

Read your book

Saw you on TV

Read about you in newspaper

Read an article you authored

Heard you speak in a seminar

Met you via cold call

Most Effective

Least Effective

Public Relations

VISIBILITY MEANS CREDIBILITY. Gaining visibility is an important challenge for any adviser. Larry Chambers, a writer focusing on media issues, points out that "celebrities earn a premium because they are better known than other members of their profession."[2] Visibility builds credibility, which brings clients. Larry's visibility hierarchy looks like the illustration above. You'll notice that four of the seven items listed in Chambers Visibility Hierarchy involve the media, and none of them is "I started noticing your paid ads after three or four repeat impressions."

Larry's hierarchy confirms just how important media exposure is for us in developing our business. Unfortunately, all too often media are equated with advertising. Few practitioners have the resources to compete with the financial gorillas in advertising. The good news is that we don't have to.

Courting the Media

NO MATTER THE LEVEL TO WHICH YOU FEEL you need to take your visibility, you are going to want some media exposure. The more formalized you make your approach to the media, the better success you'll have. First, recognize that there are different kinds of media to target. Aside from the obvious printed media, there are broadcast and Internet media as well.

In my book *Deena Katz on Practice Management* (Bloomberg Press, 1999) I described how my partner Harold approached print media by writing letters to reporters, commenting on their articles. He did this consistently until one day they started calling him for comments on their developing stories. He then worked hard to become a valuable resource for the reporter. If he didn't have the answer, he'd find someone who did. This worked for us, but there are certainly plenty of other ways that you can catch the eye of the media.

Lou Stanasolovich of Legend Financial Advisors, Inc. in Pittsburgh compiled a list of reporters in publications that he'd like to reach, then sent each of them a letter similar to the one below:

> This letter is to introduce you to our firm, Legend Financial Advisors, Inc. Attached is a fact sheet about the firm and our services as well as biographies of our financial advisors.
>
> Also attached are several "Briefs" (story ideas) on current financial planning and investment market issues. We make Briefs available on a monthly basis with hope that you will find them valuable in identifying emerging issues. Each Brief lists how to contact us directly by phone if you require more information, want to follow up one of the topics, or want to discuss any other topic that you may be interested in for a story.

Lou reports that he gets several calls a month from reporters following up on an interesting idea he's sent their way. You can get ideas for stories by jotting down issues that your clients have asked you to address over the past few days or weeks. Look for trends in their queries, as well as items that you thought were different or challenging to tackle. Lou cautions that this approach takes work. Each month you need to come up with some substantive ideas to send.

Tucker Hewes of Hewes Communications in New York City agrees that sending story ideas to the media is a good way to stimulate interest. Tucker cautions, though, that cultivating media relationships is not for everyone. "Most advisers don't know why they are doing it. Ask yourself, what are you going to get—higher visibility, credibility, and article reprints to send your clients? Is this what you are aiming for? Are you really going to get new clients from this effort?" Tucker also believes that planners seldom stay with their public relations plan. "They sit down one weekend, write a few press releases, then next month they get busy and forget all about it." Tucker's tips:

➲ **If it's news**, such as hiring a new somebody, issue a press release.

➲ **If it's an idea or a comment,** one-on-one contact is the best.

➲ **Forget the *Wall Street Journal*.** Make a list of a handful of newspaper writers in your hometown, contact them, get to know them and send them ideas. Reporters like to feel that they are getting exclusive information. They know that when a press release shows up, everybody has it. If you call or e-mail them with a good idea, they know you've singled them out.

➲ **Watch your expectations.** There are really very few planners who are quoted on a regular basis by the financial press.

➲ **Keep a current press list.** Reporters move around a lot so you need to periodically check the phone numbers, addresses, and e-mail addresses to keep them current.

➲ **Follow up, follow up, and follow up.** Like everything else, this plan takes constant attention.

➲ **Be sure you have the skills for this.** Just because you want to talk with the press doesn't mean they want to talk with you. Be brutally honest about your ability to communicate effectively. Don't try it if you don't enjoy it.

➲ **Have patience.** Courting the media is all about cultivating relationships, and this takes time.

Here are some other ideas for getting media attention:

⮱ **Regularly attend professional conferences and conventions.** Reporters and correspondents are there to get a perspective on these meetings, and they want new contacts.

⮱ **Speak at these professional gatherings.** The media tend to be interested in profiling a good speaker who has a good story.

Broadcast Media

MANY PUBLIC TELEVISION STATIONS around the country have cable programs. As a professional you have unique knowledge that can be a valuable commodity for their programming. It's your job to let them know you're available and how you might be a resource. In Miami the local PBS station provides community-access programming. Students are the camera and crew. A few years ago, through this program, I produced my own series, *Financial Fitness*, in conjunction with the local chapter of the IAFP (now the FPA). The IAFP members were talk show participants. We covered such topics as "You Can't Take It with You, But Who Gets It When You Go?" (estate planning issues) and "The Taxman Cometh" (end of the year tax planning). Explore what's available in your area.

Bob Glovsky of Mintz Levin Financial Advisors, LLC, appeared on his own radio program every week for eight years. Bob says that certain people like the anonymity of radio or TV to ask questions they might feel intimidated to ask an adviser face-to-face. A radio show, he says, also gives an opportunity to reach a wide range of people and to "feel them out" before they visit in a formal appointment.

The Internet

THERE'S A WHOLE NEW WORLD OF MEDIA that you can target on the Internet. In many ways this contact is easier—simply leave an e-mail with comments, ideas, and issues. Here are some favorites of planners I know.

Morningstar www.morningstaradvisor.com

Pro2Net www.pro2net.com

Horsesmouth www.horsesmouth.com

Bloomberg L.P. www.bloomberg.com

The Street.com www.thestreet.com

Money Watch www.moneywatchtv.com

SmartMoney www.smartmoney.com

Media Referral Programs

THE FOLLOWING ORGANIZATIONS have media referral programs. Essentially, you can sign up, declaring areas in which you consider yourself an expert. When they get specific media calls, they'll refer to you.

CFP Board www.cfp-board.org (800-433-4292)

AICPA www.aicpa.org (212-596-6111)

FPA www.fpanet.org (800-322-4237)

NAPFA www.napfa.org (800-FEE-ONLY/800-333-6659)

SFSP www.financialpro.org (610-526-2521)

Preparing for Media Calls

ONCE YOUR NAME HAS HIT A REPORTER'S computer screen, you'll need to start brushing up on events of the day that might be newsworthy.

➲ **Skim the financial press** each morning, making notes on interesting items.

➲ **Choose a financial Web site** that gives you up-to-the-minute news in a format you like. I use www.bloomberg.com, but there are plenty of others.

➲ **Visit the financial professional sites** listed above to see what professionals are talking about.

➲ **Keep a resource file** with interesting articles and information that you can get to quickly if your phone rings and a writer wants a comment.

➲ **Read what your prospective clients read,** not just the *Journal* and *Barron's*. Successful, media-savvy planners read the publications their clients read—*Money, SmartMoney, Kiplinger's Personal Finance,* and similar publications—cover to cover.

Preparing for Interviews

A FEW YEARS AGO SCHWAB INSTITUTIONAL gave a few of us advisers an opportunity to spend a day with their PR consultant, Edelman Public Relations. The workshop leaders for Edelman gave some interesting advice about interviews. "An interview is only an opportunity if it provides a platform to showcase your expertise and firm." This was a different perspective for me. I thought the object was to get your name in the paper. They were telling us that we should "grant" interviews only if it suits our purposes. The second bit of advice I found valuable was, "the point of the interview isn't to answer the reporter's questions. The point of an interview should be because you have something to communicate. Determine your objective, then balance everything you say against it." Frankly, this discussion helped many of us present ourselves as less "desperate" for media exposure. Some other gems from the Edelman pros:

➲ **Know who your audience is,** and direct your answers to them when you speak to reporters.

➲ **Focus on the message you have,** not on the messenger (reporter).

➲ **Anticipate the questions.** Few people handle impromptu questions effectively.

➲ **Keep it simple and to the point.** Sound bites are good.

There are plenty of public relations books out there, but two I believe are essential are Larry Chambers's *The Guide to Financial Public Relations—How to Stand Out in the Midst of Competitive Clutter* (St. Lucie Press, 1999), and Beth Chapman's *Get Media Smart!: Create News Coverage that Builds Business* (Ink & Air, 1997). Larry has shared some great material on gaining credibility to be found later in this chapter. You can get Larry's book at your local bookstore or through online booksellers on the Internet. Monthly retainer fees for Larry's public relations and media services average between $5,500 and $10,000 per month, plus expenses.

Beth's resource guide comes with a video, audiotape, and resource guide to walk you through your own self-directed media program. She details how you should include a PR plan in your marketing plan. You can get a copy of this or any of her many products by contacting her at

Ink & Air (I love that name!) (617-983-0393) or www.inkair.com. Monthly retainer fees for her full service public relations and media strategies average between $3,000 and $5,000 per month, plus expenses. Her "Get Smart!" professional development program is currently $79.95. Both Beth and Larry's products and services are well worth the money (and I don't get a cut). Explore them now.

Press Releases

EARLIER IN THIS CHAPTER, TUCKER HEWES warned against overuse of press releases. But there are times when they are very useful for a specific event. For example, we sent out the following press release several years ago during the weeks preceding Desert Storm. We did it because it seemed like the right thing to do. We got calls from military personnel and, as a fringe benefit, calls from the media because it was timely—and it was a "story."

FOR IMMEDIATE RELEASE   Please contact:
                                         Harold Evensky
                                         305-448-8882

Financial planning firm offers free consultation for pressing financial matters to military reservists being sent to Operation Desert Shield and their families.

Deena Katz, CFP, President of Evensky, Brown & Katz, a fee-only financial and investment planning firm in Coral Gables, Florida, announced that the firm's partners will provide free counseling on pressing financial matters to military reservists and other military personnel being sent to Operation Desert Shield and to their families. This will be done without any costs, commitment, sales pressure, or future obligation of any kind.

Ms. Katz said that it seemed a small return for the commitment the military and their families are making on our behalf.

-###-

ANNOUNCEMENT CARD

Continuing the practice of fee-only financial planning and investment management

BUDROS RUHLIN

James L. Budros CFP, ChFC
Peggy M. Ruhlin CPA, CFP

BUDROS & RUHLIN, INC.

are pleased to announce

Daniel B. Roe, CFP

has joined the firm's executive staff
April 1, 1996

1650 Lake Shore Drive Suite 150
Columbus, Ohio 43204.4895

telephone (614) 481.6900
facsimile (614) 481.6919

Notice that a press release is in a specific format, with the contact person's name at the top right-hand corner, and cross-hatch marks at the end. Try to keep your press release to one page. Larry Chambers's book has a great section on press releases, including a checklist to make sure you do it right.

Announcements

ANNOUNCEMENT CARDS WORK well, particularly if you have an event to publicize. Budros & Ruhlin sends a simple announcement card (see illustration at left), accomplishing two things at once: announcing the milestone, and reminding us of what they do.

Jack Blankinship of Blankinship & Foster sent the following letter, similar to a press release in format, to his clients and professional acquaintances. Jack's letter subtly lets people know that they have been honored before, which adds even more prestige for the firm.

PRESS RELEASE   August 15, 2000

Once again a national magazine has honored our firm.

The August issue of *Medical Economics* is now on the newsstands with its exclusive list of the "150 best financial advisers for doctors."

A total of nine planners were named, including Blankinship & Foster for the state of California. Two of the nine are in San Diego.

This is the second time *Medical Economics* has published its list of "best financial advisers." The first was in 1998.

We are honored to be named again in 2000.

> **OFFBEAT ANNOUNCEMENT**
>
> ## THE DWEEB, THE CURMUDGEON, AND THE DRAGON LADY
>
> [HAROLD EVENSKY, PETER BROWN, AND DEENA KATZ]
>
> ANNOUNCE THE RENAISSANCE OF
>
> ### EVENSKY, BROWN & KATZ
>
> FINANCIAL ADVISORS
>
> 241 Sevilla Avenue, Suite 902   305-448-8882
> Coral Gables, Florida 33134   FAX 305-448-1326
> January 1999   EBK@EVENSKY.COM

Announcements are still announcements, so if you really want to get some attention, you might want to consider something a bit more offbeat. When we returned to our former name after a named partner left, we sent this announcement (see illustration *Offbeat Announcement* above) to some (not all) of our clients. We got lots of attention and plenty of laughs.

Do It Yourself

I LEFT ONE OF THE BEST RECOMMENDATIONS FOR LAST. All of the earlier strategies depend on getting the media to accept your expertise and write about it. Why not take control yourself?

Years ago, a professor in one of my marketing courses gave us a project. We each had $5,000 to market our business. (OK, so this was quite a few years ago.) Our job was to figure out how we were going to spend it effectively. Some set aside money for newspaper advertising, while some spent money on fancy brochures and fine stationery. Not one of us came up with the professor's solution, "Publish a book. It will make you an authority and give you instant credibility." In hindsight, I believe he was right. Being quoted in the press can give you instant credibility, but being an author gives you instant celebrity, or at least an instant of celebrity when you need to draw on it. You can self-publish a booklet, eighty pages or so, to hand out to your prospects and use in seminars. It's impressive and you'll distinguish yourself from others in the business.

"If you can't commit to a book," says professional financial writer Larry Chambers, "write articles." Larry has developed an interactive CD that walks you through writing an article with the ease of a professional. Larry's advice on writing about problems in an industry may help you target a certain market. For example, you could write an article about financial issues for a physician. When I asked Larry for some material about writing an article for this book, he graciously allowed me to adapt a piece from his book, *The Guide to Financial Public Relations—How to Stand Out in the Midst of Competitive Clutter* (St. Lucie Press, 1999). This is good stuff.

HOW TO WRITE A PROBLEM SOLUTION ARTICLE

How does your service solve industry or consumer problems? A published article in a targeted periodical that educates, informs, or solves a problem can be very effective in generating new business. Readers are much more likely to respond favorably to a solution to a problem from someone who communicates expertise than from someone who is pushing a firm or product.

Design the article to explain the complexities of a problem in a certain industry. This draws readers and increases your chance of getting published. Your goal should be to create a feeling within the reader that he or she has discovered something new and useful.

Don't write self-serving articles. If an article sounds like you're trying to sell something or be manipulative, you are! Instead, address a problem, pose a question or series of questions, or explain an opportunity. Begin with a brief introduction of only a sentence or two, and then get right into the "how-to" of the article. Educate, solve a problem, or reveal an advantageous situation. Success sells success. Highly educated professionals are always looking for timely information that will increase their wealth of knowledge.

— Outline the article. Carefully determine who your readers are and what the point of the article will be. Identify the main premise you want the readers to learn.

— Identify the problems or concerns that the readers have in common.

— State the problem.

— Identify three related problems that are a result of the main problem.

— Provide steps/action to correct the problem.

— Discuss any relevant discoveries or recent developments that the readers wouldn't likely have heard about yet.

— Write a personal experience story that shows the problem and how you solved it.

— Use a call to action, when appropriate.

— Summarize your article.

— Re-read. Does the ending answer the question that you posed at the beginning? That's the built-in test.

So, What's the Story?

IN THE FUTURE, THE NEED FOR MARKETING and public relations will become much more important as the competition for clients becomes fierce. You won't have the luxury of making mistakes, so carefully plan your approach, track your progress, decide what's working for you, and keep at it.

customer **profile**

PLEASE FILL IN (YOU CAN TYPE RIGHT ON THE LINE)

Complete this form based on the similar characteristics of your best customers.

	EXAMPLE	
AGE RANGE:	35-49	
GENDER: • Male • Female	Male	
HOUSEHOLD INCOME (Average)	$175M	
NET WORTH (Average)	$400M	
EDUCATION: % of total • High School • College • Graduate	Graduate	
OCCUPATION: • Professional • Self-employed • Business executive	Professional	
BEHAVIORAL PROFILE: • Conservative • Moderate • Aggressive	Aggressive	
INVESTMENT TIME HORIZON: • Long term • Short term	Long term	
INVESTMENT CHARACTER: • Family needs/obligations (education, etc.) • Personal freedom/comfort • Relieve financial worries • Influence/power/prestige • Make money • Risk level • Challenge	Make money	
NOTE OTHER IMPORTANT CHARACTERISTICS OF THIS CUSTOMER		

SOURCE: FIDELITY INVESTMENTS INSTITUTIONAL BROKERAGE GROUP

1
page
on CD-ROM

CHAPTER 2

OLD AND NEW MARKETING TRICKS

Aunt Deena, I founded you on the SpiderWeb at school.

– LOGAN WELLS (age 5)

If you have not yet found the Internet to be an indispensable resource, better start looking for another career, because technology has taken this profession by storm. In the not-too-distant future you will be able to rely on dozens of sites to support your client relationships. Currently, portfolio management, separate account custody, financial planning, analytical tools, research, and trading (just to name a few) are all available for your use on the Web. Some Internet sites are prepared to be your virtual back office. The key is to figure out how to incorporate and personalize these various functions to support your prospects and clients.

Life Service Providers

YOU'LL PROBABLY JUMP UP AND DOWN screaming when you read where I think our profession is going. I believe that we will become the quintessential Life Service Providers (LSP) of the future. Think about it. Our clients' lives are like enterprises, and they are the CEOs. You know how corporate life is. CEOs want to save time and money and utilize the expertise of others to get where they want to go. Somebody must facilitate these tasks for individuals, and I think that should be you. You will be able to do it efficiently, effectively, and at low cost by using and leveraging the support you'll get from the Internet. In essence, our clients will be "outsourcing" their lives to us.

I don't know any advisers today who don't have Web sites. Many are contracting with Web service providers to set up the sites and provide some meat for them. These include links to sections providing portfolio data, bank statements, and other material the client would find useful. For example, Andrew Gluck of AdvisorSites (www.advisorsites.com) designs customized Web sites for you, then provides articles for the site each month to keep it fresh and interesting. Andy believes the key to "branding" (a hot business buzzword) is in your Web site. "Your fourteen inches of screen depth is potentially every bit as influential as the fourteen inches at Salomon, Smith, Barney," he says. "If you're using a cookie-cutter site, that's not helping you create a brand nor is it telling someone who visits your site much about you." This is important because one of the worst errors we've all made is to set up a site and subsequently forget about it. Occasionally someone e-mails us about it, but running to update the Web site has never been high on anybody's list of work priorities. Until now.

"Co-opetition"

ACCORDING TO 1999 STATISTICS, 74.5 million Americans were then using the Internet.[1] That number is growing exponentially. According to Jupiter Communications,[2] 37 percent of those using the Internet will be utilizing online financial services. To my mind, that means that advisers will have to explore various ways of "co-opetition" with other financial institutions in order to effectively care for our clients' needs.

Co-opetition is a way of working with, instead of against, your competitor, of discovering new ways to cooperate for everyone's benefit. For example, in the early days of auto manufacturing, companies were suffering because no one was buying cars. They discovered that the roads in many areas were so bad that cars couldn't operate on them. In some cases, there just weren't any roads at all. So, car manufacturers got together and started building roads. They built the roads so *all* of the companies could sell cars. Co-opetition. Think about what that can mean for you.

Your Value Net

I BELIEVE THAT STRATEGIC ALLIANCES with others who can support, supplement, and complement our profession will be much more important in the future. Many of these relationships will be facilitated through the Internet. It's up to you to figure out your "Value Net," mining those relationships both within and outside the Internet world. Take a look at the illustration below.

Your complementors may be others who can provide information and resources for you to synthesize in useful ways to serve your

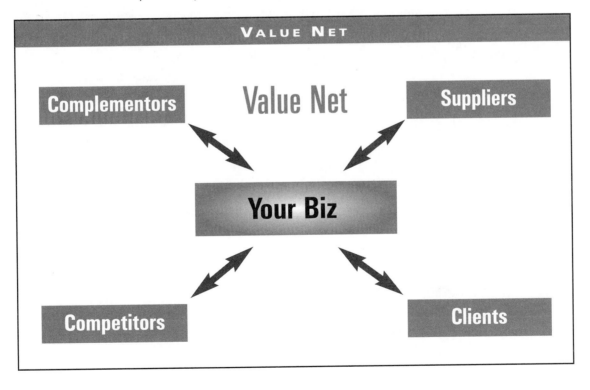

client. You may use real estate sites, for example, to search the housing market in a particular area of the country for your retiring client (see illustration *Value Net Complementors* above). You may add health care, social and community information, along with cost of living figures, to prepare a complete relocation package for your retiring (and moving) client.

Next you'll want to explore ways you can work with suppliers to enhance your client relationships (see illustration *Value Net Suppliers* at right). For example, utilizing support systems such as those developed by PIE Technologies (www.pietech.com), Morningstar Advisors (morningstaradvisor.com), or Financeware (www.financeware.com), will give you financial planning and analytical tools that can be used interactively with your clients. You may offer to beta-test some of the newer programs being developed by your vendors, in an effort to help create new and more useful systems.

You'll also want to make the best use of your clients and their capabilities (see illustration *Value Net Clients* at right). It is in our clients' best interest to help us be successful. They can be the best representa-

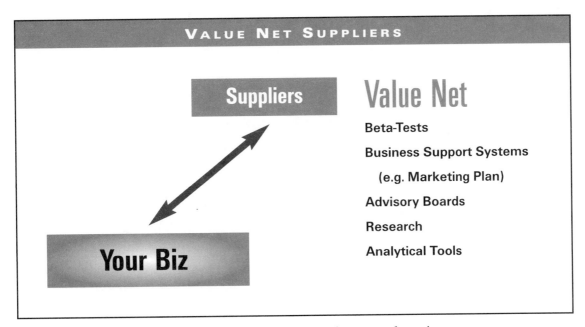

tives for us if they are happy with us and we give them good service. They have opinions on how we can work with them, what kinds of services we should offer, and how we can give them an "exceptional experience." Ask them. Use their skills and ideas.

Finally, seek out your competitors to find ways that you can work together for the benefit of everyone (see illustration *Value Net Competitors* on the following page). Your Value Net can be created by

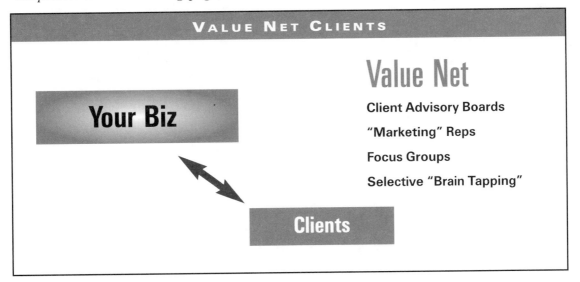

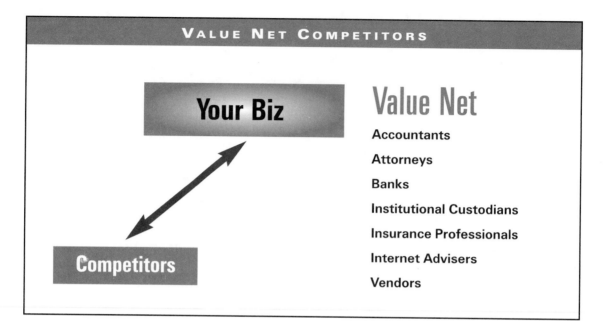

using the Internet as a vehicle of communication and action. For example, using the Web you might, with your client's approval, drop financial data into an accountant's designated site to avoid anyone having to reenter the information to prepare tax forms. You've already gathered the data, it's just a matter of making it available in a meaningful way to the other professionals your client may use.

Using the Internet

KNOWING HOW YOU CAN BEST UTILIZE the Net is important, especially when using the Internet to market your services. I have in the past felt that a Web site should be a slick brochure for prospects and a resource for existing clients. I've changed my mind. I believe now that our Web sites will be the windows from our "world" to others. However, it won't be a closed window; we'll fling it open and communication will be interactive.

Currently, many advisers allow their clients access to their portfolios through their Web sites. We have started to provide personal Web connectivity through our Web sites. Our clients will be able to design what *they* want to see on *their* own sites, through us. Instead of designing one site that we think everyone can use, we let each client customize. So Dr. Jones won't go to www.evensky.com to see his portfolio, he will go to jonesfamily@evensky.com, his customized site, to see his portfolio and any other information that he finds useful.

Aside from portfolio access, many advisers include links to useful sites such as Schwab, Fidelity, Morningstar, the Internal Revenue Service, the Social Security Administration, and e-magazines like *Money, Worth,* and *Bloomberg Personal Finance.* Joel Isaacson & Co., Inc.'s site (www.joelisaacson.com) has often-used forms, such as IRA distribution request forms, transfer forms, and limited power of attorney forms in .pdf (Acrobat) format so that prospects and clients can download them easily for themselves. They even include an Acrobat download link in case the client does not have that software on his system.

Keats, Connelly and Associates, Inc. (www.keatsconnelly.com) has links to articles of interest that are updated monthly. Tom Connelly reports that Andy Gluck of AdvisorSites designed his site and in addition to writing its articles, Andy provides the links to others of interest each month.

Probably one of the best sites I've seen is Garrett Financial Services's site at www.gfponline.com. (AdvisorSites also designed this one, and no, I don't get anything for talking about them.) Garrett Financial is located in Kansas City. The neat thing about this site is that the pictures across the top of the screen are of Kansas City, so anyone looking in will recognize the places on the page and feel right at home.

One of the best ways to set yourself apart from all the other advisers will be through the use of aggregation providers on the Net. It is estimated that an average person has thirteen relationships with various financial institutions, including a brokerage, credit card providers, banks, and mortgage lenders. People do not have time to track all these relationships effectively. Through account aggregation, your client will be able to access *all* his password-protected accounts, including airline mileage accounts, through your site. Currently, the top aggregation providers are Yodlee (www. yodlee.com), By All Accounts (byallaccounts.com), Cash Edge (www.

cashedge.com), Corillian (www.corillian.com), and ezlogin (www. ezlogin.com). Large institutions such as Citibank, Yahoo!, Quicken, Wells Fargo, Chase, and E*Trade are offering this service. You will too if you want to stay competitive.

Andy Gluck and I discussed the value of Web sites for advisers. "I was speaking on a panel a few months ago," says Andy. "One adviser asked me, 'How can I make money from my Web site?' I told him, that's like asking how you can make money from your fax machine. It's a tool—a different kind of tool, sort of a cross between a book and a TV."

The more useful those who visit your Internet site find it, the more likely they will keep coming back for more resources and services. The big hitch in all of this is that cyberspace is beyond huge, so unless someone knows how to get to your site, all the good stuff you do will be lost. This may be one place where existing clients can be extraordinarily useful in spreading the word about the services you offer through the Internet. It's also useful for helping new acquaintances to check you out. You just might get the next client by attending your kid's soccer game and handing out your Web address. Use your imagination.

Tips on Seminars

BARRY FREEDMAN, CHAIRMAN OF Freedman Financial Services, is one of the best seminar presenters I know. His presentation style is warm, comfortable, and knowledgeable without being overwhelming or complicated. Barry feels that seminars are the cornerstone of marketing and client retention programs. Barry says that one of the key reasons is that he knows why he's giving a seminar. Here are his four seminar tips:

➲ Don't give the seminar to educate; give it to disturb.

➲ Don't give it to inform; define problems.

➲ Don't give the seminar to offer solutions; provide just a foretaste of solutions.

➲ Don't do it to sell products; do it to sell YOU and your style.

Many advisers told me that the hardest job in preparing a seminar is to design and outline the content. The worst thing you can do is to walk into a seminar and "wing it." You should go in with well-defined expectations, and you should be prepared to communicate those expectations to your audience. The next worst thing you can do is to use a seminar that was prepared by others, without making it uniquely your own. For example, there are some great PowerPoint slides and pre-written seminars you can buy, but you can immediately lose the audience if you are not familiar or comfortable with the presentation.

You don't have to make this process complicated. Start with a simple outline. I find it is best to use keywords for my outlines so I can trigger the point of my message for each section. When I first started speaking publicly, I wrote everything down. Unfortunately, this encouraged the temptation to read everything because I wanted to make sure that I did not miss a point. It was awful. Have you ever sat in a meeting where the speaker read his talk? You're bored; he's bored. I think of seminars like live theater. If you've ever attended a great theater presentation, you'll note that the actors draw their energy from the reactions of the audience. Chemistry exists while the actors and audience feed on the experience. I believe that a good seminar presenter has got to be part thespian.

Let's take a brief look at the format for a good seminar outline. The following is one on retirement planning, titled "Issues in Retirement Planning." This was actually a two-hour workshop. Notice that it begins by talking about the "soft" issues of retirement—health, housing, and what will keep you occupied. If, as Barry Freedman suggests, we need to "disturb," then we probably want to avoid more technical information and offer, instead, issues to stimulate the attendee's thinking.

The second section of this outline discusses investment aspects for retirement, including identifying and prioritizing goals and determining resources available to meet those goals. The section also includes an explanation of asset allocation and how it works for a retirement portfolio. These are the tools that give more detail to the issues of retirement. The next section of the outline describes the capital needs analysis process. This explains how an individual's unique personal circumstances can have a great impact on the expectations for the success of a retirement portfolio to meet their goals. We then show the individuals how the tools apply to individual circumstances. It's a good idea to use examples (such as those listed under sample cases in the outline), so the audience can identify specific circumstances. The final section of this outline covers special needs such as long-term care and Medicare. This last subject matter is related to retirement issues, but is not the main point of the talk. I like to have a filler part at the end so I can adjust my talk to the time. If I am running short of time, I breeze through this; if not, I can take my time and explain more fully. The topic is actually broad enough for a short seminar.

When I did seminars frequently, I also had a "take away," an informational form or brochure that gave some generalized advice or tips. For example, if I did a seminar on long-term care, I would give out a checklist labeled, "How to Evaluate a Good Long Term Care Policy," that simply offered some information about long-term care policies. Many seminar presenters provide a card for the attendees to complete before they can get their free take-away. This way, the presenter gets the names and addresses of attendees, and an opportunity for another contact.

ISSUES IN RETIREMENT PLANNING PRIVATE

I. **Retirement Planning Overview**
   A. Fitness
      — How will you feel?
      — Developing a wellness approach to health
   B. Attitudes and Role Adjustment
      — A philosophy for living fully at any stage of life
   C. Housing
      — Where will you live?
      — Matching your desired lifestyle to your retirement housing
   D. Time
      — What will you do?
      — Developing a positive, contributing lifestyle
   E. Financial Planning

F. Work

— Will you?

— Factors to decide on whether or not to work in retirement

G. Legal Issues

— Estate planning

— Estate preservation

— Living estate planning and planning for disability

II. Financial Planning for Retirement

A. The Investment Process

1. Goals

— Interim vs. life goals / uniqueness

— Institutions vs. individuals

— Time and dollar specificity

— Priority

2. Resources

— Current savings

— What you have now

— Future income

— Additional savings

— Social security, pension, inheritance

3. Economy

— Past, present, future

4. Constraints

5. Asset allocation

— Select asset categories

— Fixed income (debt)

— Short, medium, and long term

— Growth

— Commercial

— Real Estate

— Natural Resources

— Tangibles

B. Investment Planning Fundamentals

— Time value of money

— Constraints

— Liquidity

— Marketability

— Reduction

— Liquidity

— Preservation

— Risk

- Taxes
- Income
- Regular
- AMT
- S.S.
- Catastrophic
- Health
- Estate

- No safe investment
- Psychology
- Risk adverse vs. loss adverse
- Absolute Risk
- Unsystematic
- Systematic
- Risk volatility
- Diversification

III. Capital Needs Analysis

   A. Assumptions

      - Mortality

      - Inflation

      - Investment growth rates

   B. Investments

   C. Pre-retirement Savings and Distributions

   D. Income after Retirement

   E. Expenses after Retirement

IV. Sample Cases

   A. Age 50: children's education, home addition, pension retire at 65

   B. Age 62: child's wedding, inheritance, retire at 65

   C. Age 68: mortgage, travel, retired

V. Special Issues

   A. "Medicare Catastrophic Act"

   B. Long-Term Health Care

   C. Investment Evaluation

If you are going to use visuals such as PowerPoint presentations and are designing them yourself, make them simple, visually attractive, but not so overdone that the automation or clipart attracts more attention than the message you want to convey. Don't try to put more than one thought on a PowerPoint slide, and remember, if you are addressing larger crowds you will have to use larger fonts. If you are using material supplied by someone else, be sure you are comfortable with the aspects of each slide. If something does not make sense to you, don't use it. There are few things worse than trying to fake it through a slide.

Using PowerPoint slides makes your presentation colorful and interesting. There is also another benefit: it keeps your speech on track. There is nothing that can lose an audience faster than an unprepared or undisciplined speaker whose talk meanders all over hell and half of Georgia. Finally, a prepared presentation (if you follow it) will never let you run on too long. Take a cue from the words of Will Rogers and "never miss a good chance to shut up."

I thought it might be useful to see how other advisers prepare PowerPoint presentations, so I asked Bill Knox of Bugen Stuart Korn & Cordaro for a sample. Let's look at some of the slides in Bill's presentation on estate planning. You'll find the entire presentation on the CD-ROM as Form 2-01.

The first slide tells the audience that Bill is going to talk about estate planning (see illustration *Presentation: Beginning Slide* on the following page). The slide also makes it clear that this is a subject that everyone needs to address. Bill is managing expectations; we're going to talk about estate planning, make no mistake about it!

The next slide sets up the problem (see illustration *Presentation: Setting Up the Problem* on the following page). This is the "disturbing" element that Barry Freedman recommends. There are many unknowns, and estate planning is not a "one-shoe-fits-all" solution, nor is it one that should be considered cavalierly. Bill then creates a scenario to help his attendees identify and make the experience more personal for them. Throughout the presentation, he illustrates both good and not-so-good planning alternatives so his attendees can see the consequences of making poor estate planning decisions.

Bill then presents the more technical aspects of the seminar, discussing different types of trusts and how each type works in an estate

---

PRESENTATION: BEGINNING SLIDE

You should be somewhere else if
you're pretty sure that . . .

You'll live forever, or

If you happen to die, you will
have spent everything, or

You're taking whatever's left with you.

Otherwise, We're Glad You're Here !

Bugen Stuart Korn & Cordaro,Inc.   **BSKC**

PRESENTATION: SETTING UP THE PROBLEM

Why Two Such Different Futures ?

Estate Planning !   (surprise)

- with some effort and modest expense,
  the parents can eliminate the $2,000,000
  estate tax coming due at the survivor's
  death

- gifts to descendants can be "packaged" in
  trusts to further increase their value

- favorite charities can be remembered
  and a permanent legacy established

Bugen Stuart Korn & Cordaro,Inc.   **BSKC**

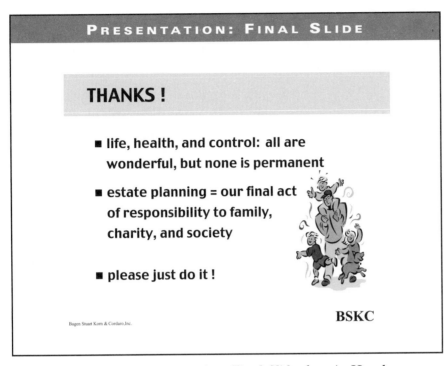

PRESENTATION: FINAL SLIDE

THANKS !

- life, health, and control: all are wonderful, but none is permanent

- estate planning = our final act of responsibility to family, charity, and society

- please just do it !

Bugen Stuart Korn & Cordaro, Inc.

BSKC

plan (see illustration *Presentation: Final Slide* above). He also covers family partnerships and sheltered accounts, highlighting how they fit into the estate-planning scenario. He has given his attendees a disturbing problem and a taste of possible solutions. The final slide simply appeals to their sense of duty. This ending practically screams of Mom, apple-pie, and flag waving. If these attendees don't do something now, they are letting *everyone* down.

This presentation sets up the problem, provides generalized but possible solutions, and then leaves attendees to ponder their own circumstances.

New Marketing Environment

MANY OF US HAVE STOPPED GIVING SEMINARS in recent years; clients were falling in the door and we had no need to gear up for a speaking engagement. The new competitive environment will demand that we find ways of reaching prospects that really work. I truly believe that seminars will still be a useful prospecting tool in the future. I also believe we will need to augment the traditional tools with others, like marketing through the Internet. In fact, I think the key to success will be a blend of the old techniques of giving seminars coupled with very new marketing tools like useful Internet sites, or sites that will give us the ability to present online. Check out www.placeware.com for a Web site that will allow you to show material to several people at once.

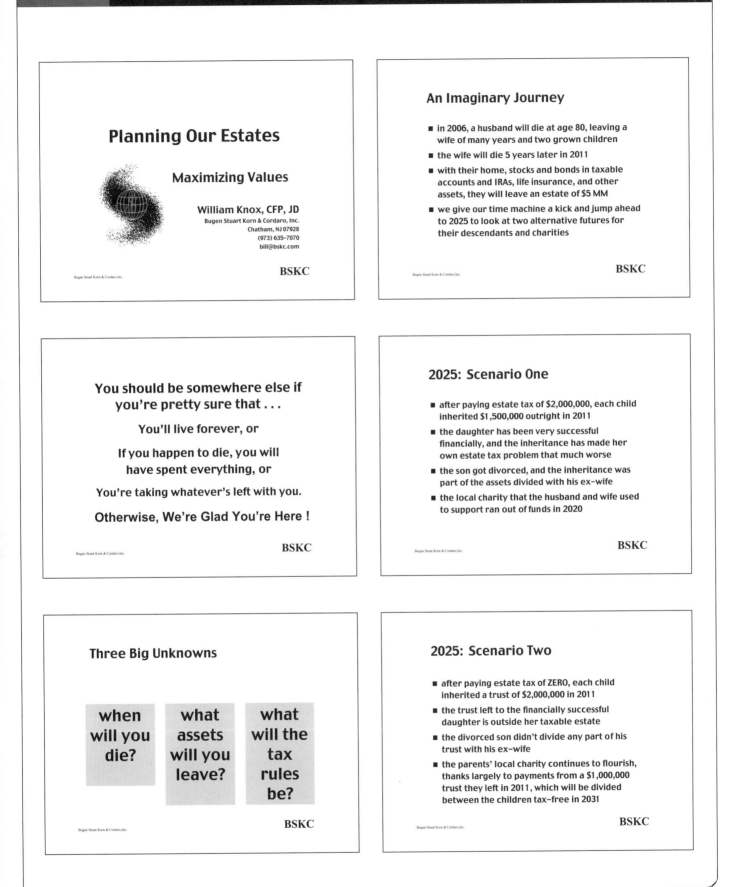

Planning Our Estates

Maximizing Values

William Knox, CFP, JD
Bugen Stuart Korn & Cordaro, Inc.
Chatham, NJ 07928
(973) 635-7070
bill@bskc.com

BSKC

Bugen Stuart Korn & Cordaro, Inc.

An Imaginary Journey

- in 2006, a husband will die at age 80, leaving a wife of many years and two grown children
- the wife will die 5 years later in 2011
- with their home, stocks and bonds in taxable accounts and IRAs, life insurance, and other assets, they will leave an estate of $5 MM
- we give our time machine a kick and jump ahead to 2025 to look at two alternative futures for their descendants and charities

BSKC

Bugen Stuart Korn & Cordaro, Inc.

You should be somewhere else if you're pretty sure that . . .

You'll live forever, or

If you happen to die, you will have spent everything, or

You're taking whatever's left with you.

Otherwise, We're Glad You're Here !

BSKC

Bugen Stuart Korn & Cordaro, Inc.

2025: Scenario One

- after paying estate tax of $2,000,000, each child inherited $1,500,000 outright in 2011
- the daughter has been very successful financially, and the inheritance has made her own estate tax problem that much worse
- the son got divorced, and the inheritance was part of the assets divided with his ex-wife
- the local charity that the husband and wife used to support ran out of funds in 2020

BSKC

Bugen Stuart Korn & Cordaro, Inc.

Three Big Unknowns

| when will you die? | what assets will you leave? | what will the tax rules be? |

BSKC

Bugen Stuart Korn & Cordaro, Inc.

2025: Scenario Two

- after paying estate tax of ZERO, each child inherited a trust of $2,000,000 in 2011
- the trust left to the financially successful daughter is outside her taxable estate
- the divorced son didn't divide any part of his trust with his ex-wife
- the parents' local charity continues to flourish, thanks largely to payments from a $1,000,000 trust they left in 2011, which will be divided between the children tax-free in 2031

BSKC

Bugen Stuart Korn & Cordaro, Inc.

---

33 slides on CD-ROM

CHAPTER 3

DESIGNING PROSPECT PACKAGES

If a man smiles all the time he's probably
selling something that doesn't work.

— GEORGE CARLIN

Your brochure is one of your first opportunities to let people know about you and qualify them at the same time. There are a couple of choices you can make for an initial information brochure. You can get a big, slick, professionally printed one, or you could create your own with desk-top publishing, printing only what you need, when you need it.

The Big Brochure

MANY ADVISERS PRODUCE A slick brochure with information and pictures of the principals and key personnel. These can be very impressive, but there are a few things you must think about before deciding to make this commitment. Budros & Ruhlin in Columbus, Ohio have gone this route. Peggy Ruhlin advises:

➲ **Get a professional.** Unless you have talent in this area, hire a professional to design your image, including the logo, then lay out the brochure to speak to your target market. Peggy says their target is high-net-worth individuals, so they wanted a "rich" look.

⮕ **Be sure the copy speaks in your voice.** A copywriter will probably do the work, but you will need to inspect it carefully to be sure that it is in keeping with your personality and style. Peggy advises that it is not necessary to use a professional who has done other financial brochures. In fact, sometimes a fresh new look emerges from someone who has not.

⮕ **Get ideas from clients (a client advisory board, perhaps) about the content.** For example, you may interview several clients and ask what issues about your relationship and services are important to them.

⮕ **Consider the costs of the design you choose.** Peggy notes that the costs of printing their Big Brochure were "astronomical." This was in addition to the costs for the design. She and her partner, Jim Budros, decided to order thousands of copies to get a price break. "Unfortunately," reports Peggy, "we have new partners in the firm who are not even in the brochure. We handle this by including bios on all of us when we send it out." She suggests that in the future they might consider one with "moving parts" so that they can update pieces periodically.

RTD Financial Advisors, Inc. in Philadelphia also has a professional brochure. Roy Diliberto, the firm's president, decided to hire a financial writer to design and pen the copy for the brochure. As a result, Roy feels that the depth of knowledge from someone who knows the business well can add a great deal to the content.

Simpler Brochure Options

THERE ARE ALTERNATIVES TO MAKING the expensive leap Peggy made. Ron Tamayo, Susan Spraker, and Charlie Fitzgerald of Spraker, Fitzgerald & Tamayo in Maitland, Florida, have written a snappy brochure using Microsoft Word. When it needs updating, they simply revise the document and reprint it. To give it a little distinction, they use a heavy, more polished-looking paper stock. Ron's suggestions for producing the brochure include the following:

➲ **Keep it simple.** Don't try for fancy graphics or pictures. Unless you use a pro, it will probably look homemade.

➲ **Include a page on your company philosophy.** A clear explanation of your mission avoids misunderstandings later.

➲ **List the principals.** Give partners' background and education as part of the material.

➲ **Keep it businesslike, not gimmicky.** Cartoon characters and stick figures may show off your sense of humor but don't make a serious impression.

➲ **Include explicit descriptions of your services and fees.**

Susan, Ron, and Charlie have shared their five-page Word document for your use as a model to customize (see FORM 3-01, "Public Relations Material," on page 56). I like their format because, although the style is simple, it's classic-looking and covers all the material that I think you should impart to prospective clients. Notice how the information goes from broad to specific. That is, they talk about their firm and their philosophy, then lead in to specific details like indexing and tax planning. Then they discuss the planning process and the fees. Finally, they introduce you to the players—a section with short bios to impress the prospects with their experience and credentials. You'll also find this file on the CD-ROM as FORM 3-01.

Greenbaum and Orecchio, Inc. in northern New Jersey once had nice preprinted brochures but have since elected to desktop-publish their own on demand. "For one thing," reports Tom Orecchio, "we like to make our informational packages more customized to the client's interests and the type of work he wants us to do." Tom credits their flexible design and high-end color printer with making the package look more professional. "You can have the best-written material in the world, but the design and print quality make a big difference in the presentation." Tom also advises not to make the informational package too technical. "Our old brochure even had pictures of the efficient frontier." Along with a warmer style, their new format includes a client profile sheet. This can be found on the CD-ROM as FORM 3-02 (also see "Client Profiles" on page 57). Tom and his partner Gary Greenbaum decided that prospects would be more comfortable with them as advisers if they could identify with other clients of the firm. This is a great idea because my experience has shown that prospects will usually ask what types of clients we have. This pre-empts the question.

Among the other materials that Greenbaum and Orecchio provide in their initial package is a one-page description of services (FORM 3-03 on the CD-ROM and on page 58). This page outlines the services available and explains whether each is a one-time matter or an ongoing function. The at-a-glance format makes it easy for the prospect to grasp whether the services are what he is looking for.

Brochure Supplements and Alternatives

ALONG WITH THE MATERIAL IN OUR prospect package, we include a rather detailed philosophy statement, (see FORM 3-04, "Investment Philosophy," on page 59). We also use it separately for reinforcement during the client relationship. We include detailed information about investment theory, client-related concepts, and implementation. I am positive that most clients do not read our statement when we send it out initially, but we always walk new clients through it during our education process.

We also may include a reprint of an article or two that gives us some credibility. We choose an article that either describes our services well or is a current quote from a national source, such as the *Wall Street Journal* or the *New York Times*. Generally, if we know what interests the prospect has, we will include a pertinent article as well. Since I have covered public relations in Chapter 1, I won't go into any other detail here. The entire package is placed in a linen-type, colored folder with our name embossed on the front. You can purchase these from a local office supply store or alternatively, try www.paperdirect.com for some very nice specialized paper for stationery, folders, and envelopes. We do our own embossing, but a local instant printing office can probably do it as well. As a courtesy to the prospect, we also include a detailed map of Coral Gables to assist in locating our office. MapQuest (www.mapquest.com) is a great Web site to use in making highly customized maps and directions.

Along with the package, we include the following simple prospect letter explaining what we've sent and indicating that we will contact them later to see if they have questions or want to make an appointment. The whole experience is very low-key, which is our style, but many advisers are much more proactive in attempting to set an appointment.

Dear PROSPECT:

It was a pleasure speaking to you regarding our services. As I mentioned, I have prepared a packet of information describing the nature of our firm's practice and our philosophy.

Once you've had the opportunity to review our material and would like to consider establishing a relationship with us, please fill out the enclosed data-gathering booklet and return it in the self-addressed envelope. This information will assist us to better understand your needs so that we can make our preliminary meeting more productive. I will call you in about one week to see if you have any questions and to schedule an appointment at your convenience.

Should you have any questions in the interim, please call me at 305-448-8882.

Cordially yours,

Financial Planner

A few years ago we became a bit frustrated at the cost of sending our expensive brochures to anyone who happened to find our phone number, so we developed what I call the "tire-kicker" brochure (see FORM 3-05 on page 60). It folds to business-envelope size and has the "quick-and-dirty" information about us, including lists of services, fees, and philosophy. We use it for people we think are not yet serious about our services. It has saved us time and money over the years. I have reproduced it here for you, and you'll also find it on the CD-ROM so you can customize one for yourself.

The Targeted Brochure

DAVID NORTON OF NORTON PARTNERS in the United Kingdom designed a brochure aimed at entrepreneurs. The first page reads like this: "You're an entrepreneur. Do you run your personal finances as if you were a business? In your business, you'll seek to increase your income, spend and invest effectively, protect yourself from disaster, and plan for the future. We'll help you do the same for yourself personally. Read on to see how the 'Entrepreneur as a Business' Programme can meet your needs." David then gives a list of problems his target market might have:

➲ My accountant advises the business, but I'd like someone who specializes in advising directors to assist me personally.

➲ I'd like to increase my after-tax income.

➲ My financial affairs could be better organized.

➲ I want to run my business and leave personal finance to someone who knows what he is doing.

➲ I'm not sure how my pension schemes work or what they are worth.

➲ I'd like to plan how I'll exit from my company.

➲ If I die tomorrow, I don't know how secure my family would be.

➲ I wish I had more time.

➲ I wonder what my company is worth.

➲ I haven't got anyone I can really talk to about my finances.

➲ I'd love to do something different, but I don't know if I can afford it.

➲ I'd love to find a financial adviser I can trust.

If a prospect identifies with any of the problems, he suggests they see if they qualify for the "Entrepreneur as a Business" Programme.

David reports that he has had good success with this brochure because it is customized to the prospects he's seeking. They can immediately identify with the material, and David can be sure that those people he wants to see have gotten the message he wants them to get.

Video and Audio Brochures

I HAVE SEEN AUDIO AND VIDEO "BROCHURES" used as different approaches to telling clients about you and your services. I have never been a fan of these, primarily because I don't think anything can replace a personal explanation of what we do, supplemented by written materials that can be later referenced. Some advisers have had great success with these, though, so you might want to investigate www.audiobusiness-card.com or www.miamisolutions.com. For a real change, try putting a "talking head" on your Web site to explain your services. A short video clip of you or other key personnel in your office may be a unique way to personalize your Internet impression.

The Second Impression

THERE IS NO QUESTION THAT the second impression is made with the material you provide to a prospect. (The first, I maintain, is in the voice of the person who attends to the call when the initial contact is made.) If your material is haphazard and disorganized, or if it looks amateurish, it will affect what the clients feel they can expect from you. If it makes a good impression from the day they receive it, you'll be managing their expectations of an excellent experience with you.

SPRAKER, FITZGERALD & TAMAYO FINANCIAL PLANNING & WEALTH MANAGEMENT

OUR FIRM provides comprehensive fee-based wealth management services to corporate executives, professionals, business owners and other affluent clients. We utilize a team approach in analyzing and planning a client's investment portfolio, estate plan, cash flow, income taxes, and retirement. Recommendations are based solely on your specific needs, circumstances and goals. The firm and its partners are registered with the U.S. Securities and Exchange Commission. The partners are Certified Financial Planner licensees with over thirty years planning and investing experience. All are active members of The Financial Planning Association, The Central Florida Estate Planning Council and other professional organizations.

OUR MISSION is to partner with clients to establish and achieve financial goals through objective planning and management of investment assets. Our purpose is to help build, manage and preserve your wealth. We put our client's interest first, act with integrity and honesty, and strive for excellence in every facet of our practice. Our success is not measured by performance statistics but rather by our clients' success in achieving their goals.

OUR CLIENTS share in the realization that by coordinating and managing today's financial decisions they can achieve their goals for tomorrow. They are individuals and businesses who expect excellence and have made a firm commitment to achieving it themselves. Our clients usually have no desire to manage their financial affairs on a daily basis, want to simplify their lives, and are willing to enter into a long-term relationship that is mutually beneficial. They are highly motivated to work with a professional advisor, not a sales representative.

OUR PHILOSOPHY is to provide our clients with the highest level of service and technical expertise in the management and preservation of wealth. The entire staff of Spraker, Fitzgerald & Tamayo is firmly committed to this philosophy.

5
pages
on CD-ROM

Introduction

CLIENT PROFILES

Greenbaum and Orecchio, Inc. provides wealth management services to a wide variety of high net worth individuals, trusts, foundations, and endowments. All client information is held in the strictest confidence. Presented below are a number of Greenbaum and Orecchio, Inc. client profiles which fairly represent the wide variety of clients which the firm serves. We currently represent 74 clients with total assets under management of nearly $125 million.

Executives
- Total number of clients: 19
- Average age: 51, ranging from 38 to 66
- Assets under management: $55,000,000
- Current client status: 2 working, 7 retired

Business Owners
- Total number of clients: 16
- Average age: 51, ranging from 41 to 66
- Assets under management: $16,000,000
- Current client status: 11 working, 5 retired

Professionals
- Total number of clients: 8
- Average age: 57, ranging from 44 to 67
- Assets under management: $13,000,000
- Current status: 5 working, 3 retired

Widows
- Total number of clients: 6
- Average age: 69, ranging from 58 to 86
- Assets under management: $10,000,000
- Current status: 1 working, 5 retired

Consultants
- Total number of clients: 7
- Average age: 65, ranging from 55 to 78
- Assets under management: $5,000,000
- Current status: 2 working, 5 retired

Corporate Employees
- Total number of clients: 7
- Average age: 59, ranging from 47 to 70
- Assets under management: $4,000,000
- Current status: 2 working, 5 retired

Trusts & Foundations
- Total number of clients: 11
- Assets under management: $19,000,000

Introduction
DESCRIPTION OF SERVICES

Features and Benefits of Our Services

	Consulting	Investment Counsel	Wealth Management
Define how we will work together with you You will get full disclosure of risks and fees so that by understanding how we work together, you avoid unpleasant surprises.	One time	Ongoing	Ongoing
Learn about you and your goals and answer your questions. We learn about you, your goals, and your constraints so we both understand where you are starting from and where you want to go.	One time	Ongoing	Ongoing
Analyze financial planning strategies to help you make informed decisions We evaluate alternative solutions and make specific written recommendations so you can understand how to best achieve your goals.	One time	----------	Ongoing
Analyze investment choices and allocation strategies to help you make informed decisions We evaluate investment options and different allocation choices with you so that you understand the risks you are about to take and the risks you can expect	One time	One time	Ongoing
Implement the financial planning strategies that best achieve your goals We help you to implement the written recommendations we present to you and we consult your other advisors so that we work toward a coordinated, comprehensive strategy for you	----------	Ongoing	Ongoing
Measure, manage, and report to you your progress towards your financial planning goals Quarterly, you receive a financial goals report which details your progress toward those goals	----------	----------	Ongoing
Measure, manage, and report to you your progress towards your investment goals You get ongoing investment management and communications. Quarterly, you receive a performance report that monitors your progress towards achieving your investment goals. We rebalance your portfolio periodically so that you stay on track and earn what you need to achieve your goals. This strategy causes you to systematically buy low and sell high.	----------	Ongoing	Ongoing
Update your financial plan to accommodate changes During our comprehensive review we answer any new questions you may have, we integrate new research, products, and tax law, and we learn about your updated goals. We do this so that you can continue to make informed decisions and we can update your strategy so that it stays optimized, prudent, low cost, and tax smart.	----------	----------	Ongoing
Update your investment strategy to accommodate changes During our comprehensive review we answer any new questions you may have, we integrate new research, products, and tax law, and we learn about your updated goals. We do this so that you can continue to make informed decisions and we can update your strategy so that it stays optimized, prudent, low cost, and tax smart.	----------	Ongoing	Ongoing

1 page on CD-ROM

INVESTMENT PHILOSOPHY

The following summarizes our firm's core beliefs. These provide the basis for your Investment Policy. The entire staff of Evensky, Brown & Katz participates, at different levels, in the development of our philosophy. All members of the firm are committed to its consistent implementation. Policy design, implementation, continuous monitoring and, as necessary, modification, are integral parts of the wealth management process. Our success is measured not by performance statistics but rather by our clients' success in achieving their goals.

CLIENT RELATED ISSUES

Goal Setting
We believe that clients must set their own goals. It is our responsibility to educate them in the process and to assist them in defining, quantifying, and prioritizing their goals

Cash Flow
We believe that clients need total return, not dividends or interest. The traditional concept of an 'income' portfolio is archaic and places unnecessary and inappropriate restrictions on portfolio design.

Expectations
We believe that 'conservative' assumptions are a dangerous myth. Return requirements should be based on real rates of return. An investment policy should not be prepared based on a client's unrealistic expectations. If necessary, we will refuse the engagement.

Risk Tolerance
We believe that a client's risk tolerance is a significant constraint in the wealth management process. Success can be measured by our clients' ability to sleep well during turbulent markets.

Tax constraints
We believe that tax considerations must be considered. However, the goal of tax planning should be to maximize after-tax returns, not to minimize taxes. Neither reported turnover nor holding period calculated from reported turnover is a useful measure of tax efficiency. Annuities should generally only be considered when asset protection is an issue (in those states where the law protects annuity assets).

Evensky, Brown & Katz

Evensky, Brown & Katz is nationally known for its skill in wealth management and financial planning. The firm provides its clients with traditional wealth management service as well as comprehensive tax, insurance, and estate planning services; generational wealth transfer and charitable planning advice. Taking responsibility for providing and/or supervising all aspects of the members' financial planning needs enables the firm to provide it clients with cost effective, 'one stop' hassle-free personal financial planning and management.

Implement and Monitoring

The Company's strategy for providing many services is to enter into alliances with established service firms and outsource providers (e.g. attorneys, accountants, banks, trust companies, insurance firms, mortgage financing, auto leasing, bill paying, college planning) to seamlessly provide products and service to clients.

Evensky, Brown & Katz
241 Sevilla Avenue, # 902
Coral Gables, FL 33134
(800) 448-5435
(305) 448-1326 fax
www.evensky.com

*Uncared for wealth
is one risk you can't afford*

Private Family Office. We developed our Private Family Office to offer our clients comprehensive solutions to their financial and related personal needs. The Evensky Group Private Family Office provides an exceptional experience and a level of sophistication and service that, until now, has been impossible to obtain for individual investment portfolios of less than $50 million.

A Private Family Office...

Evaluates

- Client Objectives
- Investment Issues
- Risk Management
- Tax Issues
- Estate and Gifting
- Income Needs
- Other Financial Issues

Plan Design

- Investment Planning
- Risk Management
- Tax Planning
- Estate Planning

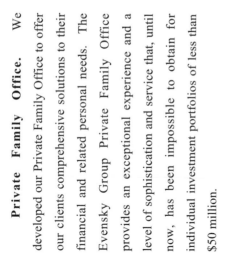

2 pages on CD-ROM

There's an old story about a man who picks up the phone at work one day.

"Son," says the voice on the other end, "I haven't been feeling too well."

"I'm sorry to hear that, Mom," he says. "What's the matter?"

"Well," she begins, "my leg hurts when I walk. The doctor says it's arthritis, and I'm just going to be in pain all the time."

"I'm sorry to hear that, Mom," says the man again.

"When are you coming to see me?" she asks.

"Gee, Mom," he replies, "I am awful busy with work. I've got some new contracts, and they really need some attention."

"But, son," she says, "you haven't been here in so long, and I really would like to see you."

"I know, Mom," he says, "But the kids play soccer on the weekends, and then there are the dance lessons, the skating lessons, the music lessons—you know."

"I understand," she says, "But I really miss you. And when you visit you really brighten my otherwise lonely day."

INTERVIEW 'EM

"OK, Mom," he acquiesces, "I'll be there Saturday. I'll bring those cinnamon rolls you always love, and Jill will bake a chicken for you."

"Jill? Who's Jill?" asks the old woman.

"Why, Jill is my wife, Mom, you know that," says the man.

"No, your wife is Karole Sue," counters the old lady. "Isn't this Buddy?"

"Buddy?" says the man. "No, this is David. David Rhinehart." There is absolute stillness at the other end of the line.

"Oh," exclaims the old lady, "I must have the wrong number."

"That's OK," assures the man, preparing to hang up.

"But," she continues, "does this mean you aren't coming Saturday?"

Chapter 4 offers some tools and tips for qualifying and interviewing prospects. On the surface, many prospects may seem just right for you and your practice, but digging a little deeper avoids misunderstandings like the one in the story above and assures that you don't begin inappropriate relationships and waste your time on unproductive meetings. Chapter 5 gives you some ideas for data gathering.

4

CLIENT QUALIFICATION TOOLS AND THE FIRST INTERVIEW

*It don't take a genius to spot a goat
in a flock of sheep.*

— WILL ROGERS

We try to screen our prospects as much as possible before they waltz in the door. We have used a qualification questionnaire for years, one that we fondly call "the pink sheet" because it is printed on pink paper (see FORM 4-01 on page 79). Pink was chosen in deference to my partner, Harold, because it's easily identifiable on a messy desk.

The form is two-sided. One side is used to record the identity of the caller and to record the disposition of the call. We use this side as an input form for our Client Relationship Management (CRM) database, which will be explained in Chapter 9. It is here that we note whether we will be sending a "puff package," and a preliminary data guide (see FORM 4-02 on page 81). We can also customize this data guide (note FORM 4-01 section under Result of 1st Communication: "a," #1-6) if we don't want to include all the pages. This pink sheet also documents whether we will be putting the name on our newsletter mailing list or referring them to someone else. If we make an appointment, we note with whom, the date, and the time. That information is then entered into our corporate calendar and the calendar of each responsible party. The flip side of this form gives us plenty of room to record details about our conversation with the prospect.

For me, there are a few essential questions to ask a prospect:

⮑ How did you hear about us? This is obviously an important question if you're to track the success of your marketing efforts. If you have no marketing plan, you'd better get one (see Chapter 1). Our days of getting clients for free are about over. If you have a marketing plan and aren't tracking it, start now.

⮑ What prompted you to make this call? It's important to identify the caller's professed as well as hidden agendas. One day I got a call from a doctor who wanted an appointment with me. When I asked this question, he said, "My wife keeps hounding me to have a professional look at our portfolio." "How do you think you are doing?" I asked. "I think we're fine, but my wife is unhappy," he replied. "Do you think sitting down with a professional will make her more comfortable?" I asked. "I have no idea, but I'm sure my life will be more comfortable. She'll stop hounding me to see a professional," he said.

⮑ Have you worked with a professional financial adviser before or are you now working with one? The last thing I want is someone else's problem. Originally, we did not ask this question. Then, one day we took on a new client. He seemed pleasant, and our first meeting was a pleasure. Early in the second meeting he asked me to recommend a securities attorney because he was planning to sue his last financial planner. I asked about the problem. He told me that the planner put him into some bad investments and he wanted to be made whole. I asked how much he'd lost, and he said, nothing. His complaint was that the investments recommended by the adviser were too conservative and he didn't make the money that he thought he was going to make. The investments? A 50 percent allocation to large cap core, 25 percent to small cap core, and 25 percent to core international. "Everybody else is making a fortune and my portfolio just sat there." This was during 1998 when Nasdaq left everything sitting in the dust. I decided that we didn't need a client with this kind of 20/20 hindsight. Another warning: Be sure you know your own motivation for selecting a client, and don't delude yourself. I once took a client from one of the big, high-profile brokers in town, simply because the client said he was unhappy, and I thought that I could do a better job than the broker. OK, it was an ego thing. Well, that client turned out to be a big pain. Six months into the relationship he was complaining and fussing, saying all the things to me that he had said about the broker.

➲ **If you are no longer working with a professional, what led to the change?** Often people who have worked with an adviser before have a much better idea of how the engagement will go and what they can expect from it. Some of my best clients are physicians who have had poor experiences with a "hot shot" who pandered to their ego, not their long term financial well-being.

➲ **What do you think we can do for you?** Better know in advance if the client expects a 35 percent return and wants you to walk his dog, too.

Pre-Data Gathering

ALTHOUGH I WILL COVER DATA GUIDES more in Chapter 5, there are a few clever "pre–data-gathering" ideas that I thought I'd introduce here. Lou Stanasolovich of Legend Financial Advisors in Pittsburgh, Pennsylvania, tells me that he uses a rather detailed data-gathering form on the phone with prospects before he schedules the first meeting. He wants to sit in front of only serious prospects. Their willingness to complete the form before they have their first meeting demonstrates their intentions to follow through. David Bugen of Bugen Stuart Korn & Cordaro agrees. "It's like visiting a new physician," he maintains. "We want to make the best use of our time together and we can only do that by having some advance information." David's firm uses a short data guide that they send out with the puff package.

On the other hand, I have a close personal friend who believes that a prospect's phone call should be rewarded with an appointment. She firmly believes that asking too many questions in advance of a first meeting discourages people who need help but who are uncomfortable with the process. She charges a nominal fee for the first visit, and if she's not going to work with them, she gives them a personal referral to a planner who can meet their needs. She also maintains that neither she, nor the prospects, think they are wasting their time if they are not a good fit.

Still, most advisers agree that the more you prescreen, the better the first appointment goes. It's much easier to help the client zero in on his issues once you have some background.

The Client Fit Ratio[SM] System

CHRIS DARDAMAN OF POLSTRA AND DARDAMAN, LLC has devised a Client Fit Ratio[SM] system to help the firm qualify clients (see FORM 4-03 on page 82). You might consider using their process to develop your own client fitness test.[1]

Chris and his partners, Dave Polstra and Alan Gotthardt, have defined what they believe to be the attributes of their "ideal" client. They express these attributes in terms of four criteria:

- ⮱ Available investment resources
- ⮱ Desire and ability to delegate
- ⮱ Reasonable expectations
- ⮱ Personality/chemistry

Chris explains the genesis of their system: "Last year, a large Atlanta-based corporation we have worked with for ten years offered an early retirement package to hundreds of people. We knew it would be impossible for us to take all of the people who might call and were forced to be extremely focused as to whom we could accept as new clients. Even after referring out over 50 percent of the inquiries, we still ended up with a six-month waiting list to complete financial plans for new clients. The Client Fit Ratio[SM] system is a simple tool, designed to focus on what makes a good client-adviser relationship. Our firm has three partners. Having determined that each partner only wants to have about fifty to sixty clients, the Client Fit Ratio[SM] system forces us to look at each new prospect more closely."

Chris asserts that the "expectation gap," that is, the difference between what the client expects and what you provide, is narrowed considerably using this method. "The wider the gap, the more tension and friction in a relationship." Not only is everyone happier working with clients they like, but the company is more profitable because the principals are not spending valuable time with troublesome people.

Chris maintains that following this process is really the key to accepting better client relationships as you are consciously evaluating prospects and making concrete decisions about the fit. I have included a couple of Chris's examples so you can get an idea of how this process works.

In the following example, Chris determines that these potential clients will have investable assets available within a short period of time, do not have a strong relationship with anyone else, and have reasonable expectations of Chris and his firm. Additionally, other clients know these prospects, giving Chris a stronger reason to accept them as clients. They are accepted.

CLIENT FIT RATIO: ACCEPT

	POTENTIAL SCORE	TOTAL SCORE
1. Available Investment Resources > $2 million	20	20
Within 6 months	20	
Within 6–12 months	12	
Over 12 months	8	

He is retiring in 3 months and will have $3 million to roll over.

	POTENTIAL SCORE	TOTAL SCORE
2. Desire and Ability to Delegate		
Do they desire to outsource their personal finances?	10	10
Are they busy with other things?	10	9
Are we the sole trusted advisor?	10	7
Are they comfortable paying for advice?	10	8

He does not want to spend time on finances in retirement. He has a stockbroker but not a strong relationship.

(continued on the following page)

	POTENTIAL SCORE	TOTAL SCORE
3. Reasonable Expectations		
Of us and our services	10	9
Of investment markets ability to meet their cashflow needs	10	10

He is an experienced investor and has plenty of cash flow.

	POTENTIAL SCORE	TOTAL SCORE
4. Personality/Chemistry		
At peace with themselves and their life?	10	10
Responsible and responsive to us?	10	9

The prospect and his wife seem happy, organized, etc., and have close family ties with children. They are longtime friend of our good clients, Sally and John Smith, who think they will be easy to work with.

	POTENTIAL SCORE	TOTAL SCORE
TOTAL SCORE	**100**	**92**

TOTAL SCORE	CLIENT FIT
93–100	Excellent
85–92	Good
77–84	Average
70–77	Below Average
Below 70	Unacceptable

PDLLC Partner _____

__X__ Accept

_____ Reject

_____ Refer to _____

In this next example, Chris decides he has a closet "do-it-yourselfer" who does not have a good relationship with his spouse. In fact, they are talking of divorce, and she explains he abuses drugs. The husband has unrealistic expectations about returns and Chris feels uncomfortable with them. They are rejected.

From our experience, if you do not have a formal way to evaluate prospects, you will inevitably wind up with some clients who are inappropriate. This is not profitable, but more importantly, not fun.

CLIENT FIT RATIO: REJECT

	POTENTIAL SCORE	TOTAL SCORE
1. Available Investment Resources > $2 million	20	5
Within 6 months	20	
Within 6-12 months	12	
Over 12 months	8	

They will have $900,000 in the next 12–24 months if he retires then:

	POTENTIAL SCORE	TOTAL SCORE
2. Desire and Ability to Delegate		
Do they desire to outsource their personal finances?	10	2
Are they busy with other things?	10	3
Are we the sole trusted advisor?	10	1
Are they comfortable paying for advice?	10	4

He is an engineer, changes his own oil, and does his own tax return. He did their will from a $25 software package. His favorite show is CNBC Squawk Box. He reads numerous financial magazines and has accounts at 5 brokerage firms and 8 different mutual fund families.

	POTENTIAL SCORE	TOTAL SCORE
3. Reasonable Expectations		
Of us and our services	10	1
Of investment markets ability to meet their cash flow needs	10	3

He is looking for a one-time analysis of his stock options, etc., not an ongoing relationship. He said he expects a 20% return with little downside risk, and wants to take 10% withdrawals from his account each year.

	POTENTIAL SCORE	TOTAL SCORE
4. Personality/Chemistry		
At peace with themselves and their life?	10	1
Responsible and responsive to us?	10	2

(continued on the following page)

	POTENTIAL SCORE	TOTAL SCORE

They yelled at each other in our meeting and are planning to get divorced. He complained about every other adviser they have ever had, suing them for negligence. She said he has a problem with drugs.

TOTAL SCORE   100   22

TOTAL SCORE	CLIENT FIT
93–100	Excellent
85–92	Good
77–84	Average
70–77	Below Average
Below 70	Unacceptable

PDLLC Partner _____

_____ Accept

__X__ Reject

_____ Refer to _____

The First Interview

IN THE EARLY DAYS OF OUR PROFESSION, the first appointment was sales oriented. We would ask about their financial needs then tell the clients what we could do for them. Today, advisers have a more professional approach. The first meeting is now generally what I call the "tape recording session": You ask about them, and they ask about you, all for playback later. I spend more time listening to what the prospect says (or sometimes doesn't say) than anything else.

Preparation

AS I NOTED EARLIER, DAVID BUGEN and his partners at Bugen Stuart Korn & Cordaro send out a preliminary data questionnaire, requesting the client bring it with them or mail it in advance of the first appointment. Many advisers have found this to be a good way to avoid "tire-kickers."

    Lou Stanasolovich has a very good confirmation letter that is sent to prospects after the first appointment is scheduled. Lou also uses this opportunity to ask for documents for the first meeting by including a page with a financial document list. This lets the prospect know that this meeting is more than a "getting to know you" session. The letter and list appear below.

Dear PROSPECT:

Thank you for inquiring about our services. As you requested, I am enclosing some background information on myself and my firm.

You may find of interest the enclosed article reprinted from *Barron's* entitled "Planning Your Financial Future: Meet The Alpha Group, The Nation's Most Powerful Financial Planners." As you will read in the article, I am one of the founding members of the Alpha Group. I have also enclosed my personal biography. You might also wish to know that I was selected by *Worth* magazine as one of the "Best Financial Advisors in America" in their October, 1996; October, 1997; September, 1998 and September, 1999 issues. I have also been chosen by *Medical Economics* magazine as one of "The Best Financial Advisors for Doctors in America" in their July 27, 1998, and November 8, 1999, issues. Furthermore, our investment process has been profiled in *Business Week, Morningstar Investor, USA Today*, and on the Internet publication TheStreet.com.

It should be noted that Legend Financial Advisors, Inc. is a fee-only, Securities and Exchange Commission-registered investment advisory firm. We provide two primary services:

1. Asset management services where we assist you in creating an investment portfolio designed to help you achieve your financial goals. We then manage your investable monies on an ongoing basis and provide regular periodic performance reporting on the portfolio's performance, and;

2. Development of a customized financial plan that will address all major areas of your finances.

We charge fees for both services so that we will provide you with unbiased advice.

As we discussed, I am enclosing directions to our offices as well as a list of documents for you to bring to our first meeting on _____ at a.m./p.m.

Please call me if you have any questions. I look forward to meeting you.

Cordially,

Financial Planner

FINANCIAL DOCUMENT LIST

— Your most recent income tax return

— One month's worth of pay stubs

— A listing of all assets and liabilities

— The amount of money you will save and invest within retirement plans this year

— The amount of money you will save and invest outside of retirement plans this year

— Copies of the latest confirmation and/or monthly statements of any investments you own

— Insurance policies: life, disability, medical, long-term care, homeowners, auto, umbrella liability

— Wills, trusts, powers of attorney, if any

— Employee benefits information

— Your latest retirement plan statements, if applicable

— A listing of all family members, ages, official names, nicknames, grade in school, and health problems, if any

— Be prepared to talk about any obligations you might have with regard to other family members such as parents or grandparents now and in the future

— Include a list of any expected cash windfalls such as inheritances, gifts, business successes, and invention or publishing royalties, etc., if any

— A prioritized list of all financial goals: short-term (next 12 months), intermediate (12 months to 5 years), and long-term (example: retirement, college funding, debt reduction, new home or second home purchase, etc.)

Many advisers I know confirm the first appointment via telephone a day or two before the meeting. This personal contact lets the prospect know that you expect them, respect their time, *and* respect yours, too. Some contact manager software such as ACT or Outlook will allow you to e-mail your clients reminders of upcoming meetings and appointments.

What Brings You Here?

MY PARTNER HAROLD HAS A VERY sophisticated opening: "What brings you here?" This open-ended question is great for getting dialogue going. Ron Tamayo says of their first meetings, "We strongly encourage both spouses to attend. At the beginning of the meeting we ask them if they have any specific questions they would like to ask us right away. We listen a lot and try to find out what their goals are or what motivated them to come see us. We also show them a sample client binder which contains a financial plan, investment policy statement, newsletter, and quarterly report."

Many advisers I know have a sample binder to show the prospects. It gives people a sense of what's to come. In our office we have a selection of various types of reports in the binder so that when the prospect becomes a client, he can select from among the various formats to customize his own reviews. (More about reviews in Chapter 9.)

Follow Up

DAVID NORTON OF NORTON PARTNERS in Bristol, U.K., devised a short questionnaire that he completes with the client during the first meeting (see FORM 4-04 on page 83). He feels this helps him to narrow the client's focus since often they have not clearly defined their objectives prior to their meeting. It definitely helps David get a better picture of the client.

We like to follow up our first appointment with a confirmation letter that recaps what we've discussed and outlines the work that we will do. We refer to the issues that the client has raised and how we will address those issues. I have included a sample letter here.

Dear PROSPECT:

As a follow-up to our meeting on February 12, this letter will outline the services Evensky, Brown & Katz (EBK) would provide to you. We would be honored to be chosen as your investment adviser and look forward to what is, hopefully, the first step in a long relationship together.

As we discussed, we propose to provide certain services and information pertaining to your investment portfolio. We will recommend that your assets be segregated into two pools. The first is those assets which are restricted or to which we will not act as fiduciary. This includes _____ 401(k) and _____ 403(b) portfolio. We are not making a judgment regarding these investments, however, we understand you do not wish to liquidate these assets. We will consult with you on these securities if requested but will not take fiduciary responsibility. The second pool would be the remaining assets of approximately $_____ and shall be referred to as the "managed assets." We would recommend that institutional accounts be established in your name with Fidelity Investments. Our services are independent of Fidelity. We do not receive any commissions or other compensation from any vendor, including Fidelity. Based on our discussion, for the managed assets, we will provide the following services to you:

1. Analyze the current position: The investment management process begins with a thorough understanding of your current situation and future needs. The typical examination will include discussions with you, risk and return statistics for the managed assets, and a discussion of capital market history. We will discuss the requirements of the Uniform Code of Fiduciary Conduct.

2. Design the portfolio: It is generally agreed by theoreticians and practitioners alike that the asset allocation decision is by far the most important decision made by the investor. Based on the information gathered above, EBK will prepare the portfolio's asset allocation. The allocation is very dependent on four factors: risk tolerance, asset class preferences, time horizons of major disbursements, and the expected returns.

3. Develop an Investment Policy Statement (IPS): The most important duty of the fiduciary or trustee is the development and ongoing maintenance of this policy. The IPS provides a paper trail of policies, practices, and procedures for investment decision. The document can be critical evidence used in the defense against litigation or accusations of imprudence. It serves as an excellent example of compliance for auditors. The IPS negates second-guessing or "Monday morning quarterbacking," and ensures continuity of the investment strategy. The IPS reassures corporate and public contributors as well as individual donors affected by the investment performance of investment stewardship. The IPS provides a baseline from which to monitor investment performance of the overall portfolio, as well as the performance of individual money managers. EBK will prepare the IPS in consultation with your other professional advisers, continue to monitor the IPS, and maintain documentation as to investment decisions.

4. Implement Manager Search and Selection: Investment returns and risks are largely determined by asset allocation decisions. This will include decisions regarding active versus passive investment strategies, due diligence, and portfolio structure. EBK will search for, select, and upon approval by the Trustees, hire and monitor investment managers. EBK has access to most investment managers: however, due to the size of the portfolio and minimum requirements of world-class portfolio managers, we would recommend the universe of no-load and institutional mutual funds.

5. Monitor the Portfolio: Once the portfolio has been designed and the investment policy statement prepared and implemented, the final critical step is the ongoing monitoring and supervision of the investment process. We will continue to update you regarding fiduciary requirements, maintain performance attribution, recommend terminating managers when appropriate, measure money manager performance, update the asset allocation, rebalance the portfolio, compute performance calculation, prepare for meetings with you on a quarterly basis, and create performance measurement reports.

The fee for providing these items and conducting quarterly meetings with you shall be based on the total of the managed assets. Our fee shall be XX% (basis points) of the total billable assets (approximately

$_____) payable quarterly in advance and subject to a minimum of $_____ quarterly.

For disclosure purposes, we are, with this letter, providing you with a copy of Part II of our Form ADV that has been filed with the Securities and Exchange Commission. Also attached is a selection of actions required of a fiduciary from Harold Evensky's book, *Wealth Management.*

Thank you for the opportunity to submit our proposal to you for investment management services.

Cordially,

Financial Planner

Remain in Control

HOWEVER YOU QUALIFY CLIENTS and whatever you cover in the first appointment, you'll want to remain in control of the relationship. We've found the dialogue goes better when we direct the questioning with open-ended questions and let the conversation flow. There's an old Sir Arthur Conan Doyle story about Sherlock Holmes who solves the mystery because something expected did not happen: the dog didn't bark. Listen to what your prospects *aren't* saying, too. That may be telling you a great deal about them. If you manage the relationship from the first "touch," you will have more rewarding experiences and so, I believe, will your clients.

EVENSKY, BROWN & KATZ PROSPECT FORM

Person taking call:	Date:
Partner Assigned:	Advisor Assigned:
Name of caller:	

Address:	Telephone home:
	Telephone work:
	Fax #:
	E-mail address:

Communication preference: ___ regular mail ___ telephone ___ e-mail ___ fax

Result of 1st Communication:

    a. Send puff package & Data Gathering Guide - **CIRCLE PAGES TO INCLUDE**

        #1. Client Info Sheet

        #2. Qualitative Survey

        #3. Assets

        #4. Cash Flow

        #5. Professional Advisors

        #6. Client Documents

    b. Who are we referring this prospect to: _____

    c. Follow-up phone call. When:_____ Who: _____

    d. Not compatible/do not need to send information.

Receipt of Data Gathering Questionnaire

    Date received in office: _____

    Does it meet our requirements: Yes _____ No _____

    Date prospect called: _____   By Whom: _____

      a. Set an appt. with:___ HRE ___ DBK ___ PB Time: _____ Date: _____

      b. Other: _____

          _____

Action:	Initials and date of person taking action:
a. Puff sent (including Data-Gathering & Return Envelope)	_____ _____
b. Added to Client Relationship Mgr Database	_____ _____
c. Marked as prospect & Newsletter	_____ _____
d. Thank you card sent to referral for sending prospect	_____ _____
e. Letter/e-mail sent to referral informing them of our referring a prospect	_____ _____
f. Take off of prospect &/or Newsletter List	_____ _____
g. Is any pertinent prospect information in the notes?	_____ _____

          ARE ALL THE BASES COVERED?

How did you hear about us?

What kind of issues made you call us?

What prompted you to make this call?

What kinds of issues do you have?

Are you managing your own portfolio or is someone assisting you?

What are you hoping we can do for you?

2
pages
on CD-ROM

CLIENT INFORMATION SHEET

CLIENT INFORMATION

CLIENT NAME _____   D/O/B _____   S.S.# _____

SPOUSE/PARTNER _____   D/O/B _____   S.S.# _____

Status (circle one):   Married   Single   Not Married/Together   Other

Home Addres _____   Other address _____

City, State, Zip _____   _____

Phone _____   Fax _____   _____

Where would you like your mail sent?   Home   Business   Other

CLIENT

Occupation _____   U.S. Citizen: Y   N

Employer _____

Address _____   Approximate net worth $ _____

City, State, Zip _____   Approximate income $ _____

Phone _____   Fax _____   Email

PARTNER

Occupation _____   U.S. Citizen: Y   N

Employer _____

Address _____   Approximate net worth $ _____

City, State, Zip _____   Approximate income $ _____

Phone _____   Fax _____   Email

DEPENDENT CHILDREN

_____   D/O/B _____   S.S.# _____

_____   D/O/B _____   S.S.# _____

_____   D/O/B _____   S.S.# _____

_____   D/O/B _____   S.S.# _____

Please list any special interests or hobbies:

PRIOR INVESTMENT EXPERIENCE

Indicate H, M, or L   *H = high   M = moderate   L = low*

Listed stocks and bonds _____   Insurance _____   Public limited partnerships _____

Mutual funds _____ _   Annuities _____   Tangible Assets _____ _

Other: (please indicate)

CLIENT SIGNATURE _____   DATE _____

PARTNER SIGNATURE _____   DATE _____

ADVISOR ACKNOWLEDGEMENT _____   DATE _____

© EVENSKY, BROWN & KATZ

POLSTRA & DARDAMAN, LLC
Client Fit Ratio^{sm} **For:** _____

As of: _____

	Potential Score	Total Score
1. Available Investment Resources > $2 million	20	_____

    Within 6 months   20
    Within 6-12 months   12
    Over 12 months   8

2. Desire and Ability to Delegate	Potential Score	Total Score
Do they desire to outsource their personal finances?	10	_____
Are they busy with other things?	10	_____
Are we the sole trusted advisor?	10	_____
Are they comfortable paying for advice?	10	_____

3. Reasonable Expectations	Potential Score	Total Score
Of us and our services	10	_____
Of investment markets ability to meet their cash flow needs	10	_____

4. Personality/Chemistry	Potential Score	Total Score
At peace with themselves and their life?	10	_____
Responsible and responsive to us?	10	_____

TOTAL SCORE   100   _____

Total Score	Client Fit
93-100	Excellent
85-92	Good
77-84	Average
70-77	Below Average
Below 70	Unacceptable

PDLLC Partner_____

_____ Accept

_____ Reject

_____ Refer to_____

SOURCE: CHRIS J. DARDAMAN, JR.
CLIENT FIT RATIO^{SM} IS A TRADEMARK OF POLSTRA & DARDAMAN, LLC

1
page
on CD-ROM

CLIENT OBJECTIVES

A key to successful financial planning is to identify your personal objectives, so that you are better placed to achieve them. Norton Partners have found that clients wish to set many of the following objectives. Which apply in your own case?

INCREASE my net spendable income

IMPROVE my quality of life

SAVE tax (including income tax, capital gains tax and inheritance tax)

INCREASE the return on my investments

SAVE money by using it effectively

INCREASE my expected income in retirement

GAIN peace of mind by feeling financially comfortable

REDUCE paperwork

IMPROVE my insight into present and future values of my pension schemes

INCREASE my financial security

REDUCE time spent worrying about my financial affairs

ACHIEVE financial independence

IMPROVE my business performance

SAFEGUARD my family and dependants

IMPROVE the organization of my financial affairs

INCREASE my financial awareness

REDUCE personal, business and investment risks

INCREASE the net amounts I give to charity

CHAPTER
5

DATA GATHERING

This writing business, pencils and what-not.
Over-rated, if you ask me. Silly stuff. Nothing in it.

—EEYORE

from *Winnie the Pooh*

Data gathering is one of the more critical aspects of planning. You get it wrong and all your work from then on is worthless. I'm beginning to see a resurgence of comprehensive planning software use among senior planners. I think this is because many planners, looking to add value in their relationship with their clients, feel a more formalized approach will enhance the experience. Second, and perhaps more important, there's much better stuff out there than there used to be. Consider Naviplan, www.naviplan.com, developed by EISI, a Canadian company that has built a comprehensive, cash-flow–based program that has attractive reports and good analytics. A fringe benefit of good software is that it provides a printable comprehensive data gathering guide that reduces the chance of missing important information.

More and more companies are producing Web-based comprehensive planning software. PIE Technologies (www.pietech.com), for example, has built a completely interactive planning system that allows you and your client to view the plan simultaneously over the Internet. It also allows the client to create and change scenarios on his own, so that he can discuss it with you later. Earlier I spoke about our client's need to have some control over his financial life—the CEO model, if you will. Some people will turn to planners to create the plan, but they'd like to have the control of creating and tweaking their own scenarios. An interactive system fits this need. More about plans in Chapter 7.

Getting the Data

HOW YOU COLLECT YOUR DATA is a question of style. Do you sit down with the clients and gather the data, or do you give the form to them to complete and bring in to you? When I started out in practice, particularly since I was working with little old ladies, I went to their homes, fished around in their cabinets and drawers to find source material, and completed the data-gathering on my own. These days, I have neither the time nor the inclination to help clients sort through shoeboxes of statements and receipts. I'm now a firm believer in sweat equity. I mentioned in Chapter 4 that we send an abbreviated data guide (FORM 4-02) at the initial contact. When the client sets the appointment we ensure that we have the completed data form at least one week before the meeting. At our first "in person" meeting, we fill in the blanks, double-check the data, and determine what additional information we may need. As I've said, Lou Stanasolovich often sends his full-length questionnaire, along with a list of documents for the clients to bring to the meeting. Lou's cover letter lets them know exactly what will be happening at the meeting and manages their expectations:

> Dear CLIENT:
>
> We are looking forward to seeing you on _____ at ___:___ A.M./P.M. in our office to start the information gathering process. To obtain a complete financial picture, we will ask many questions which may seem inappropriate at first. The purpose is to ascertain whether each type of asset or liability does or does not exist. Many questions seek a response regarding your goals and your atti-

tudes toward various aspects of personal finance:

- **Savings philosophy and investment risk tolerances**
- **Career, lifestyle, hobby, and retirement goals**

No one has all of this information readily at hand, nor have they even considered many of the factors. Please do the best you can with the information form and the gathering of the appropriate documents. Do not worry about any omissions.

Whenever you are not certain an item applies to you, simply place a large question mark in the margin. It will be covered in the meeting. Items which we discuss will all be covered in the written interview notes which you will receive subsequently.

Cordially,

Financial Planner

Data-Gathering Guides and Worksheets

➲ **Plain Vanilla Data Guide.** Spraker, Fitzgerald & Tamayo has a comprehensive data guide that I have included on the CD-ROM in an Excel file (see FORM 5-01 on page 94). I like it because it is so complete. For example, it asks for information regarding insurance for long-term care, major medical expenses, property/casualty, as well as all the usual information about assets and income. A unique and particularly useful part is the "Planner Use Only" (see FORM 5-01 on the CD-ROM). This four-page section of the worksheet allows the planner to make notes about specific tax treatments, such as holding periods for capital gains and marginal tax rates. I like the idea of a guide that clients complete with an additional section for the planner to make notes and observations, including unique assumptions such as returns or inflation factors.

➲ **Data gathering using a tax return.** My friend, Ben Tobias of Tobias Financial Advisors in Plantation, Florida, feels that he can accomplish all the data gathering he needs simply by analyzing the client's individual tax return. He believes that this is an excellent way to gather additional information or just to recheck the data the client provided you in other forms. He also reports that he frequently finds errors in the returns that can benefit the client. Here's Ben's description of how it works:

> I find that the 1040 form is a very useful tool for not only uncovering clients assets and income sources, but also to use as a checklist to determine clients' risk tolerance levels as well as attitudes toward investing.
>
> The 1040 is used in my office as the primary data-gathering document, especially during a prospect meeting. It, of course, is supplemented with a checklist and various other forms, especially the ever-versatile lined yellow pad, but the individual income tax return becomes the focus of the data-gathering component of the financial planning process. It is virtually useless without the taxpayer present. More questions arise when reviewing a return than can be answered by the return itself.
>
> **The Form.** Starting off with prospects or clients, you're given the name, address, and Social Security number of the taxpayers. I will add, next to the Social Security numbers, the birth dates.
>
> **Filing Status and Exemptions.** This area lets us know the family unit, whether or not there are minor children. If there are children, we ask the question of birth dates; we ask where they are in school; we ask what plans are for college, public or private, etc. It is important at this point to ask whether or not there are any other dependents that are not indicated in the return. This may be an elderly parent or a sibling whose situation requires financial outlays.
>
> Depending on the age of the client, we'll ask if there is a chance of increasing family size. We will also ask if there are any children of other marriages. This accomplishes two things. One, we immediately find out if there have been other marriages, which will start a whole new slew of questions, and two, we will be able to determine a client's attitude towards extended family members and his or her feelings of responsibility.
>
> **Line 7: Wages.** This tells us how much taxable income someone

earns from a job. However, that's all it tells us. We would ask for a W2 to find out if there are tax-deferred plans, such as 401(k)s, reducing the income. I also use this time as an opportunity to discuss a person's job. This may also be done while going over a Schedule C.

It is important to note that the order of questions will vary from interview to interview. A lot of what we do here is intentionally redundant, and questions are asked in numerous ways at different times of the process. I warn clients to expect redundant questions. Frequently we find that a client remembers additional information as we are going along.

We try to find out about a person's occupation at this point—whether or not it looks as if they will be staying in their position, whether they will be retiring soon, what their goals or desires are along those lines.

Line 8: Interest. This tells us if a client has taxable interest. We then are able to estimate the size of a bank or bond portfolio and confirm those estimations right there and then with the client. Also with a quick glance at Schedule B we are able to see where the client invests, in what companies the client invests, or which brokerage firm the client uses.

Line 9: Dividends. This tells us essentially the same as the interest number, but it brings up clients' attitudes. We have the opportunity to discuss the difference between stock and bonds, and guaranteed investments versus variable investments. Discussion at this time goes a long way to determine a client's risk tolerance. When we look at Schedule B and we see, for example, a line item that may say the name of a brokerage firm, I will ask for a copy of their brokerage statement to see the individual types of securities that are contained therein.

Line 11: Alimony Received. If we have not discussed previous marriages, at this point, we do.

Line 12: Business Income. Here we again discuss a person's work. At this point, it is not financial planners' real interest to see if income is shown on a Schedule C or on a W2. We are simply data-gathering to find out income sources as well as the individual's thoughts about the current position.

Line 13: Capital Gains. Here we will take a look at Schedule D. If there is a lot of trading on Schedule D, we will ask questions and try to tie that in with information we already found out about a client's portfolio and its size. If we see pages and pages of transactions from E*trade or something along those lines and we're dealing with a day trader, we know it's best to walk away very politely from the engagement. Also, for future tax planning purposes it is very important to peruse Schedule D to determine if there are any Short-Term or Long-Term Capital Loss carryovers.

Lines 15 and 16: IRA, Pension and Annuities. As we know, much of many individuals' worth is not reflected in a current income tax return. Amounts of IRAs, annuities, or pensions that they may be receiving at some time in the future do not appear anywhere on the original tax return. It is very important to remember this and at this point as well as in other points during the process, it is a good idea to ask the questions: Do you have an IRA? If so, where and how much? Do you have annuities? Do you have any type of pension at your place of employment or previous places of employment that may be coming to you?

Line 17: Schedule E. If anything was written in on line 17 relating to gains or losses, we immediately must go to Schedule E to see the origination. At this point, we ask the client what types of other investments they may have made over the years or trusts that they are part of. It is important to know which type of trust they are a part of, for example, and whether or not they are beneficiary on an estate that has yet to distribute dollar one.

Line 18: Farm Income. I use this as another opportunity to talk about real estate in addition to their primary residence. I bring up the question of vacant land and what their current values are.

Line 20: Social Security Benefits. I try to get an idea of what the benefits will be if they have not yet been paid out, but I also will ask about, more important than the Social Security benefits, disability and income protection for those clients who are still working.

Lines 23–31: Adjustments for adjusted gross income. I see what a person's IRA situation is. Again, this is redundant to earlier questions, but it is surprising how many times new IRAs will pop up. I also will ask if they've ever paid penalties on early withdrawals of CDs. Almost everybody has, but they seem to forget about it. I think this is a good way to point out that CDs should not be considered liquid investments.

Page 2 of the tax return serves as a review, as a checklist for other items, and as confirmation of what we have already learned.

I will go over Schedule A in detail and ask questions. For example, in looking at the mortgage interest question, I will ask at that point about their home owners and automobile and personal liability insurance. I will ask if there are other debts that are not recorded. For example, credit cards debts are not recorded on a Schedule A.

We will review the tax preparation fees and see if the clients feel that they are getting their money's worth. When I reviewed Al Gore's return I found that he was paying $4,400 for a return that probably was worth $700 to $900. Pointing out these inflated fees is becoming more important since CPAs are no longer just a referral source but now represent competition. We will also find out about a client's charitable intent, whether through the use of cash, securities, or donated property. I will always have a discussion at this time about charities, to find out if it would be pertinent to bring up philanthropy conversations later concerning estate planning.

I find that about 20 percent of the returns contain errors in presentation or treatment. About half of these errors benefit the client.

We have been using Ben's method in our office to double-check against our own gathered data. It has been a great supplement to the process.

Data Guide for Business Owners

LOU STANASOLOVICH TOLD ME THAT he hasn't found any planning software that effectively handles closely held small-business data. That's why he created his own small business data guide. I like it because it asks questions that often take us many months of dialogue just to get to. I've included it for you at the end of this chapter in its entirety (see FORM 5-02 beginning on page 95); it is on the CD-ROM as FORM 5-02 as well.

Cash Flow Worksheet

OFTEN CLIENTS HAVE NO IDEA of their own spending habits. Many advisers I know provide their clients with Quicken or Microsoft Money. We have also. But, for those clients who are unwilling to do the in-depth preparation, we devised FORM 5-03, a one-page worksheet to help them determine their cash flow needs and to remind them of where they are spending their money (see FORM 5-03 on page 109).

Life Insurance Design Questionnaire

LARRY RYBKA OF VALMARK SECURITIES has a nifty questionnaire for walking your clients through a life insurance analysis and matching them with a generic insurance solution(see FORM 5-04 on page 110). This isn't a capital needs analysis; it's a tool to assist your having meaningful discussions with your client about his insurance requirements. It also helps facilitate discussions about the types of insurance available that fit his needs. Larry provides this assessment tool to all his firm's representatives, but he has graciously agreed to let me include it in this book. It's on the CD as FORM 5-04 so you can print it off as needed. Here's how it works.

The first page is an easy-to-understand chart, describing the various types of life products. This helps you acquaint the client with the different products available, including a price comparison of products at different ages.

The twelve questions presented on pages 2 to 4 are designed to help you get a clear picture of the client's needs and preferences. For example, on page 2 you ask the client how long he wishes to pay premiums and what type of rating he would like the insurance company to have. Page 4 is focused on asset allocation, inflation, and cash value issues.

Question 12 on page 4 helps the client prioritize and rank those issues that are most important to him when selecting insurance.

When you total the score for all of your client's responses, the questionnaire helps you determine what types of insurance would be most appropriate to use. The questionnaire also provides a ranking for the client's answers to determine whether a variable life product is appropriate. If a variable product is used, the information helps determine what asset allocation within the product is most suitable.

As I noted earlier, the best part of this questionnaire is that it provides a good framework for having insurance discussions with your client. My friend Ben Baldwin, planner and insurance expert, maintains that all insurance is term; the rest is just packaging. Larry's Life Insurance Design Questionnaire reinforces that.

Asset Titling Matrix

JERRY NEILL OF NEILL & ASSOCIATES in Kansas City, Missouri, devised this little Excel chart years ago for titling assets (see FORM 5-05 on page 115). He feels this spreadsheet method makes it easy for clients to see how the assets are divided and whether retitling may be necessary for estate planning purposes. It's also helpful in totaling the assets to be sure you didn't miss anything in your general data gathering. I think you'll find it useful.

Vary Your Approach

GOOD DATA GATHERING IS THE ESSENCE of a good plan. Sometimes you need to vary the way you ask the questions to get the best answers. We usually have two advisers in the initial data-gathering meeting. We each hear something different and we each have a different perspective about what we heard. We each write up our notes, then compare them before we actually begin the analysis. Try it yourself.

Spraker, Fitzgerald & Tamayo, LLC
Financial Planning and Wealth Management

Confidential Personal Financial Profile

Date Completed: _____

	Name	Age	Life Expectancy	Date of Birth	Social Security #
Client 1				/ /	- -
Client 2				/ /	- -
Children & Dependents				/ /	- -
				/ /	- -
				/ /	- -
				/ /	- -

Home Address

Email

Home Phone ( ) -
Home Fax # ( ) -

OCCUPATION	Client 1	Client 2
	# of Years	# of Years
Business Name		
Business Address		
Business Phone	( ) -	
Fax Number	( ) -	
Email		
Retirement Age		

Miscellaneous Information:

Marriage Date	/ /		Insurance Agent	
Referral Source			Stockbroker	
# of Years in Current Home			CPA	
Client 1: US Citizen	Yes	No	Attorney	
Client 2: US Citizen	Yes	No	Other Advisor	

CONFIDENTIAL

Data Gathering is the first important step in financial planning process and proper data gathering is required per the Practice Standards of the CFP Board. Unless required by law, information provided in this profile will not be released without client consent.

BUSINESS INFORMATION

Full Legal Name of Business _____

Address _____

Phone Number _____

Fax Number _____

Principal Business Activities _____

Employer Identification Number _____

Form of Business Entity

_____ Sole Proprietorship   _____ Non-Profit Organization

_____ General Partnership   _____ Professional Corporation

_____ Limited Partnership   _____ Limited Liability Company

_____ C Corporation   _____ Other

_____ Subchapter S Corporation

Accounting Basis: Cash _____   Accrual _____

Date Business Began _____

Date of Incorporation _____

State of Incorporation _____

Fiscal Year Ends _____

Related Corporations or Entities (Names, nature of enterprises, relationship of enterprises)

_____

_____

_____

Capitalization

	Number of Common Shares	Voting	Number of Preferred Shares	Voting	Other	Voting
Outstanding	_____	Y N	_____	Y N	_____	_____
Authorized	_____	_____	_____	_____	_____	_____
Dividend Rate	_____	_____	_____	_____	_____	_____

SOURCE: LEGEND FINANCIAL ADVISORS, INC.

18 pages on CD-ROM

DISTRIBUTION OF OWNERSHIP

Name of Owner	Birthdate	Date Employed	Employment Agreement	Position	Salary	Bonus	Currently Active
			Y N		$	$	Y N
			Y N		$	$	Y N
			Y N		$	$	Y N
			Y N		$	$	Y N
			Y N		$	$	Y N

Common

Name of Owner	Number of Shares	Purchase Date	Cost

Preferred

Number of Shares	Purchase Date	Cost

Other

Number of Shares	Purchase Date	Cost

OTHER KEY EMPLOYEES

Name	Birthdate	Date Employed	Employment Agreement	Position	Salary	Bonus
			Y N			
			Y N			
			Y N			
			Y N			
			Y N	Personnel Mgr.		
			Y N	Controller		
			Y N			

18 pages on CD-ROM

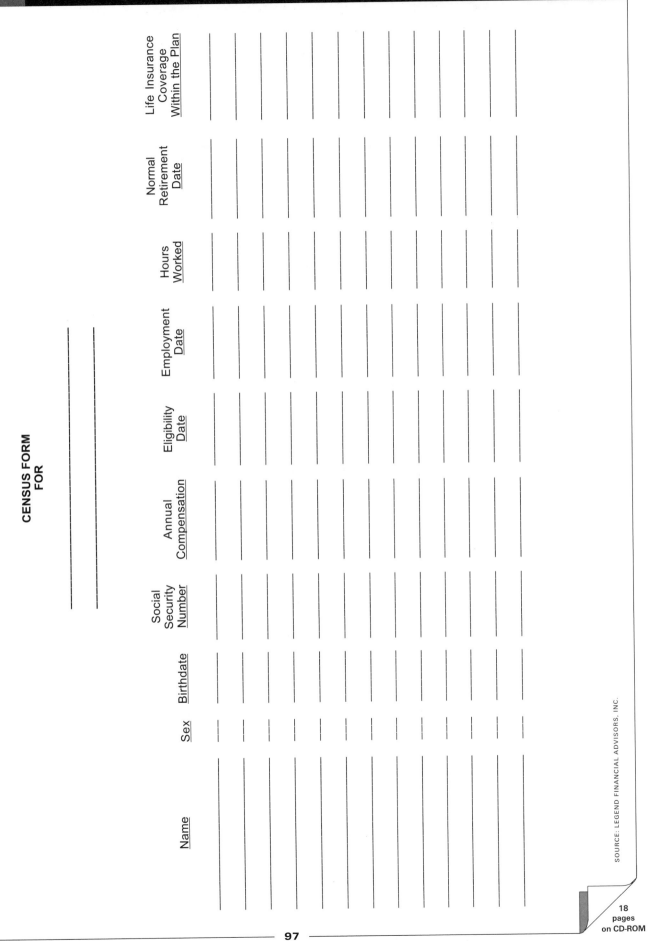

**CENSUS FORM
FOR**

Name Sex Birthdate Social Security Number Annual Compensation Eligibility Date Employment Date Hours Worked Normal Retirement Date Life Insurance Coverage Within the Plan

SOURCE: LEGEND FINANCIAL ADVISORS, INC.

18 pages on CD-ROM

LOANS
(Complete one page for each loan. Do not include credit cards.)

Asset Description (If applicable) _____

Borrower(s) (Is loan personally guaranteed by anyone? If so, whom?) _____

Type of Loan (Plant & Equipment, Lines of Credit, etc.) _____

Balance Outstanding $_____

Last Annual Reset Balance Date _____

(Variable Rate Only)

Original Amount Borrowed $_____

Minimum Payment
(If mortgage, exclude taxes and insurance) $_____

Actual Payment $_____

Frequency of Payment _____

Date of 1st Payment _____

Issue Date _____

Maturity Date _____

Current Interest Rate _____

Institution (Bank, S&L, etc.) _____

Address _____

_____

_____

Phone _____

Loan Account No. _____

Comments _____

_____

_____

_____

18
pages
on CD-ROM

FUTURE BUSINESS PLANS

Where is the business going?

_____

_____

Are there any plans to go public?

_____

_____

If so, when? _____

Are there any material acquisitions or dispositions anticipated in the next few years?

_____

_____

Are there any new product lines or services, which will be provided and will change your profit structure?

_____

_____

Will there be any material capital requirements in the next few years?

_____

_____

Have you formally put together a business plan?

_____

If so, for how long of a period? _____

What is your anticipated rate of growth in sales profits?

_____

_____

What are the most important factors in making your business successful?

_____

_____

_____

How many additional employees do you anticipate adding and in what areas of the business?

_____

_____

_____

Are any of your employees unionized? Give details.

_____

_____

18
pages
on CD-ROM

FUTURE BUSINESS (cont.)

Is there any current attempt by your employees to become unionized? Give details.

_____

_____

What has been the company's policy concerning salary increases, bonuses and employee fringe benefits?

_____

_____

What has been your rate of employee turnover?

_____

_____

Do you presently have an accumulated earnings tax problem? (C Corporations Only)

_____

Do you have any loss carryforwards available?

_____

_____

Is any property owned by the shareholders being leased to the business?

_____

_____

_____

Have any reorganization plans been implemented or are about to be implemented because
of the planned retirement, death, disability, divorce, bankruptcy, or estate tax problems of one of the
owners?

_____

_____

BUSINESS CONTINUATION

Do you want your business interest retained or sold if you:

Owner	Insurable	Retire?	Become Disabled?	Die?	Other?
_____	_____	_____	_____	_____	_____
_____	_____	_____	_____	_____	_____
_____	_____	_____	_____	_____	_____
_____	_____	_____	_____	_____	_____
_____	_____	_____	_____	_____	_____

If the business interest is retained, who will end up with each owner's interest and how will they acquire it? Also, who will replace you in your job?

Owner	New Owner of Interest	Method of Acquisition	Replacement
_____	_____	_____	_____
_____	_____	_____	_____
_____	_____	_____	_____
_____	_____	_____	_____
_____	_____	_____	_____

If sold, list the purchaser, purchase price and funding arrangement.

Owner	Purchaser	Price	Funding Arrangement
_____	_____	_____	_____
_____	_____	_____	_____
_____	_____	_____	_____
_____	_____	_____	_____

18
pages
on CD-ROM

BUSINESS CONTINUATION (cont.)

Is there Key person insurance on all key owners and employees?

_____

_____

Estimate the lowest price for which the entire business might be sold as a going concern today.

_____

What would you sell your interest for?

_____

Does a buy-sell agreement exist?

_____

If a buy-sell agreement does not exist, how do you intend to dispose of your interest?

_____

_____

Type of agreement: (Circle One).. Cross Purchase

.... Stock Redemption/Entity Purchase

.... Combination

Method for determining value: (Circle One)   Book Value $_____

Earnings Multiple $_____

Appraisal $_____

Agreed Value $_____

Other $_____

How is the agreement funded and for what amount?

_____

_____

Will the business have to be liquidated upon your death?

_____

_____

Have you purchased disability overhead insurance?

_____

_____

_____

18
pages
on CD-ROM

EMPLOYEE BENEFITS

Department Head: _____ Phone: _____

Does your company provide any of the following?

Benefit	Employees Covered	Details
Group Term Insurance	_____	_____
Split Dollar Insurance	_____	_____
Accident Insurance	_____	_____
Medical Insurance	_____	_____
Medical Reimbursement	_____	_____
Dental Care	_____	_____
Vision Care	_____	_____
Sick Pay Plan	_____	_____
Long-Term Disability Insurance	_____	_____
Company Car or Van	_____	_____
Club Memberships	_____	_____
Educational Reimbursement Plan	_____	_____
Group Legal Service Plan	_____	_____
Financial Planning Services	_____	_____
Child or Dependent Care Assistance	_____	_____
Other:	_____	_____
_____	_____	_____
_____	_____	_____
_____	_____	_____

Have you established a Cafeteria Benefits Plan?

_____

_____

SOURCE: LEGEND FINANCIAL ADVISORS, INC.

18
pages
on CD-ROM

RETIREMENT PLANS

Benefit	Employees Covered	Details
Pension Plan	_____	_____
Profit-Sharing Plan	_____	_____
SEP	_____	_____
SAPSEP	_____	_____
401(k) Plan	_____	_____
401(a) Savings Plan	_____	_____
Employee Stock Ownership Plan (ESOP)	_____	_____
Non-Qualified Deferred Compensation Plan	_____	_____
Incentive Stock Options	_____	_____
Non-Qualified Stock Options	_____	_____
Stock Appreciation Rights	_____	_____
Performance Units	_____	_____
Employee Stock Purchase Plan	_____	_____
Stock Bonus Plan	_____	_____
Restricted Stock Plan	_____	_____
Phantom Stock Plan	_____	_____
Formula Price Shares	_____	_____
Salary Continuation After Death	_____	_____

18 pages on CD-ROM

ADVISOR QUESTIONNAIRE

	Name	Firm & Address	Phone/Fax Number

ACCOUNTANT

**RETIREMENT PLAN
ADMINISTRATOR/ACTUARY**
(if you own a business)

ATTORNEY

BANKER -
(loans)

INSURANCE AGENT -
(Life & Disability)

INSURANCE AGENT -
(Property & Casualty)

18
pages
on CD-ROM

ADVISOR QUESTIONNAIRE (cont.)

EMPLOYEE BENEFITS -

_____   _____   _____
_____   _____   _____
                       _____   _____
                       _____   _____
                       _____

OTHER

_____   _____   _____
_____   _____   _____
                       _____   _____
                       _____   _____
                       _____

OTHER

_____   _____   _____
_____   _____   _____
                       _____   _____
                       _____   _____
                       _____   _____

18
pages
on CD-ROM

BOARD OF DIRECTORS

What are your annual directors' fees per director? $_____

Name	Address	Phone Number

CHECKLIST OF DATA/DOCUMENTS

Tax and Financial Information (3 years)

_____ Tax Returns for all Affiliates
_____ Financial Statements
_____ Copy of Your Latest Business Plan
_____ Loan Agreements
_____ Lease Agreements
_____ Corporate Minutes and Communications
_____ Investment Confirmations for All Corporate Investments

Retirement and Compensation Plan Documents

_____ Qualified Plan Documents
_____ Non-Qualified Deferred Compensation Agreements
_____ Employment Agreements
_____ 5500 Federal Tax Forms (3 years)
_____ Personal Services Contracts
_____ Investment Confirmations for Qualified and Non-Qualified Plans

Employee Benefits

_____ Medical Plan Information
_____ Disability Plan Information
_____ Life Insurance Plan Information
_____ Split Dollar Insurance Policies
_____ Latest Billing Statements for All Employee Benefits
_____ Copies of All Employee Benefit Books and Brochures

Ownership Transfer Information and Insurance Policies

_____ Listing of All Owners and the Percentage of Ownership
_____ Copies of All Buy-Sell Agreements
_____ Information on Funding Arrangements and All Insurance Policies
_____ Disability Overhead Insurance Policies
_____ Key Person Life Insurance Policies
_____ Property and Casualty Insurance Policies

SOURCE: LEGEND FINANCIAL ADVISORS, INC.

18
pages
on CD-ROM

CASH FLOW WORK SHEET

Monthly Income

	Current	Retirement
Wages, salary, tips		
Cash dividends		
Interest received		
Social Security income		
Pension income		
Rents, royalties		
Other income		
Total Monthly Income	**$0.00**	**$0.00**

Fixed Monthly Expenses

	Current	Retirement
Mortgage payment or rent		
2nd home mortgage		
Automobile note		
Personal loans		
Credit cards		
Life insurance		
Disability insurance		
Medical insurance		
Long-term care insurance		
Homeowner's insurance		
Automobile insurance		
Umbrella liability insurance		
Federal income taxes		
State income taxes		
FICA		
Real estate taxes		
Other taxes		
Savings (regularly)		
Investments (regularly)		
Retirement Plan Contributions		
Total Fixed Expenses	**$0.00**	**$0.00**

Variable Monthly Expenses

	Current	Retirement
Electricity		
Gas		
Telephone		
Water		
Cable TV		
Home repairs and maintenance		
Home improvements		
Food		
Clothing		
Laundry		
Child care		
Personal care		
Automobile gas & oil		
Automobile repairs, etc.		
Other transportation		
Education expenses		
Entertainment/dining		
Recreation/travel		
Club/association dues		
Hobbies		
Gifts / Donations		
Unreimbursed medical, and dental expenses		
Miscellaneous		
Total Variable Expenses	**$0.00**	**$0.00**

Net Cash Flow

	Current	Retirement
Total monthly income	$0.00	$0.00
Total fixed expenses	$0.00	$0.00
Total variable expenses	$0.00	$0.00
Discretionary Income (Income - Expenses)	**$0.00**	**$0.00**

The Life Insurance Design Questionnaire

The Life Insurance Family Trees

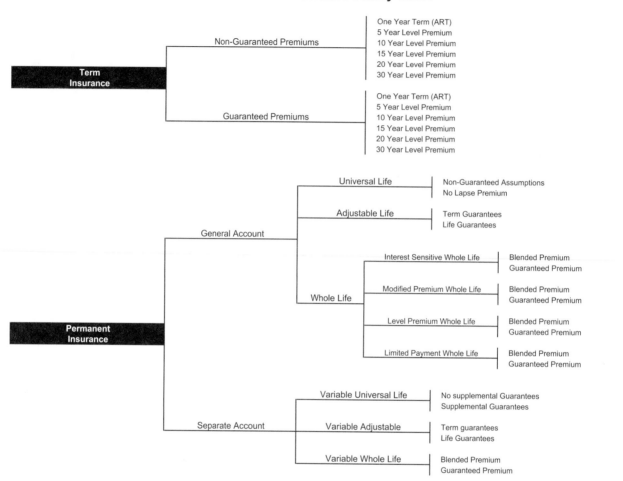

Life Insurance Premium Comparison

How Much Does One Million Dollars of Life Insurance Cost?*								
MALE - AGE	**35**	**40**	**45**	**50**	**55**	**60**	**65**	**70**
Term	$300	$330	$440	$680	$1,070	$1,820	$2,630	$3,740
Minimum Premium UL	$2,440	$3,049	$4,878	$5,727	$8,282	$10,291	$15,589	$19,316
Guaranteed Premium UL	$5,161	$7,129	$9,377	$12,551	$15,842	$20,279	$25,520	$34,254
Traditional Whole Life	$11,110	$14,070	$17,910	$22,960	$29,620	$38,420	$50,000	$65,130
Single Premium Life	$97,914	$132,425	$169,812	$217,665	$259,566	$309,397	$359,817	$428,038

*As of 4/19/99, based on preferred non-smoker rates where available. Term products are represented by Lincoln Life and First Colony Life. Insurance Company.

Minimum premium UL is represented by Jefferson Pilot Life and Lincoln Life. Guaranteed premium UL is represented by Lincoln Life. Traditional Whole Life

represented by Metropolitan Life. Single Premium Life represented by Lincoln Life.

Securities offered through ValMark Securities, Member NASD, SIPC
3690 Orange Place, Suite 310 Beachwood, Ohio 44122 216-765-1999

6
pages
on CD-ROM

The Life Insurance Design Questionnaire

Design Considerations

Client Name(s): _____

Date(s) of Birth: _____ Sex: _____ Nicotine Use? (Y/N): _____

Type of Death Benefit
        Individual: _____
        Survivorship: _____   Amount of Death Benefit: _____

Purpose (check each that applies)
    ☐ Death Benefit   ☐ Living Benefits / Cash Flow

Briefly describe the purpose of this life insurance: _____

---

1 **How Long Will You Require The Death Benefit?**

Today — Life Expectancy — Age 100 — Beyond 100

Years _____

2 **How Many Years Do You Wish to Pay Premiums?**

1 Year — 5 Years — 10 Years — 20 Years — Life Expectancy — All Years

Years _____

3 **Company Quality: What Percentile Ranking* Would You Prefer?**

Top 5 percent _____
Top 10 percent _____
Top 20 percent _____
Top 50 percent _____
All Companies _____

4 **Other Client Specifications**

■ Premium Flexibility? _____

■ Increasing Death Benefit Need? _____

■ Other? _____

*Based on the Comdex rating system produced in Vital Signs by LifeLink corporation.

Securities offered through ValMark Securities, Member NASD, SIPC
3690 Orange Place, Suite 310 Beachwood, Ohio 44122 216-765-1999

6
pages
on CD-ROM

The Life Insurance Design Questionnaire

Allocation of Cash Values

Enter Score

5 — Indicate the pattern that best matches your desires with regard to the returns on your policy values.

Year	Pattern 1	Pattern 2	Pattern 3
1	2.0%	6.7%	6.5%
2	74.5%	2.2%	6.3%
3	-9.5%	31.1%	5.8%
4	1.7%	-4.2%	5.0%
5	59.5%	4.2%	4.3%
6	-13.5%	21.2%	4.5%
7	-22.7%	-10.8%	4.5%
8	52.2%	2.7%	5.0%
9	37.1%	15.5%	4.5%
10	-0.2%	33.1%	4.8%
Average:	13.78%	9.32%	5.10%

Points:	11	5	1

_____

6 — I'm willing to accept large variations in in annual returns as I seek higher long term returns

Strongly Agree	Agree	Disagree	Strongly Disagree
11	7	4	1

_____

7 — I'm willing to accept a substantial short-term decline in my cash value if that's what is required to obtain potentially higher long-term returns

Strongly Agree	Agree	Disagree	Strongly Disagree
11	9	4	1

_____

Total for Questions 4 - 6: _____

8 — How would you rate your knowledge of investments and money management?

Very High	High	Medium	Low
10	7	5	1

_____

9 — What has been your primary investment / savings focus?

Tangible Assets	Equities	Fixed Income	Bank CD's Money Markets
10	7	4	2

_____

10 — What is your level of concern about inflation?

Very High	High	Medium	Low
10	7	5	2

_____

11 — How long before you need access to the cash values of this policy?

More than 25 years	16 to 25 years	6 to 15 years	Less than 6 years
11	9	2	0

_____

Overall Total Score: _____

Securities offered through ValMark Securities, Member NASD, SIPC
3690 Orange Place, Suite 310 Beachwood, Ohio 44122 216-765-1999

SOURCE: VALMARK SECURITIES, INC.

6 pages on CD-ROM

Priorities

12 Life insurance policies involve trade-offs between performance, guarantees and the low initial premiums. In some cases, it is possible to get two of these together, but no policy can offer all three simultaneously.

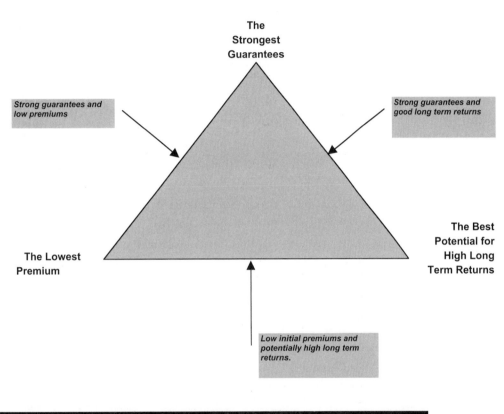

The
Strongest
Guarantees

Strong guarantees and low premiums

Strong guarantees and good long term returns

The Lowest
Premium

The Best
Potential for
High Long
Term Returns

Low initial premiums and potentially high long term returns.

Prioritize these objectives in order of their importance to you:

Rank

I want the best potential returns in the long term

I want the strongest possible guarantees

I want to pay the lowest possible premium

The Life Insurance Design Questionnaire

Recommended Cash Value Allocation

Your Score*	Portfolio	Description
21 or Under	Conservative*	Lowest Risk / Lowest Return
22 - 34	Moderately Conservative	
35 - 48	Moderate	
49 - 61	Moderately Aggressive	
62 or Over	Aggressive	Highest Risk / Highest Return

These allocations only apply to variable life insurance policies. If your goals and preferences indicate that a non-variable product is more suitable for you, the table above does not apply to you.

*Note: If your total score for questions 4 - 6 is less than 13, you should focus on general account life insurance rather than variable life.

Verification

The answers to this questionnaire correctly reflect my beliefs, preferences and goals with respect to the life insurance under consideration. I have discussed these responses with my agent.

I understand that all illustrations contain both guaranteed and non-guaranteed pricing assumptions. I further understand that sales illustrations are an estimate of actual product performance. The above data will be used to help me evaluate ledgers and select an appropriate product type and design. The actual performance and ultimate cost of cash value policies will vary to the extent that they are based upon non-guaranteed elements.

Signature(s): _____   Date:_____

_____   Date:_____

Securities offered through ValMark Securities, Member NASD, SIPC
3690 Orange Place, Suite 310 Beachwood, Ohio 44122 216-765-1999

ASSET TITLING MATRIX

CLIENT:

SPOUSE :

Date: _____

	CLIENT TRUST	SPOUSE TRUST	IRREVOC. TRUST	CLIENT PERS.	SPOUSE PERS.	JOINT	TOTAL
CASH/CASH EQUIVALENTS							
Personal Checking							0
	0	0	0	0	0	0	0
SECURITIES							
Fidelity Investments							0
	0	0	0	0	0	0	0
RESIDENCE & OTHER ASSETS							
Residence (net of debt)							0
Florida Home							
Personal Property							0
	0	0	0	0	0	0	0
RETIREMENT PLANS							
IRA - Fidelity							0
IRA - SEI							0
							0
	0	0	0	0	0	0	0
LIFE INSURANCE							
							0
	0	0	0	0	0	0	0
TOTALS WITHOUT INSURANCE	0	0	0	0	0	0	0
TOTALS	0	0	0	0	0	0	0

FIGURE 'EM OUT

MY FIRST FINANCIAL PLAN was 103 pages. You can't even imagine how many data guide pages you must fill out to put that much stuff in a package for a client. In those days we didn't ask the client to fill in anything—we sat pen in hand, writing interminable notes about the client's financial life and circumstances. Then we had to transcribe all that data into planning software to produce a plan. Somewhere in between those activities, we needed to educate the client to what we were doing. Truthfully, educating the client often boiled down to hoping they'd read your tome once it was finished. My first

Section

client never read the plan, but assured me she would have her plan bronzed for the living room coffee table.

Today we have some choices in the way we gather data from the clients, in the way we educate them, and in the way we produce our plans. We've covered some ideas for data gathering in Section 2. Now we'll see how to use that data. In particular, Chapter 6 deals with client education. I've collected some unique tools that may assist in getting your client on the same page with you. Finally, in Chapter 7 I've included some sample plans and policies you can adapt to deliver advice to your clients in a new way.

CLIENT EDUCATION

*Few things are harder to put up with than
the annoyance of a good example.*

— MARK TWAIN

[Samuel Langhorne Clemens] (1835–1910)

Educating your client from the first day he walks in your office ensures a better relationship and helps manage his expectations. A 1999 Gallup poll[1] shows that investors today expect a more than 20 percent return each year for the next ten years. Right, we can do that.

To compound the problem, today your client can get extensive investment research on the Net. Without your guidance, this abundance of information will only create more confusion for your client and higher expectations for your performance. As I've said, information is not knowledge, judgment, or empathy. If you are to have a successful long-term relationship, good client education is the key. The client who trusts you and with whom you have a good relationship will rely on you to provide the knowledge, judgment, and empathy.

Risk Coaching Questionnaire

I BELIEVE THAT THE MOST IMPORTANT client education experience in our office is our risk-coaching process, built around our risk questionnaire.

This process helps both us and the clients determine the more elusive of the two critical factors necessary to design an investment policy: their ability to withstand the reality of market volatility. (The other factor is the required return, and for this we use a traditional capital needs analysis.) After completing the capital needs analysis and the risk-tolerance questionnaire and comparing the results, if we're lucky, the conclusion is that our client can achieve his goals without taking a risk in excess of his comfort level. Unfortunately, it doesn't always work out that well. We've all had the experience of having to counsel clients who either need to reduce their expectations or accept more risk then they might like. By using our process, we help our clients understand these issues so they can decide whether they can live with the increased risk or must modify the goals. My partner Harold distills this to a simple question: "Do you want to sleep less well or eat less well?"

We have elected to use a formalized risk questionnaire to ensure that we cover all the aspects of risk that we think are important. For that reason, we call this document our Risk Coaching Questionnaire (see FORM 6-01 on pages 152–161). We also use it to help quantify the risk decisions and allow the client to participate in this critical element of the asset allocation design.

The questionnaire consists of twenty-two questions. It is designed to facilitate dialogue between the adviser and the client. Therefore, it is necessary to complete it together. Because this is such important stuff, I'll take some time and explain in detail our standard dialogue, what we expect to learn, and what we expect our client to learn from the exercise. The entire document is available on the CD. This questionnaire is completed during the second or third meeting we have with the client.

○ **Question 1.** Because it's critical that both you and the client have the same "investments" in mind as you go through the questionnaire, the first question begins the process by asking for a dollar amount of the investment portfolio. We explain that this is the total value of the assets for which we will be developing an investment policy. As we're financial planners, we also must understand how the investment portfolio fits within the framework of the total investment universe, hence the second part of Question 1. If the answer is significantly less than 100 percent, we tell our client that although we may not be handling all his assets, it is necessary for us to know where everything is and how these assets work together for his objectives, so we'll need to get additional details on his other investments.

⮑ **Question 2.** This question gives us an indication of how much the client understands about asset classes. It also helps him to look at his personal and retirement assets as one portfolio. Professor Richard Thaler, behavioral finance professor at the University of Chicago and a partner in the firm Fuller & Thaler Asset Management, has completed extensive studies on what he refers to as "separate pockets." Thaler maintains that clients often think of different portfolios as independent of each other. For example, although as planners we know it's important to plan holistically, our clients often tend to treat their IRAs as independent from their personal investments. Thaler demonstrates this thinking with a two-part story-question.

You buy a ticket for a concert. The ticket costs $100. On the way to the concert, you lose the ticket. Do you buy another one? (The client usually says, "Probably not, I'd be out $100 bucks.")

You buy a ticket for a concert. On the way to the concert, you lose $100 bucks. You could sell the ticket easily for $100 bucks at the door. Do you still go to the concert? (Clients always say, "Yes, I already have the ticket.")

According to Thaler, our clients don't equate the loss of the $100 and the loss of a $100 ticket because they tend to see the money and the tickets as separate "pockets." Using Thaler's story-question, you can help your client recognize that there's really only one-pocket—his.

⮑ **Question 3.** Many people don't realize how capricious their past investing has been. By asking clients to think back over past investing history, we frequently help them realize that they have made changes in their portfolios far more frequently than they realized.

⮑ **Question 4.** This next question is an extension of the last one and gets to the heart of your client's investment rationale. By offering your client a number of choices to explain portfolio allocation changes, you can uncover important elements of his investment philosophy and history. The responses also provide additional opportunities for discussion:

I learned more about investments. It is our experience that many novice investors begin slowly and then work up to greater equity positions. This is a good opportunity to delve into how much they do know.

I had a lifestyle change or I met a major financial goal (e.g., paying for a wedding). It is appropriate to revisit allocations at major milestones and discuss the changes and the thinking behind the changes.

I was attempting to achieve superior returns through market timing. Make 'em face it. This is a good time to ask how it went. Most timers do not have a grasp of the costs of trading or the impact of timing on their returns. Many have not tracked returns.

I did not have enough funds to invest in certain asset classes. This is where we discuss the strategy of using index funds. We talk about different asset classes and how they affect volatility and return.

I did not pursue an asset-allocation policy. Everyone has an allocation, whether it is designed analytically or just by whim. If you have not read Roger Gibson's books[2] on asset allocation, I strongly urge you to do it. His latest book, *Asset Allocation* (McGraw-Hill, 2000), has an exercise that demonstrates the power of diversification. It is an effective tool that we often use with our clients.

Other. (I have never actually had anyone check this box until recently.) One of my newest clients checked "other" then wrote beside it: "Fear." We had a good discussion about achieving an allocation that will allow her to sleep at night.

➲ **Question 5.** With this question, we get an opportunity to discuss the fallacy of the income portfolio. We don't believe in designing portfolios to spin off income. A popular but flawed strategy for retirees is to place assets in higher yielding stocks, such as utilities and/or in bonds (often munis). The need to build the portfolio around these assets limits the growth potential of the portfolio. We discuss with our clients the concept of total return and explain that we will design their investment portfolio for total (tax efficient) return. We then explain that we'll handle their cash flow needs by carving out of the investment funds up to twenty-four months of their cash flow requirements and placing that amount in a "reserve" cash account. I then go back and adjust the amount entered in Question 1 to reflect this carve-out. The balance of the portfolio is invested according to the asset allocation needed to maintain their long-term lifestyle. As we rebalance the portfolio, we replenish the reserve account as necessary.[3]

⮌ **Question 6.** I believe that an investment portfolio should have at least a five-year horizon. Therefore, it's important to know the client's lump sum needs in the near term. For example, if the client intends to withdraw $25,000 in two years for his daughter's wedding, it would be inappropriate to invest this sum in long-term investments. I would tell my client, "Let's carve out the $25,000 and decide how to invest it later. I want you to be comfortable that you're not likely to need any of the funds from your investment portfolio for at least the next five years." I would then go back and again adjust the amount entered in Question 1.

Admittedly there's nothing magic about five years. As with this entire questionnaire, it's simply a suggestion based on our experience. Customize it to your taste. For example, if you like three years better, simply adjust the questionnaire to meet your criteria.

⮌ **Question 7.** This question allows the adviser to discuss the impact of taxes on a portfolio, as well as reinforce the distinction between assets subject to taxes and assets that are not.

⮌ **Question 8.** If this seems to be asking the same thing as Question 5, you're right. In this case, redundancy is good. It's important to reinforce the time horizon of the investment portfolio, so we ask the same question in a little different way. It also helps our client realize that in reality the investment horizon is REALLY long. Here's how we use it:

Suppose my client says "Three years." My response is "Oh goodness, I'm sorry, I must have missed something earlier when we chatted about Question 6. I thought we'd pulled out of the portfolio everything you needed in the next five years." Usually the client admits that they really don't need anything in three years, they're just not used to acknowledging that fact.

If they say "five years," I ask, "What happens then?" Typically the answer is "I don't know, it just seemed like a long time." Our goal is to emphasize that in most cases the portfolio better last for the balance of their life or they'll get pretty hungry near the end.

⊃ **Question 9.** My partner Harold tells of the time that he designed an investment plan for a new client. He carefully asked questions about risk, completed a capital needs analysis, and after many days of hard work handed the client a beautifully prepared (colored charts—the works) asset-allocation recommendation. The client looked at the long-term return expectations, jumped up from the table, slammed the plan on the desk and hollered, "Ten percent! My barber can do better than that!" From then on, we've always asked in advance if the client has something in mind regarding return expectations. We also use this question as an opportunity to explain the impact of inflation on investments over time and discuss the concept of real rate of return versus nominal rate. Note that this is an optional question. By that, we mean we don't want to force the client into providing an answer unless he really has an opinion.

⊃ **Question 10.** This question requires some explanation, so I will run through it as though I am speaking with a client.

This table has a list of six phrases, each describing a common investment attribute. If the attribute or goal is extremely important to you, circle the number 6 next to it. If it is not important at all, circle 1. Circle any of the numbers in between to describe its level of importance to you. It's not necessary to prioritize these attributes. In fact, you may use any number in as many of the six categories as you wish, as long as it reflects how important or unimportant it is to you.

— *Capital Preservation.* Suppose you have $100,000 to invest today. How important is it to you that five years from now your investment will be worth at least $100,000? If your response is "extremely important," circle 6. Or would you think, "I don't care. After all, I'm investing with a twenty-year time horizon. As long as it's worth a lot more in twenty years, I don't care what it will be worth five years from now." In that case, circle a lower number.

— *Growth.* How important is it to you that five years from now your investment has some "growth?" If your response is, "That's extremely important. After all, that's why I am investing," circle 6. If instead you think, "I don't much care about growth. I just want to be sure that my original principal is preserved," circle 1. If you think that some growth would be desirable, circle 3, 4, or 5.

— *Low Volatility.* Volatility describes the reality that investment values may change daily, even from minute to minute. Ask, "Would you lose sleep if your portfolio declined in value from week to week, even if the portfolio later recovered from those short-term losses?" If the answer is yes, circle 6. If you know you would not pay attention to your portfolio in the short term, but would have confidence it would recover over time, circle 1. If you are like most investors and think you don't much like volatility, but are prepared to live with some in order to get better returns, circle a number in between.

— *Inflation Protection.* Again, suppose you have $100,000 to invest. How would you feel if, five years later, your investment had grown in value but, because of high inflation, your money now bought less than five years earlier? Choose 6 if you believe it is vitally important to avoid this, a lower number if inflation protection is less important.

— *Current Cash Flow.* Some people, particularly retired people, must take money from their investment portfolios in order to supplement their Social Security, pension, and other noninvestment income. Most working investors have enough income from sources such as wages to allow all of their investment returns to be reinvested in the portfolio for greater long-term growth. How about you? What percentage of your investment portfolio must you withdraw every year in order to maintain your current lifestyle? Divide that number by two. Use the answer to determine which number, 1 to 6, to select. For example, if you need 12 percent of the portfolio's value per year, circle 6. If you need only 2 percent less per year, circle 1.

— *Aggressive Growth.* I'm not talking about high growth, but rather aggressive strategies, such as options, short sales, and margin. Are you completely comfortable with such strategies? If so, circle 6.

If the very idea makes you break into a cold sweat, circle 1.

It's important to discuss each answer with the client. For example, in our experience we've seen clients often answer 6 to both capital preservation and growth. We never lose the opportunity to point out that although they have strong concerns about each of these, it is impossible to achieve both equally in a single portfolio.

We always ask married couples to answer separately because, according to our experience, they seldom have the same risk tolerance. This makes for a useful discussion when they disagree significantly. It is also important that by the time we finish we have either reached some consensus or we elect to design the portfolio initially around the individual with the lower risk tolerance.

Once the questionnaire has been completed, you can put the answers in the Excel risk algorithm (see Form 6-02 on the CD-ROM and on page 162). It's based on our experience with hundreds of clients and is designed to weight the combination of answers in such a way as to ultimately reach a single number from zero to one hundred. For each phrase or goal, insert the number that your client circled in Question 10. For example, if a client circled 3 for capital preservation, type a 3 in the capital preservation row beneath the 3 column. The score, or risk level, will compute automatically.

A score of zero would suggest 100 percent allocation to bonds and a score of one hundred suggests 100 percent to equities. Normally scores range from fifty to eighty, suggesting portfolios of 50 percent to 80 percent equities. This is not the final allocation; it is simply a guide. We compare this number to the other answers we receive to be sure that our findings are consistent.

⊃ **Question 11.** This is another optional question. If the client has no strong feelings we leave it blank. However, this question does provide us an opportunity to discuss different asset classes and whether or not the client has preconceived notions about them. It also allows us to "negotiate" with the client. For example, often clients will express concerns about small company and foreign stocks. It's often possible to get our client to agree to inclusion of these investments if we agree to place constraints on the size of the allocation to these asset classes. Most important, even if our client suggests no constraints, we can be assured that our client understands these investments and how they operate within a portfolio.

➲ **Questions 12 and 13.** Yep, you're right again. These are redundant, too. We just want to reinforce the importance of time horizon when designing a portfolio. We expect the answer to Question 12 to be 0 percent and to Question 13 to be 100 percent. If we get anything else, it's time for more discussion and education.

➲ **Question 14.** This has four scenarios. They must be ranked according to our client's level of concern. I usually ask our client to read through them first, then select the one that worries them the most. Since we have had the first thirteen questions to make our point, the answer we look for is, "I would be very concerned with long-term volatility ..." If this isn't the answer, we talk further. While it's possible that someone might be more concerned with a real return or even their targeted return, our experience is that, after discussing the issues, every client has ultimately acknowledged that long-term volatility is their number one worry. We then ask the client to choose the statement that worries them least. We expect them to answer, "I would be very concerned with short-term volatility...." If we get any other response, we again go into discussion mode. Even an all-bond portfolio has a reasonable probability of short-term volatility, and unless a client is willing to accept this fact, we can't be of much help.

➲ **Question 15.** Admittedly this one is a bit complicated. Sometimes it requires reading more than once. The goal of this question is to frame our client's response by providing him with historical market reality. As you can see from the boxed response at the bottom of the question, we're pretty obvious about what answers we don't expect. As with Question 14, we're looking to make clear that markets are volatile—all markets. And, unless our client is prepared to "sleep less well," they may have to "eat less well."

➲ **Question 16.** This one is almost a tongue twister. It may also require a few readings. We expect our clients to pick the second alternative. Everyone wants to pick choice number three (not included):

"I want to be in the market when it goes up and out of the market when it goes down." By not including a third choice, this question makes clear to our clients that we do not believe in market timing. If you do, you may want to delete Question 16.

⮑ **Question 17.** This question helps us understand a client's implicit time horizon and gives us an opportunity for further discussion and education. For example, if the client indicates that he looks at his portfolio more frequently than quarterly, we would want to know why. The second part of this question addresses volatility and time horizon. We discuss how the client would react to a 15 percent portfolio value drop over a one-year period. Although I maintain that most people cannot really anticipate how they will react to such an event, an answer that mentions getting upset and selling shares reflects a need for further discussion and education.

⮑ **Question 18.** This question is similar to Question 10 in that it results in a quantifiable response. I explain to my client that many people think of their risk tolerance in terms such as "low" or "moderate." The first column, "Overall Risk Level," lists our interpretation of those descriptions in terms of differing portfolios. The first adjective refers to their tolerance over a relatively short period (i.e., a few years); the second, over a longer time frame. The second column, "Expected Compounded Return," is our estimate of the compounded total annual return of each portfolio over the next three to five years, assuming inflation is 3 percent. Since returns don't come nice and even, the next column provides an estimate of the range of returns our client might expect most of the time (our euphemism for one standard deviation). Finally, the last column is an indication of how bad it might be if we have a really rotten year. We use quotes around the descriptor "worst case" (our user-friendly term for two standard deviations) because it only reflects 95 out of 100 years. There's a slim chance that it could be even bloodier.

As an example, I'll tell the client that if they're really, really conservative, I think we can design a portfolio that will give them a 6 percent return, and most of the time the worst I'd expect their portfolio to do is break even. In a really rotten environment, I'd expect it to be down only about 4 percent. If that seems too puny a reward, I think a return of 8.5 percent is reasonable if they can live with an occasional annual loss of 6 percent and a "worst case" loss of 20 percent. I'm always careful to remind them that this is a one-year estimated loss, not the loss the day after a crash. That short-term loss could look a lot uglier.

After all of this explanation, I hand my client the pen and ask him to pick one or two of the portfolios that best reflect his balance between risk and return. In most cases the response is consistent with the results of Question 10 and his other answers. If not, it's an opportunity to delve deeper and resolve the differences.

○ **Question 19.** This is my favorite; here's how it works. I explain to a client that I'm going to give him a two-part quiz. I then show him Number 1 (covering Number 2) and ask that he choose (a) or (b). Next I cover Number 1 and ask him to pick an answer for Number 2.

Almost all of my clients pick (a) for Number 1 and (b) for Number 2. I point out that, on the surface, this response seems contradictory, because the probability is the same in both cases. I then compliment them on passing the test. (If they "fail," I compliment them on being unique and proceed with my story.)

I explain that these responses confirm our experience that most investors are not "risk averse," they're "loss averse." Selecting Number 1(a) in effect says, "I don't want to take a risk to make more money." Selecting Number 2(b) says "I will take a risk in order not to lose money." Translating this conclusion to terms relating to our services, I point out that if a conservative investor were to walk into a brokerage office with $100,000 from a maturing CD, the adviser's recommendation is likely to be, "Whoa! You've been too conservative, let's put half of your investments in stock so we can make you some money." The conservative investor is likely to respond, "No thanks, I don't like taking risks!" If that same investor were to show up on our doorstep and our planning indicated that he needed to invest half of his funds in stock in order to maintain his standard of living, we'd make exactly the same recommendation, but for a totally different reason! We're not telling them to invest half the portfolio in stock to make them rich; we're trying to make sure they don't lose their lifestyle.

This is a powerful educational tool. After taking the test in Question 19, we've had many very conservative investors respond, "I get it now! I may be uncomfortable investing in stock, but I'm likely to be a lot more uncomfortable eating cat food. Let's go ahead with your recommendations."

⊃ **Question 20.** For a long time we equated risk with downside market volatility and portfolio loss. As a result, all of our coaching was focused on that interpretation of risk. At the end of the last century we began to realize that our process was missing a significant risk; I guess you'd call it "tracking error risk." That's the risk that you're doing the smart thing (i.e., diversifying), but the stupid market is rewarding the dumb thing (not diversifying). "Stupid" investors were making out like bandits while our clients' "smart" portfolios had performance numbers that would look abysmal when compared to "the market." As a consequence, we added a number of questions to anticipate the possibility of this form of market divergence in the future. Question 20 is the first of these new questions. It is a simple graphic that allows our client to chose between a series of risk/reward portfolios.

⊃ **Question 21.** This builds on the response to Question 20 and addresses the problem of "performance envy." If a client answers that they would switch, we know that we need to discuss a potential tracking error risk with the client.

⊃ **Question 22.** This last question helps reframe the prior response by reminding the client that the go-go portfolio A might well have taken a significant tumble instead of a rocket rise.

Post Questionnaire

AT THE COMPLETION OF THIS COACHING exercise, we begin to see how compatible a client will be with our recommendations and how our investment plan will take form. We have two questions that help to quantify the client's risk: Questions 10 and 17. Look over the answers the client gave you. Do these seem to be consistent? Now look at the answers to the other questions you've discussed. If these answers are not consistent with the quantifiable ones, you may need to revisit some of these concepts with the client. The idea is to get him on the same page with you regarding his risk parameters so that your investment policy will be useful to him.

Card Tricks

IT IS NOT EASY TO EXPLAIN MANY OF THE investment concepts so important to the well being of our clients in a way that's meaningful. While we can explain the issues, and our clients may intellectually understand concepts such as market volatility and real cash flow, getting the idea across at an emotional level is really tough. Over the years I've learned that as much as we would like a client to know how he will react in volatile times, he does not. No matter how you pose the question, he is only guessing at how he will feel when his investment drops.

Our friends from PIE Technologies (www.pietech.com) worked with us to write the Monte Carlo Card Game, a program to demonstrate returns, risk, and volatility in a manner that allows our clients to experience how these attributes might feel in the future. The Monte Carlo Card Game comes closer than anything I have seen to giving the client a sense of virtual volatility. Although originally designed for our own use, PIE has graciously consented to give you access to this program so that you can use it with your clients. This program has proven to be a powerful education experience for our clients. I'm going to run through it with you the way I would with a client.

The Monte Carlo Card Game

WELCOME TO MONTE CARLO! STEP RIGHT UP and pick a table. The link http://wealth.bloomberg.com/cardgame will take you and your clients to the Monte Carlo Casino where they can play the Monte Carlo Card Game.[4] Like a real casino, this one offers your clients a wide range of

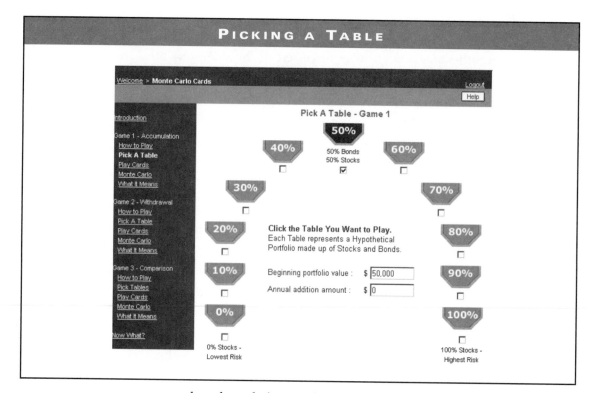

games based on their taste for risk. In effect, each table represents the return profile for portfolios ranging from 100 percent bonds (Table 0%) to 100 percent equity allocation (Table 100%). The higher the number, the higher the risk. Prior to beginning play, we discuss with our clients the different risk and return expectations for each table. We then invite them to play a series of games, occasionally changing tables (i.e., changing their risk and return expectations) so that they get a different set of possible returns. The games are such fun, you're likely to find your client asking you to move over, leave them alone, and let them play by themselves.

We've used these games with many different clients, but they're particularly powerful when clients need visual impressions that they can own. For this book, I have created a number of scenarios to illustrate how you might use it as a teaching tool with your clients. But first, let me take a minute to describe the mechanics of the Monte Carlo Card Game and the elements of the basic screen.

You'll see that there are numerous descriptive lines in the column

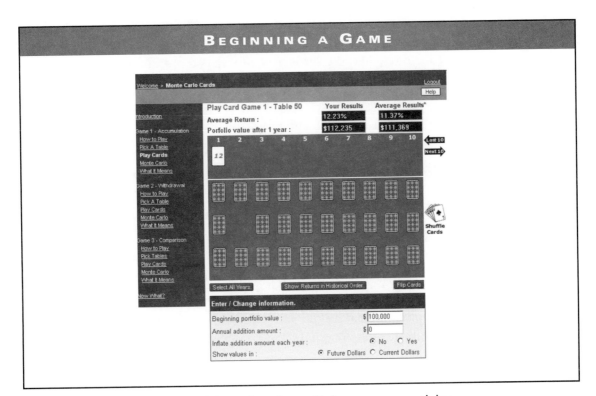

to the left. Each underlined item is a hyperlink to a new activity. Sandwiched between the "Introduction" (this is where you entered the program) and "Now What?" (a wrap-up commentary) are options for three different games. There are a number of games you can play—accumulation, withdrawal, or comparison. The format for each game is the same. For this discussion, select "Pick A Table" under "Game 1" in the menu.

Now, you'll have to decide what table you're going to play at (see illustration at left). Remember, the higher the number, the higher the risk. If you decide to change tables (i.e., allocation) later on, it's easy to do from anywhere within the program by simply clicking "Pick a Table" on the left side of the screen. You can also change the value of the beginning portfolio. I'll use a beginning portfolio value of $100,000 and the Table 50% as an example.

At the beginning of a game, face down on the table, are thirty cards (see illustration above). Each card has a number that represents the actual annual return for one year during the past thirty years for a portfolio allocated between bonds and stock in the percentage you selected. Taken together, the cards have numbers representing all of the annual returns for the past thirty years. The idea of the game is to allow clients to experience market volatility the way it might actually happen, and by using actual returns for the past thirty years the client can accept that the numbers are credible. By shuffling these real numbers we allow our clients to invent and experience a hypothetical but credible future.

You play the game by clicking on a card (any card). Your selection will tell you your portfolio's return for the next year. Each subsequent click adds a new year's return. Unlike our real world, if you don't like your return (or would like to see what a different future might look like) once a card has been displayed, you can put it back in the deck by simply re-clicking on it. Although not shown on the cards, included in the program is data reflecting the inflation rate for each year for the past thirty years. This data, linked to the return data, is the basis for calculating inflation adjusted values.

On the main part of this screen you'll also see the following items, approximately in the order discussed:

⮑ **Play Card Game 1–Table 50%.** This lets you know what game and subsequent table is active.

⮑ **Average Return.** This displays the annualized returns for the number of years the game's been played.

⮑ **Your Results.** This first return is the annualized return based on the random sequence of cards you've selected. This will change constantly with each game and each card selected.

⮑ **Average Results.** This second return is the historical annualized return for the past thirty years of a portfolio allocated between bonds and stock in the percentage noted in the left panel. You'll notice that as you play the average results do not change.

⮑ **Portfolio Value after X year(s).** This appears once you begin selecting cards and displays the portfolio values for your hypothetical portfolio (based on the cards you've selected) and for a portfolio achieving average historical returns.

⮑ **Last 10/Next 10.** These arrow tabs let you toggle between the

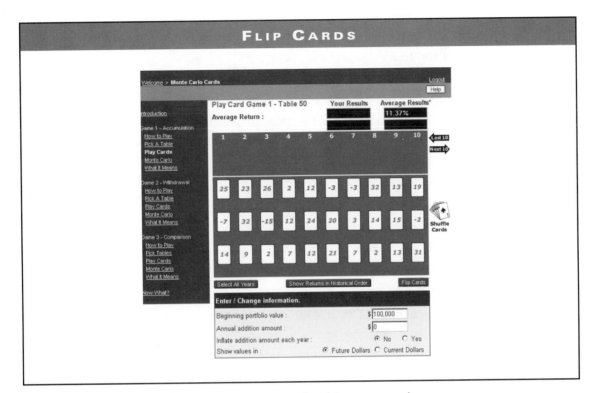

first, second, and third ten-year segments of a thirty-year series.

➲ **Shuffle Cards.** This tab lets you create a new future by reshuffling the deck and redisplaying the cards (i.e., future returns) in a new random order.

➲ **Select All Years.** This handy tab simply saves you the time of picking cards at random and automatically selects them all in the sequence they're displayed. When the cards are shuffled they are in random order so the result is a random thirty-year sequence. By alternately shuffling and selecting all years you can generate a continuing series of random futures.

➲ **Show Returns in Historical Order.** This is very cool. It turns over all of the cards, labels them by year, and displays them in actual historical sequence. In other words, it allows the player to play a what-if-I-had-invested-like-this-thirty-years-ago scenario.

➲ **Flip Cards.** This allows you to toggle between hiding and displaying the cards on the table. If you were to click on this tab the result would look something like the illustration above.

⮑ **Enter/Change information.** This section lets you change a number of input assumptions on the fly.

⮑ **Beginning portfolio value.** How much money are you starting with? We generally change the investment amount to reflect the approximate value of the client's actual investment portfolio. We find this customization enhances the reality of the game for our clients.

⮑ **Annual addition amount.** The amount of any regular additions. This is very useful for simulating dollar-cost-averaging.

⮑ **Inflate addition amount each year.** This allows you to simulate fixed real dollar savings.

⮑ **Show values in.** This allows you to toggle the portfolio value between "Current Dollars" and "Future Dollars."

⮑ **Monte Carlo.** Each game has a Monte Carlo option located in the left side of the screen. While it's interesting and educational to play one game at a time, the results only reflect one possible reality out of an almost infinite number of possibilities. Clicking this tab instructs the program to reshuffle the deck and run the game not once, but 1,000 times. It then provides some very interesting results as well as a graph displaying the 1,000 possible outcomes for each of the next thirty years. These graphs are powerful visual reminders that although on average one might reasonably expect a certain outcome, we don't live in average times. Everyone lives in a very unique time and the range of possible outcomes can be quite large. More on this when we look at Games 2 and 3.[5]

OK, that's the mechanics, let's play some games.

Game One

Scenario One

LET'S LOOK INTO THE FUTURE

"Mr. Client, all the planning we're doing is for the future, and it's a pretty murky future. In order to get an idea of what it might look and feel like, I've got a card game for you to play. Here's how it works at Monte Carlo Casino.

"As you see, you have a choice of eleven tables. As the numbers get

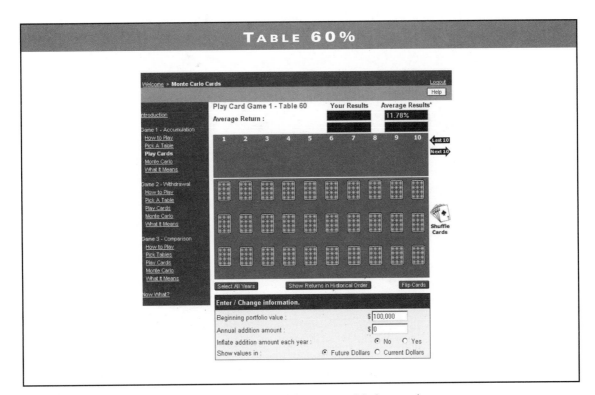

bigger, the potential winnings get bigger. Of course, this is a casino so the risk gets bigger, too. For example, Table 0% is an all-bond table. You wouldn't expect much risk, but don't expect much return either. If you're looking for action, Table 100% is all stock. Table 60% represents a 40 percent bond, 60 percent stock portfolio. OK, pick a table.

"Ah, you picked Table 60%, a portfolio with 40 percent in bonds and 60 percent in stock.

"You'll see there are thirty cards (see illustration above). As this is Table 60%, the cards have numbers representing the actual market returns for a 40 percent bond/60 percent stock portfolio, for each year over the past thirty years. We chose thirty as a representative period of time in retirement. Take a look at the number in the top right-hand corner. The number 11.78 percent represents the historical annualized return over the past thirty years for a portfolio invested 40 percent in bonds and 60 percent in stock.

"I'm going to give you a stake of $100,000. Let's see how you do in the next thirty years at Table 60%. I want you to pick ten cards at ran-

TEN YEARS OF POSITIVE RETURNS

dom. Each card's return will tell you how you're doing each year of your hypothetical future."

In this example (see illustration above), the client picks ten straight years of positive returns.[6] As each card is selected, the conversation might go something like this:

Year One Not bad, but you'd best hunker down and start doing better or you'll never get that 11.8 percent.

Year Two Much better!

Year Three You're doing fine.

Year Four Great! We ought to hire you!

Year Five Uh-oh, not negative but still well under the historical 11.8 percent. But don't worry, you have a good cushion.

Year Six Well done!

Year Seven It's OK, cushion's still there.

Year Eight Very good.

Year Nine You're back on the payroll!

Year Ten Fantastic! You're going to head the investment committee!

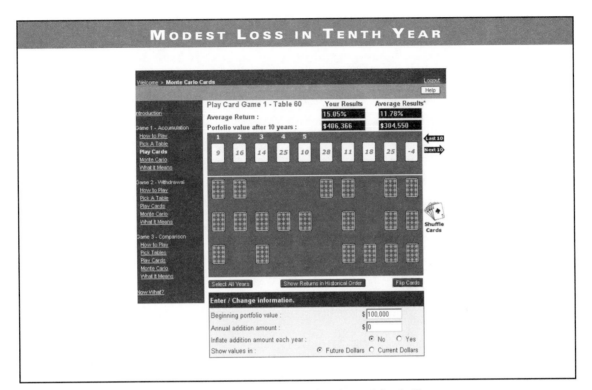

In this example, the client's really happy. He has just picked all positive returns and his total return is a benchmark-beating 18.2 percent for the ten-year period, giving him a total portfolio value of $532,480. I point out that if he'd actually realized this sequence of returns (a statistical possibility) in his personal investments, he'd likely attribute it to his skill and would be bragging to his friends how astute he was at investing. I then remind him that there could have been many other outcomes. In order to demonstrate an alternative outcome, I replace the last year with a negative return. You can do this by clicking on "Flip Cards" in order to find a losing year, then clicking on the year you want to replace, followed by clicking on the card with the return you wish to use. "Let's just see," I tell him. "What happens if after nine years of a brilliant run you had a modest loss of 4 percent in the tenth year?"

"That one change dropped your overall return by over 3 percent!" (See illustration above.)

Once we have played with the first ten years, we generally let our client play on for the next twenty years. Just click the arrow to get to each subsequent ten years. Your client will quickly discover that an extraordinary decade of great returns is likely to be followed by a decade of poor returns, and a decade of poor returns is likely to be followed by a decade of great returns, bringing the portfolio's long-term returns back into line with long-term expectations.

Scenario Two

I WANT A TWENTY-YEAR 25 PERCENT ANNUALIZED RETURN—A GET REAL EXERCISE

"Ms. Client, so does everyone. The question is, is that realistic? To achieve such a high return you'll need a high equity exposure, so select Table 90%. Keep in mind that the return for a similar portfolio during the past thirty years was 12.9 percent.

"Now, let's see how close you'll come to meeting your goal. We'll start by having you turn over ten cards to see how you'll fare for the next ten years.

"In the future you've just created, you have nine positive-return years and one year with a huge loss (see illustration at left). Your annualized return is 9.8 percent. Let's suppose you weren't so unlucky and the last year you broke even with a return of 1 percent. Your portfolio return is now 13 percent. Suppose you really aced the last year with 36 percent (the highest probability for this portfolio). The return is 16.4 percent, still far short of your desired 25 percent. (The illustrations below and on the following page show the returns remaining.) Do you really think that a 25 percent annualized return for twenty years is attainable?"

By playing with the cards, you can demonstrate that based on the historically high returns of the past thirty years, her chances of seeing a 25 percent annualized return are almost zero. Even if she were to pick every best year for the past thirty she'd drop below her target return in sixteen years, regressing to the target of 12.9 percent. Often percentages don't have the same impact as dollar amounts,

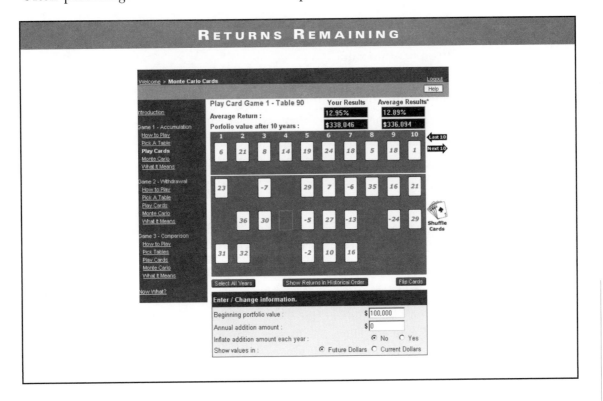

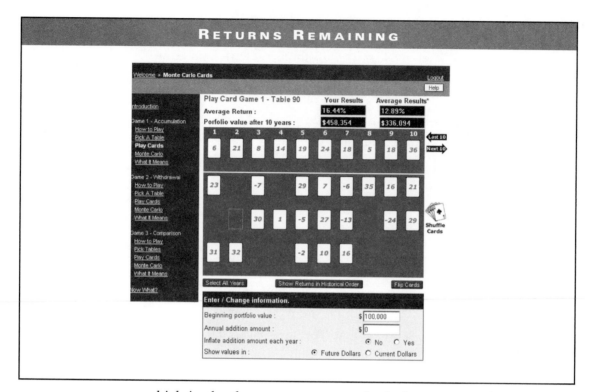

which is why the program reports both the return and the cumulative portfolio value.

As I noted earlier, a powerful additional feature is the Monte Carlo simulation. By rerunning the card game 1,000 times using random selections for future returns, your client can see a visual image of the probability of achieving a specific dollar amount at any given point in time (see illustration at right).

Scenario Three

WHAT HAPPENED TO MY 12 PERCENT RETURN?
ALL I'VE DONE IS LOSE MONEY!

Welcome to the real world of market volatility. "Mr. Client, I know how frustrating, even scary, it is to have to live through the sort of volatility we've seen recently, especially since you started investing just as everything tanked. However, as you remember, we've often discussed the fact that volatility is inherent in long-term investing. What you have to keep your eye on is the long-term game plan. Let's look at a portfolio

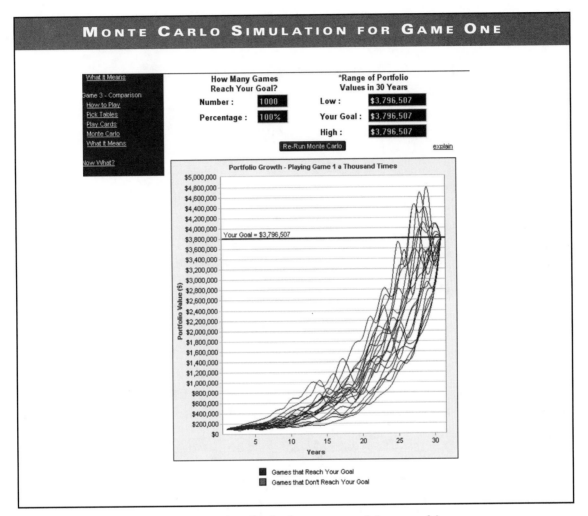

MONTE CARLO SIMULATION FOR GAME ONE

What it Means

Game 3 - Comparison
How to Play
Pick Tables
Play Cards
Monte Carlo
What it Means

Now What?

**How Many Games
Reach Your Goal?**

Number : 1000

Percentage : 100%

***Range of Portfolio
Values in 30 Years**

Low : $3,796,507

Your Goal : $3,796,507

High : $3,796,507

Re-Run Monte Carlo   explain

Portfolio Growth - Playing Game 1 a Thousand Times

Your Goal = $3,796,507

Portfolio Value ($)

Years

■ Games that Reach Your Goal
■ Games that Don't Reach Your Goal

that resembles your allocation and re-jiggle the returns of the past thirty years to see what the first few years might have looked like if you'd had some of the worst returns early on.

"Not too good: a three-year compounded loss of 8.3 percent (see illustration on the following page, top). Now suppose the markets begin to turn around. Let's see what kind of returns it would take to catch you up to the 11.8 percent of the past thirty years."

Obviously, this is not an unreasonable expectation (see illustration on the following page, bottom). The point is that markets fluctuate. No one can predict the future, but there is reason to believe that over time your portfolio returns will regress toward reasonable expectations.

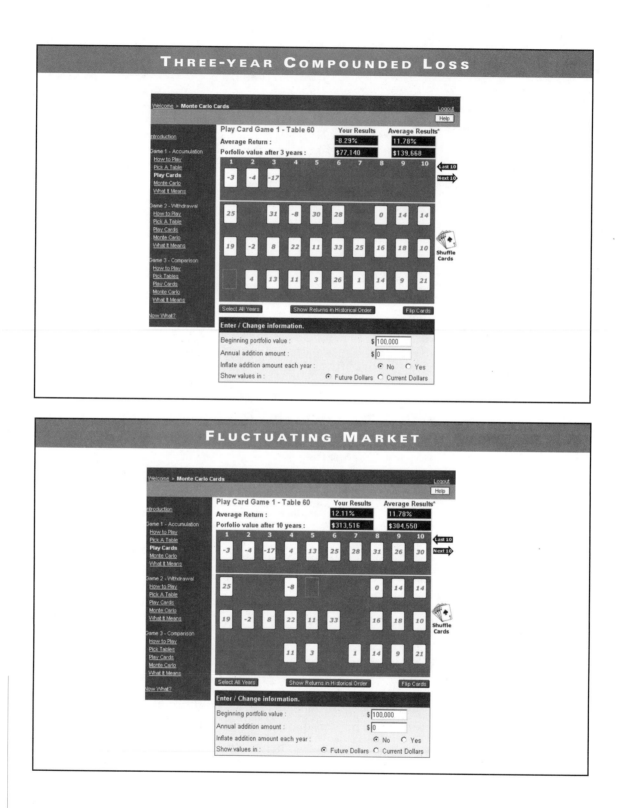

Game Two

WHEN OUR CLIENTS TELL US THEY need a certain income in retirement, they usually think in terms of a steady stream of fixed dollars. For example, suppose we suggest that it's realistic during their retirement to plan on a long-term return of 10 percent. Further, they have a nest egg of $100,000 and need $10,000 per year to supplement their pension and Social Security. It's likely that the client will conclude, happily, that they can invest, receive the necessary $10,000 like clockwork, and still pass on the corpus to their heirs. Unfortunately they're obviously missing two critical realities—investment returns don't occur like clockwork, and they need a real return, not merely a fixed cash flow.

When planning for retirement withdrawals, timing is an important factor. Although we tend to think in terms of long-term averages, our clients don't live during average years, they live during real years. If they're so unfortunate as to begin their withdrawal during a black hole[7] (e.g., a serious bear market), they may dip so heavily into corpus that there's too little capital remaining to grow during the ensuing bull market. Ask your client if any of their bills (e.g., utilities, food) ever go up as the years go by. Naturally they do, and obviously our clients want their retirement planning to take this into account.

Game 2 helps your clients see how these realities may affect their future well being. The program utilizes the same thirty years of historical returns and incorporates historical inflation. It also allows the client to enter either a fixed or a real dollar withdrawal.

Scenario Four

BLACK HOLES

Playing Game 2, select a table that reflects the allocation most representative of the one likely to be implemented by your client. For this example, I've assumed that the client is likely to utilize a 40 percent bond/60 percent stock allocation. First, determine what annual withdrawal rate your client is likely to find reasonable. As I indicated before, an effective default is a 10 percent fixed withdrawal, or in this case $10,000 per year. In the "Annual Withdrawal

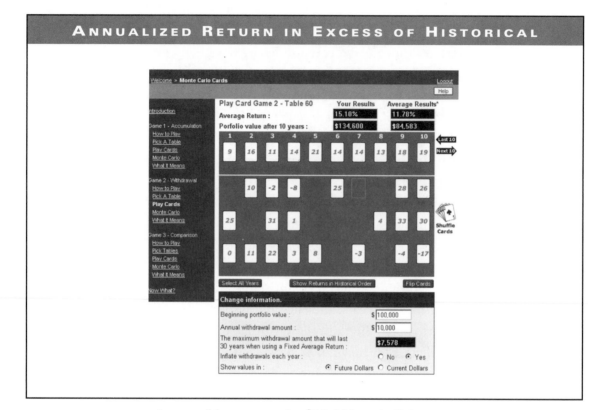

Amount" box enter the $10,000 and click next.

Now you're ready to set up the balance of the scenario. Toggle the "Inflate withdrawals each year" to "Yes." This will run the game based on withdrawals in real dollars (the kinds of dollars our clients really need). Click "Flip Cards" to display the values of all of the cards and allow you to finish your scenario creation. For this example (see the illustration above), I've selected a series of annual returns that results in an annualized return well in excess of the historical (15.1 percent vs. 11.8 percent). If you ask your client about his comfort level if this were his portfolio, he's likely to be pretty pleased. After all, it's very much as he expects, and he has a nice cushion to boot (although, unfortunately, that cushion is in future dollars).

Now let's show our client what might happen if they picked the wrong time to live and mid way through the first ten years, the market entered a mild bear period.

As in this scenario, even subsequent superior returns may not

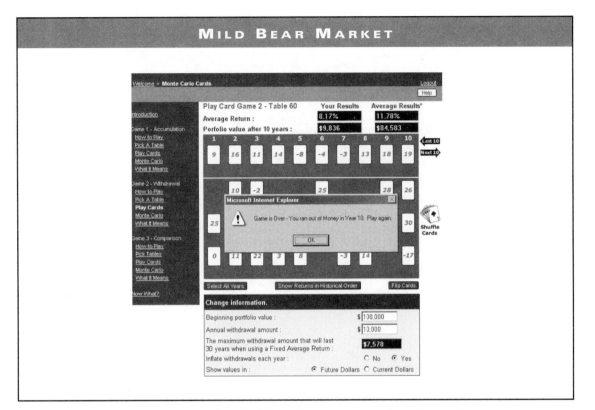

help (see illustration above). This demonstrates that if you live at the wrong time, long-term averages won't make a diddly-squat's worth of difference.

Scenario Five

FIXED RETURNS VS. REAL RETURNS

Although previous scenarios are impacted by the differences between fixed and real returns, sometimes it's useful to focus on the issue. In order to set up this game we need to determine what average fixed withdrawal rate a portfolio could have sustained over the past thirty years. That's easily determined using the game. Simply pick the appropriate table (I'll use a 40/60 portfolio) and in the "Change Information" section it will be calculated in the box labeled "The maximum withdrawal amount that will last thirty years when using a Fixed Average Return." In my example, the value is $12,213 (see illustration on the following page).

Now, in order to run a scenario using real dollars, we need to convert our $12,213 to real dollars. Do this by clicking on the "Yes" button under "Inflate withdrawals each year."

At this stage you could select a new series of cards (i.e., returns) either at random or, by showing the cards, a specific series. Alternatively you can use an additional feature of the game, the "Show Returns in Historical Order" tab. This will automatically select cards that reflect the actual series of returns over the past thirty years. For this scenario, the results are dramatic (see illustration at right, top).

It demonstrates that an investor so unfortunate to begin his investment and withdrawals in 1971 would have exhausted the entire portfolio in only seven years! If that doesn't impress your client, utilizing the Monte Carlo simulation will. With it you can demonstrate that the probability of maintaining a real dollar withdrawal equal to the historical fixed average is effectively zero percent! (See illustration at right, bottom.)

RETURNS IN HISTORICAL ORDER

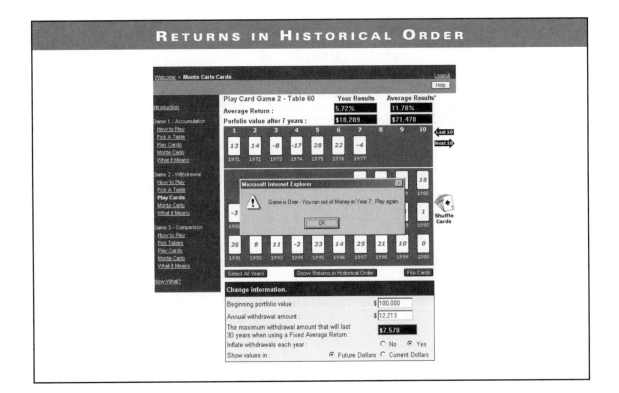

MONTE CARLO SIMULATION FOR GAME TWO

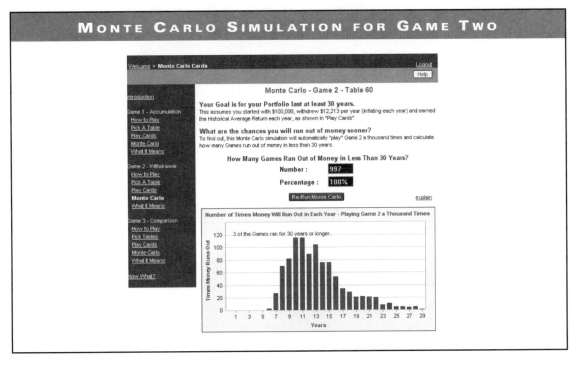

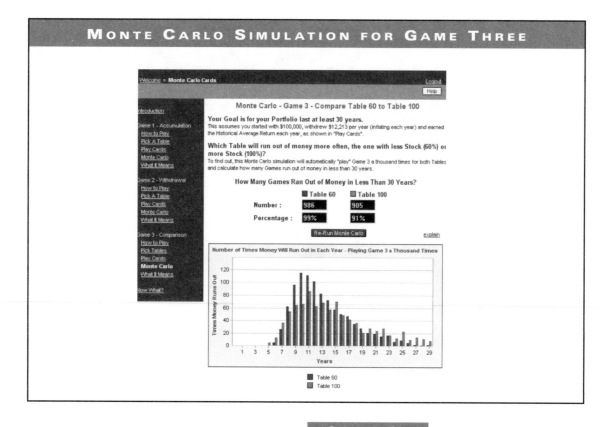

MONTE CARLO SIMULATION FOR GAME THREE

Scenario Six

THE FINAL SCENARIO—AND THE PIÈCE DE RÉSISTANCE

Once you've developed a familiarity with the card games, you'll most likely find yourself concluding your client education program with Game 3. This very powerful choice allows you to compare two alternatives. For example, many clients believe that the solution to unrealistic expectations is to simply increase their equity exposure. Rerunning the Monte Carlo simulation for scenario five in Game 3 and selecting an all equity portfolio as a second choice may disabuse them of this notion (see illustration above).

Even an all-equity portfolio results in a more than 90 percent failure rate![8]

We've used these games to demonstrate many concepts, including:

➲ No portfolio attains an average return every year

➲ Returns can vary widely from year to year

⮱ Great returns may reflect luck, not brains

⮱ Over time, returns tend to regress to the mean

⮱ The sequence of returns does not matter during the accumulation stage

⮱ The timing of returns is critical during the withdrawal stage

⮱ The use of Monte Carlo simulations can give you a better picture of the likelihood of achieving your goal than a point estimate can

However, the possible uses are unlimited. The best part is that the games are, in default mode, completely random so that each time your client plays, a different scenario affords him another opportunity to experience the volatility of real world investing. The program is also flexible, so that you can force situations to illustrate what you want.

We have literally played with this program for hours, figuring out what experiences we'd like the client to have so that when a scenario presents itself, we can change it around simply to make our point. Try it, you'll like it.

> You can get to the Monte Carlo Card Game by going to
> **wealth.bloomberg.com/cardgame.**

RISK COACHING QUESTIONNAIRE

1)   What is the approximate value of this investment portfolio(s)?

$ _____

       What percentage of your total investments are represented
by this portfolio?

_____ %

2)   Please estimate the approximate percentage of your portfolio that is
invested in each asset class. Include in your approximation checking
and savings accounts, taxable investments, 401(k) accounts, IRAs,
and Keogh accounts.

Cash/Cash Equivalents	_____ %
Domestic Bonds	_____ %
International Bonds	_____ %
Domestic Large Cap Equities	_____ %
Domestic Small Cap Equities	_____ %
International Equities	_____ %
Options/Futures	_____ %
Real Estate	_____ %
Other	_____ %

3)   How would you describe your portfolio allocations (i.e., the relative
amount held in each asset class) over time?

My portfolio allocations have remained fairly consistent over time.   O

My portfolio allocations have changed, but not dramatically, over time.   O

My portfolio allocations have changed significantly over time.   O

4)   If your portfolio allocations have changed over time, please check all
of the applicable reasons for these changes.

O   I have learned more about investments.

O   I had a lifestyle change or I met a major financial goal (e.g., retirement)

O   I was attempting to achieve superior returns through market timing.

O   I did not have enough funds to invest in certain asset classes.

O   I do not pursue an asset allocation policy.

O   Other. _____

© EVENSKY, BROWN & KATZ

10
pages
on CD-ROM

RISK COACHING QUESTIONNAIRE

5)   Is there an immediate or near term (i.e., within five years) need for income from this portfolio(s)?

Y   N

If yes, when will the income be needed?

_____ YRS

How much will be needed in after tax dollars, per year?

$ _____

6)   Will significant cash withdrawals of principal and/or contributions be made over the next five years?

Y   N

If yes, please attach a schedule.

7)   Is this a taxable or partially taxable portfolio(s)?

Y   N

If yes, what tax rate should be used for planning purposes?

_____ %

8)   What is the portfolio's Investment Time Horizon?

Investment Time Horizon refers to the number of years you expect the portfolio to be invested before you must dip into principal.   Alternatively, how long will the objectives stated for this portfolio continue without substantial modification? Please mark your choice.

Three Years...   ○
Five Years...   ○
Ten years..   ○
Over Ten years..   ○

If you have indicated less than ten years, please explain when the funds will be needed:

_____

_____

_____

9)   OPTIONAL

My (our) goal for this portfolio(s) is an annual return of:

_____ %

This is based an expected inflation rate of:

_____ %

See page #10 for a long-term historical reference.

RISK COACHING QUESTIONNAIRE

10) For each of the following attributes, circle the number that most correctly reflects your level of concern. The more important, the higher the number. You may use each number more than once.

	MOST					LEAST
Capital Preservation	6	5	4	3	2	1
Growth	6	5	4	3	2	1
Low Volatility	6	5	4	3	2	1
Inflation Protection	6	5	4	3	2	1
Current Cash Flow	6	5	4	3	2	1
Aggressive Growth	6	5	4	3	2	1

11) **ASSET CLASS CONSTRAINTS**

ASSET CLASSES	Provide Any Asset Class Limitations (OPTIONAL)	
	Minimum	Maximum
T-bills, CDs, money market	_____	_____
Intermediate government bonds	_____	_____
Intermediate corporate bonds	_____	_____
Intermediate municipal bonds	_____	_____
Long term government bonds	_____	_____
Long term corporate bonds	_____	_____
Long term municipal bonds	_____	_____
Foreign bonds	_____	_____
Domestic equities S&P 500	_____	_____
Domestic equities OTC	_____	_____
Foreign equities	_____	_____
Real Estate	_____	_____
Metals	_____	_____

© EVENSKY, BROWN & KATZ

RISK COACHING QUESTIONNAIRE

12) What percent of your investments are you likely to need within five years?

          %

13) Up to what percentage of this portfolio can be invested in long term investments (i.e., over five years)?

          %

14) Investment "risk" means different things to different people. Please rank of the following statements from 1 (the statement that would worry you the most) to 4 (the statement that would worry you the least).

I would be very concerned if I did not achieve the return on my portfolio that I expected (i.e., my target rate of return).

    1 2 3 4

I would be very concerned if my portfolio was worth less in "real" dollars because of inflation erosion.

    1 2 3 4

I would be very concerned with short term volatility (i.e., if my portfolio dropped substantially in value over one year).

    1 2 3 4

I would be very concerned with long term volatility (i.e., if my portfolio dropped in value over a long period of time (five years or longer)).

    1 2 3 4

15) Except for the "great depression," the longest time investors have had to wait after a market "crash" or a really bad market decline for their portfolio to return to its earlier value has been: four years for stock and two years for bond investments. Knowing this, and that it is impossible to protect yourself from an occasional loss, answer the following question:

"If my portfolio produces a long term return that allows me to accomplish my goals, I am prepared to live with a time of recovery of..."

Less than one year.   O

Between one and two years.   O

Between two and three years.   O

Over three years.   O

If you select less than "Between two and three years," are you prepared to substantially reduce your goals?

    Y   N

SOURCE: EVENSKY, BROWN & KATZ

10 pages on CD-ROM

RISK COACHING QUESTIONNAIRE

16) Please check the statement that reflects your preference.

I would rather be out of the stock market when it goes down than in the market when it goes up (i.e., I cannot live with the volatility of the stock market).

○

I would rather be in the stock market when it goes down than out of the market when it goes up (i.e., I may not like the idea, but I can live with the volatility of the stock market in order to earn market returns).

○

17) How often do you review the value of your mutual fund investments?

Daily	○
Weekly	○
Monthly	○
Quarterly	○
Yearly	○

Suppose that a growth mutual fund you have held for one year has lost 15 percent of its value, which is consistent with performance of similar funds. What is your reaction?

I would probably be very upset and sell all my shares.
I wouldn't be happy, but I would probably keep my shares.
I would think it was a peak buying opportunity and buy more shares.

10
pages
on CD-ROM

RISK COACHING QUESTIONNAIRE

18) Several portfolio performance projections are listed below. Assuming that inflation averages three percent, check the portfolio that most nearly reflects your goal for your portfolio.

Overall Risk Level	Expected Compounded Return (Infl = 3%)	Expected Annual Range of Returns*			"Worst Case"**	
Low/Low	6.0%	0.0%	To	11.0%	-4.0%	○
Low/Low	6.5%	-1.0%	To	13.0%	-7.0%	○
Mod/Low	7.0%	-1.5%	To	15.0%	-9.0%	○
Mod/Low	7.3%	-2.0%	To	16.0%	-10.0%	○
Mod/Low	7.5%	-2.5%	To	17.0%	-11.0%	○
Mod/Mod	7.8%	-3.0%	To	18.0%	-13.0%	○
High/Mod	8.0%	-4.0%	To	19.0%	-14.0%	○
High/Mod	8.3%	-5.0%	To	20.5%	-16.0%	○
High/High	8.5%	-6.0%	To	22.0%	-20.0%	○
High/High	8.8%	-7.0%	To	24.0%	-22.0%	○
High/High	9.0%	-8.0%	To	26.0%	-24.0%	○
High/High	9.5%	-9.0%	To	28.0%	-27.0%	○
High/High	10.0%	-11.0%	To	31.0%	-31.0%	○
High/High	10.5%	-12.5%	To	33.0%	-35.0%	○

* These estimates are based on a statistical measure of one standard deviation. This means that based on the assumptions used in developing these projections, the portfolio returns will fall within these ranges two out of every three years.

** We use the term "worst case" to describe the worst annual return that a portfolio is likely to experience 90 percent of the time.

1/1/00

10 pages on CD-ROM

RISK COACHING QUESTIONNAIRE

19)   Now you have a test to take. There are two parts to the test.
        For each question, please check (a) or (b).

Question #1. Choose (a) or (b)

(a) You win $80,000

(b) You have an 80 percent chance of winning $100,000
     (or a 20 percent chance of winning nothing)

Question #2. Choose (a) or (b)

(a) You lose $80,000

(b) You have an 80 percent chance of losing $100,000

     (or a 20 percent chance of losing nothing)

10
pages
on CD-ROM

RISK COACHING QUESTIONNAIRE

20) The following chart shows the possible range of values for four different investments of $100,000 after one year. Which investment would you be most comfortable owning?

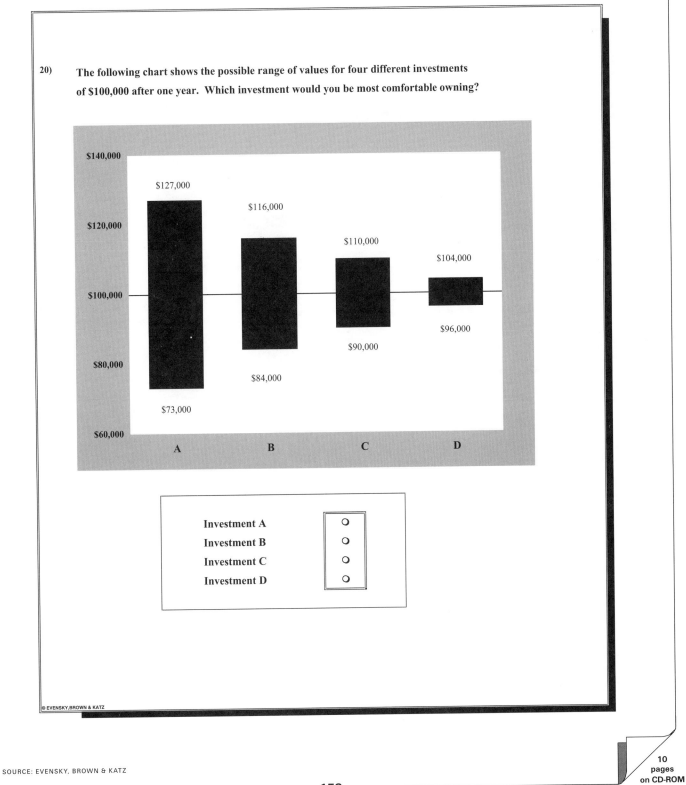

10
pages
on CD-ROM

RISK COACHING QUESTIONNAIRE

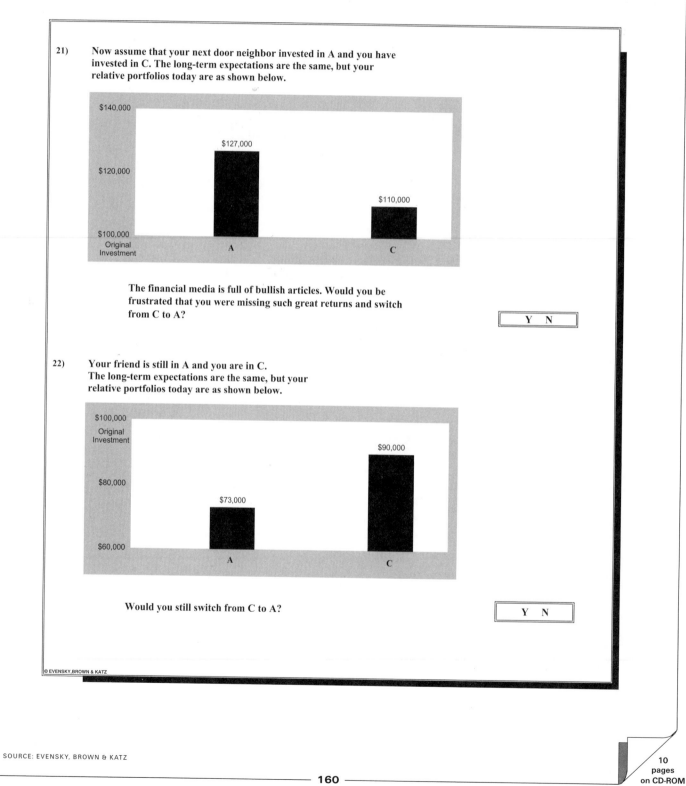

21) Now assume that your next door neighbor invested in A and you have invested in C. The long-term expectations are the same, but your relative portfolios today are as shown below.

The financial media is full of bullish articles. Would you be frustrated that you were missing such great returns and switch from C to A?

Y   N

22) Your friend is still in A and you are in C. The long-term expectations are the same, but your relative portfolios today are as shown below.

Would you still switch from C to A?

Y   N

© EVENSKY,BROWN & KATZ

10 pages on CD-ROM

SUMMARY STATISTICS

ANNUAL RETURNS   1926 - 1999

ASSET CLASS	COMPOUNDED RETURN	STANDARD DEVIATION
US TREASURY BILLS	3.8%	0.9%
INTERMEDIATE GOVT BONDS	5.2%	4.6%
COMMON STOCK	11.4%	22.1%
SMALL COMPANY STOCK	12.6%	35.3%
INFLATION	3.1%	2.0%

ACKNOWLEDGMENTS

By signing this questionnaire you agree that you received an educational experience prior to its completion with an advisor and that its contents were discussed and explained and you agree that your answers are correct to the best of your knowledge. You also understand that this questionnaire does not make or imply any guarantee regarding the attainment of your investment objective.   Please make us aware of any changes in your personal or financial circumstances.

Client _____   Date _____

Client _____   Date _____

Planner _____   Date _____

© EVENSKY,BROWN & KATZ

10 pages on CD-ROM

RISK ALGORITHM
For use with Question 10 of the Risk-Coaching Questionnaire

To use: Insert the corresponding numbers that your client circled in question 10. For example, if a client responded 5 to capital preservation, type a 5 in the capital preservation row beneath the column labeled 5. The risk level will automatically compute.

	MOST CONCERN					LEAST CONCERN
	6	5	4	3	2	1
CAPITAL PRESERVATION	0	0	0	0	0	0
GROWTH	0	0	0	0	0	0
LOW PRINCIPAL VOLATILITY	0	0	0	0	0	0
INFLATION PROTECTION	0	0	0	0	0	0
CURRENT CASH FLOW	0	0	0	0	0	0
AGGRESSIVE GROWTH	0	0	0	0	0	0

RISK LEVEL	50

SOURCE: EVENSKY, BROWN & KATZ

INVESTMENT POLICIES AND FINANCIAL PLANS

*You're not my clients. Two people with the same names ten
or twenty years from now are my clients. I don't want to let
the people with your names today mess up their life.*

— UNKNOWN

I've said before, I think the way planners deliver planning to our clients has changed markedly over time. Planning is a process, not a product, so many advisers are beginning to believe that a formal comprehensive document is unnecessary and provides only a written investment policy. Other planning recommendations are delivered orally, using a white board, or computer projector. A few advisers are beginning to use scenario software and interact with their clients via the Net.

This chapter focuses on form over substance. It will provide you with ideas you might incorporate in your investment policy and financial plan delivery. I am not going into detail about the content of the components because that has been well covered by others.[1]

Paper Plan Delivery

USING A TEMPLATE TO PREPARE THE investment policy makes it so much easier than trying to reinvent the policy with each new client. However, it's important not to use too much boilerplate. There is a fine line between standardization and useless verbiage. Ron Tamayo of Spraker, Fitzgerald & Tamayo, LLC, reports that their clients believe their policy is well constructed and easy to follow. Their document begins with a description of the Investment Policy Statement, why individuals need a written policy, and what factors were taken into consideration to develop the policy. Their IPS discusses what asset classes will be used, what the asset allocation should be, and how the monitoring and rebalancing will be accomplished. At the end of the document, they list the duties of the adviser and the investor and require signatures from both.

Our investment policy contains both Word and Excel documents. The Word file (FORM 7-01) has text that we can customize for our current client circumstances, but has enough structure so that we are sure we don't miss something. The Excel forms include the Strategy Analysis page (FORM 7-02 explained below) as well as charts with financial and retirement assumptions (FORMS 7-03, 7-04, and 7-05) so we can share our analytical assumptions with the client in an understandable way.

The policy form also has a one-page summary sheet that requires the client's signature. We think having the client's signature is essential for managing expectations. As soon as the market takes a dip, your brand-new client will be beating a path to your office, convinced that a dip like this shouldn't be happening and that the world is coming to an end. You know your client's definition of a major correction? When stocks decline for a day. A bear market is when stocks decline for a week. The more you can do to disabuse him of that thinking, the better your relationship will be. We haul out his IPS, remind him that we discussed volatility (as his signature confirms) and walk through the thinking process to assure him that the world is not coming to an end. Our experience is that when our clients are reminded that their investment plan has anticipated these dips, they feel much better.

As part of our IPS, we include a strategy analysis page that lists the client's assets, the ownership, the amount, the asset class, and asset percentage of the total portfolio. This document is written in Excel and is on the CD-ROM as FORM 7-02 for your use (see FORM 7-02 on page 171). There are hidden columns in the document that allow you to put in the CUSIP number of the asset so that you can use this document for trading as well. Since it breaks down the assets by ownership, it is a very useful tool for aggregating several portfolios. Because we also use it for rebalancing, I have elected to further discuss its uses in the rebalancing section of Chapter 9.

The strategy spreadsheet allows you to enter your asset allocation by percentage of asset class or sub-asset class. When you put a dollar amount in the money market column, it automatically distributes that amount according to the policy. (Note on FORM 7-02, I have put in $1,000,000 as an example.) Additionally, if you are reporting on a portfolio that contains more than one account (e.g., an IRA and a joint account) you can note the ownership in the "Owner" column, and hidden columns (you can open on the right of the form) will keep track of how much is owned by whom. This is also a nifty form to use for rebalancing, because it will let you balance the portfolio as a whole without over- or underallocating dollars by account.

Electronic Plan Delivery

WE RECENTLY EXPERIMENTED WITH OUR investment policy by transferring it to PowerPoint slides so we can make verbal presentations to clients without the necessity of the full written plan. I have included our PowerPoint slides on the CD-ROM as FORM 7-06 so that you can see what we think is important to include on the slides (see FORM 7-06 on page 175). So far, it seems to be a successful experiment. Clients like the interaction of this type of plan delivery and frankly, I've had my fill of reading the plan upside down while explaining it to the client.

There are many more adviser tools being delivered on the Web these days. I predict that in the near future you won't have any software resident on your system—you will just pull up your Web tools on demand. And, because of the Web format, these tools will allow you to interact with your client when and how you want to.

WHAT IF PLAN RESULTS—ALL GOALS

One of the interactive Web-based financial plans I've worked with recently is a goal planner that allows the client to create scenarios based on the personal data we've entered. Written by our friends at PIE Technologies (www.pietech.com), these "what-ifs" let our client change assumptions and financial data to get a better feel for his options, without disturbing the integrity of our original input. We either provide our client a copy of the software with their personal data or give them access via the Web. If you subscribe to PIE's program, you and your client can go through the Web site and view the data simultaneously. Above and following are screen shots showing how this works.

The illustration above is a copy of the user-friendly screen that allows the client to play with changes. Assets can be assigned to goals, which can be prioritized. The client assigns the priority. Running the program shows the client how much of his goal he can accomplish under the present scenario (see illustration at right).

To tweak the plan, the client may change nearly every variable. For example, if he wishes to extend his retirement age, he simply makes the

ASSIGNING ASSETS

Address: http://www.pietechdev.com/PWGoals/PWGoalPlanning.asp?sSessionID=10E5B7279C1D4EEF8723454B89B9A318

What If...

	Current Plan	What If Plan
Retirement Age		
Client retirement age :	65	65
Spouse retirement age :	65	65
		Calculate
Hypothetical Average Rate of Return		
Before retirement :	10.28%	12.00 %
After retirement :	10.28%	10.00 %
		Calculate
Increase Current Additions		
Total taxable	$2,000	$ 2,000
401k	5%	5 %
Plan addition amount	$8,550	$8,550

change on the screen. If he wishes to make increases to his projected retirement plan contributions, he can do that. He can even change the return assumptions (see illustration *Change in Variables* on the following page). He can also elect to increase savings at various times or increase spending on specific goals.

Finally, when the variable has been addressed, the new calculations provide the plan results in the form of an easily understandable graph. The client can view the impact of all changes, or just one at a time. This graph is a powerful visual (see illustration *Graph of Plan Results* on the following page).

And, for those engineer clients, there is a table of returns (see illustration *Table of Returns* on page 169).

The best part is that your client can play alone and go over it with you at a later time. Or, he can meet you on the Web and you can change the scenarios together, because it allows both of you to view and change it at once. You create a duplicate copy of the file so the client won't disturb the original input of the PIE Web site.

CHANGE IN VARIABLES

Address | http://www.pietechdev.com/PwGoals/PwGoalPlanning.asp?sSessionID=10E5B7279C1D4EEF8723454B89B9A318 ▾ | Go | Links »

Calculate

Increase Current Additions

Total taxable	$2,000	$ 2,000
401k	5%	5 %
Plan addition amount	$8,550	$8,550
Mutual fund Jay	$1,500	$ 1,500
Mutual fund Susan	$1,500	$ 1,500

Calculate

Save More Money in the Future

Future addition #1 : $

Start year :

End year :

Future addition #2 : $

Start year :

GRAPH OF PLAN RESULTS

Address | http://www.pietechdev.com/PwGoals/PwGoalPlanning.asp?sSessionID=10E5B7279C1D4EEF8723454B89B9A318 ▾ | Go | Links »

Goal Planner: Test 1 for Tim and Amanda   Help

Current Plan Results - All Goals
Total Portfolio Value Graph

TABLE OF RETURNS

Address http://www.pietechdev.com/PWGoals/PWGoalPlanning.asp?sSessionID=10E5B7279C1D4EEF8723454B89B9A318 | Go | Links »

$0
2000   2010   2020   2030   2040   2050
RC RS   DC   DS

■ Qualified Assets   □ Taxable Assets
■ Tax Deferred Assets   ■ Tax Free Assets

RC   Tim retires at age 65   DC   Tim dies at age 90
RS   Amanda retires at age 65   DS   Amanda dies at age 94

Total Portfolio Value Chart

Year	Beginning Portfolio Value		Other Additions	Additions	Post Retirement Income	Investment Earnings	Taxes	Goals - Funds Used			Ending Portfolio Value
	Assigned	Priority						Retirement	College - Jay	College - Susan	
2000	$199,000	$0	$0	$13,550	$0	$20,457	$2,283				$230,724
2001	$230,724	$0	$0	$13,849	$0	$23,718	$2,600				$265,692
2002	$265,692	$0	$0	$14,159	$0	$27,313	$2,939				$304,225
2003	$304,225	$0	$0	$14,479	$0	$31,274	$3,303				$346,676
2004	$346,676	$0	$0	$14,811	$0	$35,638	$3,694				$393,432
2005	$393,432	$0	$0	$15,155	$0	$40,445	$4,113				$444,919
2006	$444,919	$0	$0	$15,510	$0	$45,738	$4,562				$501,604

Not every client will want to play with these scenarios. But for those who do, you can be certain, unlike other calculators on the Web, that this input is solid and you can participate in the action along with your client.

Deliver the Goods

IT DOESN'T MATTER HOW YOU DELIVER the plan to your client. Your style should dictate what method to use. Regardless, I think it is essential to focus on the process of the plan, not the plan itself.

INVESTMENT POLICY SUMMARY
MONTH 20XX

Investor	Sample Client
Type of Assets	Trust Assets
Current Assets	Approximately $3,500,000
Investment Time Horizon	Greater Than 10 years
Return Objective	4.5% over CPI

Risk Tolerance

Intermediate Term: Moderate; Long Term: Low
Losses not to exceed 11% / year with a 90% Confidence Level

Asset Allocation

Cash Equivalents	3%		
U.S. Fixed	42%		
U.S. Large Cap	18%		
U.S. Small Cap	9%	Real Estate	3%
International	17%	Alternative	8%

Allocation Variance

	Style	Subclass	Major Class
Fixed Income			± 7%
Equity			± 7
U.S. Large Cap		± 5%	
U.S. Large Cap Growth	± 3%		
U.S. Large Cap Value	± 3		
U.S. Small Cap		± 5	
U.S. Small Cap Growth	± 3		
U.S. Small Cap Value	± 3		
International		± 5	
Emerging Market		± 3	
Real Estate	± 2		
Alternative	± 2		

Representative Evaluation Benchmarks

Cash Equivalent	Donoghue Tax MMA	**Equity**	S&P 500 Composite, Growth, Value
			Wilshire Large Growth & Value
Fixed Income	Lehman 1-3 Year Gov.		Wilshire Small Growth & Value
	Lehman Intermediate Corp./Gov.		Russell 2000 Composite, Growth, Value
	Lehman Muni		MSCI EMF ID
			MSCI EAFE ND
			Goldman Sachs Commodity
			Wilshire REIT

I have reviewed my investment policy and understand the risk and return parameters of the proposed investment strategy. I also recognize that this policy assumes at least a 5-year investment horizon. I will notify Evensky, Brown & Katz if my circumstances change.

Accepted_____   Date_____

23
pages
on CD-ROM

STRATEGY ANALYSIS

POLICY	OWNER	STYLE	DESCRIPTION		CURRENT (TOTAL %)	CURRENT	POLICY	POLICY (TOTAL %)	PROPOSED	PROPOSED (TOTAL %)	TOTAL
CASH/MMA	SAMPLE		SCHWAB MONEY MKT	SWMXX	100.0%	1,000,000	$20,000	2.0%	$20,000	2.0%	2.0%
US FIXED INCOME	SAMPLE	SHORT GOVT/CORP	DFA 1 YEAR FIXED	DFIHX	0.0%		$70,000	7.0%	$70,000	7.0%	7.0%
	SAMPLE	SHORT/INT GOVT/CORP	PIMCO-LOW DURATION FUND	PTLDX	0.0%		$40,000	4.0%	$40,000	4.0%	4.0%
		INT GOVT/CORP	BLACKROCK CORE BOND	BFMCX	0.0%			0.0%		0.0%	0.0%
		SHORT MUNICIPAL	VANG MUNI SHORT	VWSTX	0.0%			0.0%		0.0%	0.0%
	SAMPLE	SHORT/INT MUNICIPAL	THORNBURG LTD TERM MUNI	LTMIX	0.0%		$80,000	8.0%	$80,000	8.0%	8.0%
	SAMPLE	INTER MUNICIPAL	MORGAN GRENFELL MUNI BOND	MGMBX	0.0%		$180,000	18.0%	$180,000	18.0%	18.0%
FIXED INCOME					100.0%	$1,000,000	$390,000	39.0%	$390,000	39.0%	39.0%
LARGE CAP - U.S.	SAMPLE	CORE	BT EQUITY 500 INDEX	BTIIX	0.0%		$60,000	6.0%	$60,000	6.0%	6.0%
	SAMPLE	VALUE	DFA LARGE CAP VALUE	DFLVX	0.0%		$100,000	10.0%	$100,000	10.0%	10.0%
	SAMPLE	GROWTH	WILSHIRE LARGE CO GROWTH	WLCGX	0.0%		$50,000	5.0%	$50,000	5.0%	5.0%
SMALL CAP - U.S.	SAMPLE	SMALL CAP VALUE	DFA US 6-10 VALUE	DFSVX	0.0%		$60,000	6.0%	$60,000	6.0%	6.0%
	SAMPLE	SMALL CAP GROWTH	BLACKROCK SMALL CAP GRTH	PSGIX	0.0%		$40,000	4.0%	$40,000	4.0%	4.0%
INT'L EQUITY	SAMPLE	DEVELOPED	SEI INTERNATIONAL	SEITX	0.0%		$140,000	14.0%	$140,000	14.0%	14.0%
	SAMPLE	EMERGING MARKETS	MONTGOMERY EMERG MKT*	MNEMX	0.0%		$50,000	5.0%	$50,000	5.0%	5.0%
REAL ESTATE	SAMPLE	REITS	DFA REAL ESTATE	DFREX	0.0%		$30,000	3.0%	$30,000	3.0%	3.0%
ALTERNATIVE	SAMPLE	COMMODITY INDEX	OPPENHEIMER REAL ASSET	QRAAX	0.0%		$30,000	3.0%	$30,000	3.0%	3.0%
	SAMPLE	MARKET NEUTRAL	BARR MARKET NEUTRAL	BMNIX	0.0%		$50,000	5.0%	$50,000	5.0%	5.0%
EQUITY					0.0%	$0	$610,000	61.0%	$610,000	61.0%	61.0%
TOTAL					100.0%	$1,000,000	$1,000,000	100.0%	$1,000,000	100.0%	100.0%

* ONE SOURCE FUNDS

SOURCE: EVENSKY, BROWN & KATZ

1 page on CD-ROM

FIXED INCOME INVESTMENTS	ROR		STD DEV
MONEY MARKET	5.0%		3.4%
GOVT SHORT	4.3%		6.3%
CORP SHORT	4.6%		7.0%
MUNICIPAL SHORT*	5.0%		6.6%
GOVT SHORT/ INTERMEDIATE	5.7%		9.0%
CORP SHORT/INTERMEDIATE	5.8%		9.2%
MUNICIPAL SHORT/INTERMEDIATE*	6.2%		9.4%
GOVT INTERMEDIATE	6.4%		12.6%
CORP INTERMEDIATE	6.8%		13.5%
MUNICIPAL INTERMEDIATE*	7.2%		13.5%
GROWTH INVESTMENTS			
INDEX	9.8%		19.6%
VALUE	10.2%		16.0%
GROWTH	11.4%		21.3%
SMALL CAP - VALUE	11.5%		23.0%
SMALL CAP - GROWTH	12.2%		26.0%
INTERNATIONAL- DEVELOPED	11.4%		20.3%
INTERNATIONAL - EMERGING	12.5%		43.0%
COMMODITIES	9.8%		36.5%

PERSONAL INFLATION	2.5%
EDUCATION INFLATION	5.5%

*Taxable Equivalent

Month 20xx

1
page
on CD-ROM

RETIREMENT PLANNING PROJECTIONS

	BEFORE TAX RETURN	AFTER TAX RETURN
FIXED INCOME		
SHORT TERM	4.6%	3.4%
SHORT/INTER	5.6%	4.2%
INTERMEDIATE TERM	6.2%	4.7%
LONG TERM	6.0%	4.5%
GROWTH INVESTMENTS		
EQUITIES	10.6%	8.1%

INFLATION	2.7%

Month 20xx

1
page
on CD-ROM

ASSET CLASS	1926 - 1999		1990 - 1999	
	ROR	REAL ROR	ROR	REAL ROR
US T BILLS	3.8%	0.7%	4.9%	2.0%
INTERMEDIATE GOVT BONDS	5.2%	2.1%	7.2%	4.3%
LONG TERM GOVT BONDS	5.1%	2.0%	8.8%	5.9%
LONG TERM CORP BONDS	5.6%	2.5%	8.4%	5.5%
COMMON STOCK	11.3%	8.2%	18.2%	15.3%
SMALL COMPANY STOCK	12.6%	9.5%	15.1%	12.2%
INFLATION	3.1%		2.9%	

ASSET CLASS	ROLLING PERIOD 5 YR RETURNS		ROLLING PERIOD 10 YR RETURNS	
	MAX	MIN	MAX	MIN
US T BILLS	11.1%	0.1%	9.2%	0.2%
INTER GOVT. BONDS	17.0%	1.0%	13.1%	1.3%
LONG GOVT. BONDS	21.6%	-2.1%	15.6%	-0.1%
LONG CORP. BONDS	22.5%	-2.2%	16.3%	1.0%
COMMON STOCK	28.5%	-12.5%	20.1%	-0.9%
SMALL COMPANY	45.9%	-27.5%	30.4%	-5.7%
INFLATION	10.1%	-5.4%	8.7%	-2.6%

SOURCE: EVENSKY, BROWN & KATZ

1
page
on CD-ROM

Your EBK Investment Policy

DR. & MRS. JOE SURGEON

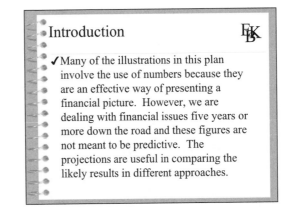

Introduction

✓ Many of the illustrations in this plan involve the use of numbers because they are an effective way of presenting a financial picture. However, we are dealing with financial issues five years or more down the road and these figures are not meant to be predictive. The projections are useful in comparing the likely results in different approaches.

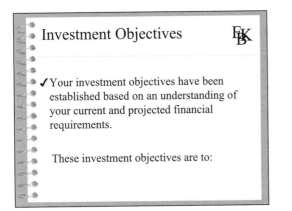

Investment Objectives

✓ Your investment objectives have been established based on an understanding of your current and projected financial requirements.

These investment objectives are to:

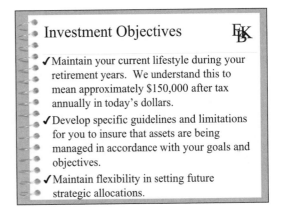

Investment Objectives

✓ Maintain your current lifestyle during your retirement years. We understand this to mean approximately $150,000 after tax annually in today's dollars.

✓ Develop specific guidelines and limitations for you to insure that assets are being managed in accordance with your goals and objectives.

✓ Maintain flexibility in setting future strategic allocations.

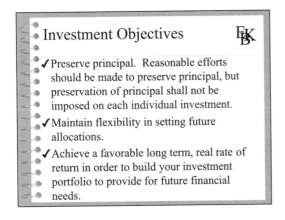

Investment Objectives

✓ Preserve principal. Reasonable efforts should be made to preserve principal, but preservation of principal shall not be imposed on each individual investment.

✓ Maintain flexibility in setting future allocations.

✓ Achieve a favorable long term, real rate of return in order to build your investment portfolio to provide for future financial needs.

Investment Constraints

• You currently have $540,000 in non-repositionable assets, consisting of

• Commercial Real Estate $450,000

• Oil/Gas Partnership $ 90,000

TAKE CARE OF 'EM

When I was setting up my financial planning practice, I visited with an attorney at his office. His desk was littered with slips of paper. On these papers were the names and phone numbers of people who'd left messages, each one asking him to return their calls. While I was explaining my situation, he was periodically grabbing messages, squashing them into neat little balls, and flipping them backward into a wastebasket behind him. After about eight of these lobs, I stopped talking and asked just what he was doing. "Excuse me," he said, "I was just answering some of my phone messages."

Sectio

Client management is all about communication. It's about responding calmly to idiotic suggestions, anticipating uneducated but opinionated observations, and knowing when to say "yes" and how to say "no." It's about *responding to,* not "circular-filing" odd requests and comments. The next few chapters just may give you an idea or two to strengthen your conversation skills. Chapter 8 offers some perspectives on communicating tough issues to clients, including agreements, action plans, and "nervous Nellie" letters. Chapter 9 addresses the issues of reviews, rebalancing, and, if necessary, terminating clients.

CHAPTER
8

CLIENT COMMUNICATION ISSUES

Yada, yada, yada.

— JERRY SEINFELD

I used to give talks on the merits and use of long-term care insurance. One of my recommendations was for advisers to determine how insurers treat existing policyholders. For example, when a new product is introduced, do they allow old policyholders to upgrade? This can give you a better idea of how the relationship with their insurers will be handled. Once while I was giving this talk, an adviser asked me, "What determines the difference between an old policyholder and a new insurance policyholder?" Without a thought, I replied, "the signature at the bottom of the contract, of course." As soon as your client signs the contract, he's an "old" policyholder, and he's usually treated very differently. Sometimes, this is what happens to our prospects once they become clients.

In the Beginning

ONCE A CLIENT HAS AGREED TO ENGAGE you as an adviser, you'll want to prepare a contract with him outlining the obligations you each have to the relationship. Greenbaum and Orecchio, Inc. has provided a contract format that is not laden with legalese (see FORM 8-01 on page 205). The Fiduciary Oath section outlines a very specific relationship with the client, with a pledge of full disclosure. We have also elected to include a Fiduciary Oath as part of our contracts. I have included our two contracts on the CD-ROM. They are FORM 8-02 for financial planning services and FORM 8-03 for investment management services only (see pages 206 and 207).

THE FIDUCIARY OATH

Evensky, Brown & Katz shall exercise its best efforts to act in good faith and in the best interests of the client. The advisor shall provide written disclosure to the client prior to the engagement of the advisor, and thereafter throughout the term of the engagement, of any conflicts of interest which will or reasonably may compromise the impartiality or independence of the advisor.

Evensky, Brown & Katz, or any party in which EB&K has a financial interest, does not receive compensation or other remuneration that is contingent on any client's purchase or sale of a financial product. The advisor does not receive a fee or other compensation from another party based on the referral of a client or the client's business.

OK, here comes the sermon: I believe that it is important for advisers to recognize their fiduciary role with clients and, more importantly, to make sure that the client is made aware of this position as well. I once thought that admitting to this role was unique to fee-only independent advisers. Then my son, David, began training with AXA under the capable tutelage of my good friend and insurance expert Ben Baldwin. David brought home his educational material one evening for my husband and me to review with him. I nearly fell off the chair when I read:

If you meet certain requirements, you will be acting as a fiduciary when using one of our three titles on your business cards, stationery and prospecting letters. The three titles are:

- **Planning Associate**
- **Financial Planner**
- **Financial Advisor**

Imagine! A huge financial planning company like AXA is teaching their planners that they are acting as fiduciaries in relationships with their clients. I believe we should all take that position.

INTRODUCTION TO THE FIRM

When a new client joins us, we immediately send a welcome letter. This letter reminds the client of our services and introduces him to the people in the firm. We list all staff members, their backgrounds, and what job responsibilities they have within the organization. Finally, we include e-mail addresses so that clients can reach them easily by electronic mail. One of the reasons we do this is to reinforce our team concept. We are politely inviting our clients to call others in our firm for services that they need, instead of constantly calling an adviser who will just have to involve others anyway.

Dear CLIENT:

I'd like to take this opportunity, on behalf of everyone at Evensky, Brown & Katz, to express how much we are looking forward to working with you. We believe it's important for you to know what to look forward to in being our client.

We all work on a team basis here. Any of our partners are available to discuss any issues with you, at any time. If Harold is unavailable, you can always speak with Lane, who will work closely with both you and Harold. Together, they coordinate all the necessary tasks—from preparing agreements and opening accounts, to placing trades and running various reports—through Michelle Grillone, Director of Operations. Michelle and her department then monitor applications, transfers, statements, and accounts for accuracy and efficiency. Our support staff then performs multiple, interactive tasks to ensure all client database information—from birthdays to IRA beneficiaries—is correct and complete. Our team approach strives to leave no stone unturned, and no questions unanswered.

Attached is a list describing our staff's diverse responsibilities. You may never have a reason to work with them directly; however, you may be greeted by one or more of them when calling or visiting our main Coral Gables office. And the entire staff of Evensky, Brown & Katz is always available to assist you with any questions, comments, or concerns you may have.

Communication means everything to us. Aside from phone calls, we often mail interesting media pieces, and use the Internet to send informational "flash" reports to keep you up-to-date with relevant current events. If you have an e-mail address, please let us know.

In addition, you will receive our quarterly *Insites* newsletter, which features articles on a variety of topics—from taxes and estate planning to insurance and retirement issues. Many of the featured articles are written by the partners and advisors of EBK, and we occasionally ask other professionals in the top of their field to share their thoughts and ideas as well. If you would like to see a specific subject discussed, feel free to let us know—your opinions and feedback are appreciated.

We want to be there for you. If at any time we fall short, please call me personally.

Cordially yours,

Financial Planner

Harold R. Evensky, CFP   Partner   harold@evensky.com

He received his Bachelor's and Master's degrees from Cornell. In his free time Harold serves on a number of national professional boards, lectures, and writes on investment issues. He is chairman of the investment committee and, along with Deena and Peter, is responsible for the firm's overall investment policy and selecting the approved manager list.

Peter Brown, CFP   Partner   pbrown@evensky.com

He earned his M.B.A. in Operations Research and Statistics from New York University, after earning his B.S. in Chemical Engineering from Massachusetts Institute of Technology. He is an arbitrator for the NASD and the American Arbitration Association and formerly sat on the board and executive loan and audit committees for a Dade County Savings and Loan Bank.

Deena B. Katz, CFP   Partner   pepper@evensky.com

Deena received a B.A. from Adrian College and is a member of the college's board of trustees. She has been active in the investment and financial planning profession, both locally and nationally, for over 25 years. Ms. Katz is also the author of various books on long-term care and retirement. Her latest achievement, published in September 1999, is titled *Deena Katz on Practice Management.*

All partners are available for questions that you feel require their attention.

Lane Jones, CFP   Advisor   lane@evensky.com

Lane earned his license from the Certified Financial Planning Education Program. He received a Bachelor of Science in Finance from the University of Florida in Gainesville. In addition, Lane is vice president of the American Association of Individual Investors. He is a candidate for his CFA designation and has successfully completed Level I.

Deana Kelly, CFP   Advisor   dkelly@evensky.com

Deana has completed her Series 7, 63, and 65 and has also earned her CFP license. She received her B.A. from Westminster College in Pennsylvania and then received her M.A. from Carnegie Mellon University.

Matt McGrath, CFP   Advisor   mmcgrath@evensky.com

Matt has received his CFP license and in addition holds a B.A. in Economics, an M.B.A. in Personal Financial Planning, and a certificate in Personal Financial Planning from the University of Miami. He is also the treasurer of the Gold Coast Chapter of the AAII.

Scott Wells, CFP   Advisor   swells@evensky.com

Scott received his CFP license and has received his degree in Accounting from State Technical Institute in Memphis. He also serves as president of the American Association of Individual Investors and president of the local FPA.

The heart of our client service team is our four advisors, Lane, Matt, Deana, and Scott. Each advisor works closely with Harold, Deena, and Peter on the management and development of your portfolio. Whether you want to know the formula for computing the Sharpe ratio or just need help opening an IRA, each advisor will be happy to help you understand your portfolio and answer any questions you may have.

Michelle V. Grillone Director of Operations mgrillone@evensky.com
As director of operations for EBK, Ms. Grillone acts as a liaison for EBK between Fidelity and Schwab. She is responsible for the maintenance of client accounts, as well as the portfolio management software database including the daily download. Ms. Grillone is responsible for establishing and maintaining all EBK accounts, which include transfers, wires, journals, and issuing checks. She also is responsible for EBK's mutual fund, bond, and equity trading on a daily basis. Ms. Grillone received her B.A. degree in business administration with a concentration in accounting from the University of Miami. A Miami native, she started with the firm in September 2000. For any operations questions, you will still want to call Matt, Lane, Scott, or Deana.

Jennifer Arbeene Operations Manager jennifer@evensky.com
Jennifer is responsible for various operational tasks, such as opening accounts and monitoring transfers. Jennifer also handles our concierge department, is the editor for the EBK Insites newsletter, and is our EBK Webmaster. She is currently working toward her Bachelor of Arts degree.

Veronica Paguaga Operations Assistant vvilchez@evensky.com
Currently, Veronica holds an A.A. in Business Administration and is working on her Bachelor's degree in International Finance. She supports the advisors with all back office procedures including preparing your quarterly reviews.

Mena Bielow Comptroller mena@evensky.com
Mena is responsible for all regulatory and compliance matters. She prepares management reports, generates financial statements, and handles all accounting-related tasks as the firm's comptroller and office manager.

Tammi Wells   Administrative Assistant   twells@evensky.com

Tammi received her Associate of Arts degree in Business from the DePaul Business School in Chicago. She is responsible for all administrative and executive tasks for Deena.

ANOTHER CLIENT LETTER

I have also included a welcome letter used by Legacy Wealth Management in Memphis, Tennessee, to give you an idea of how you might spruce up your welcome letter.

Dear CLIENT,

Legacy Wealth Management, Inc. welcomes you to our family. We appreciate your retaining us and look forward to working together with you. I will be your primary contact at Legacy Wealth and my assistant is Deborah Wilson. Deborah is fully capable of answering operations questions and can fulfill requests for information. Since I am often in client meetings, I encourage you to call Deborah with questions or requests. Please find her business card enclosed.

As our new client, please allow us to build a firm foundation with you by sharing some background information about Legacy Wealth Management, Inc.

WHY THE NAME LEGACY WEALTH MANAGEMENT?:

Our name represents exactly what we do, which is provide counsel for the overall financial well being of our clients and their heirs. The wealth management process begins with a thorough exploration of a client's goals and dreams, progressing through the identification of a client's risk tolerance and desired return, and culminating with an extensive review of his or her resources. A comprehensive list of topics can be addressed that includes education of children or grandchildren, adequacy of retirement assets, risk management, cash flow planning, estate planning, transfer of assets, and investment management.

OUR LOGO:

It's an egg. Yet so much more. It's how we view what our clients have entrusted with us. A child's future. A secure retirement. An international adventure. A backyard paradise. A wish for one more scholarship. A prayer for one less incurable disease. It's hopes and dreams. We'll provide the care and nurturing to reach them.

MORE ON CONFIDENTIALITY:

We view the confidentiality of our clients' financial affairs to be of paramount importance. Client documents are shredded at their disposal. Also, from time to time, clients have requested us to fax personal financial documents to their offices. To ensure your privacy, we will be happy to call you before sending such information.

SMART PROCEDURES:

As you know, we do not take custody of client monies or securities. If you are depositing securities or checks into your account, we ask you to send them directly to Charles Schwab & Co., Inc.

Charles Schwab & Co., Inc.
Institutional Service Group, Team 5
P.O. Box 628290
Orlando, FL 32862-9905

Also, we want to remind clients never to sign the back of stock or bond certificates. Once this is done, the certificate becomes a cash equivalent. We have stock and bond powers you can sign instead. You can then mail the certificate and the stock or bond power separately to Schwab where they can match them. These procedures serve the same purpose as signing the back of the certificate, but are significantly safer. Please write your account number on all items mailed to Charles Schwab & Co.

Another procedure we recommend to make everyone's life easier is to hold all securities at Charles Schwab & Co., Inc. in a brokerage account. We do not charge clients for this service because we are not currently charged. Dividends will then be paid into a money market account automatically so you will not have to cash numerous individual dividend checks. The value of your accounts is at our fingertips if you or we need that information quickly. Lastly, each client account at Schwab is insured up to $100,000,000.

FRIDAY DRESS:

If you should drop into our offices on a Friday, you may notice that we are dressed in more casual clothes. As they are for many other businesses, Fridays are casual days for both our advisors and staff.

WE HAVE VOICE MAIL AND E-MAIL:

During regular business hours, a receptionist will answer the telephone and will direct your calls. Additionally, we have voice mail and e-mail systems in our office to enhance communication. We ask that you provide as much information as possible on voice mail or e-mail so we can respond promptly and efficiently.

	VOICE MAIL EXTENSIONS	E-MAIL ADDRESSES
		Legacy@legacywealth.com
John Ueleke	1	JohnU@legacywealth.com
Hallie Peyton	7	HallieP@legacywealth.com
Dick Vosburg	2	RichardV@legacywealth.com
Amery Staub	8	AmeryS@legacywealth.com
Sarah Haizlip	3	SarahH@legacywealth.com
Melissa Still	9	MelissaS@legacywealth.com
Deborah Wilson	4	DeborahW@legacywealth.com
Duncan Miller	10	DuncanM@legacywealth.com
Donna Brewer	5	DonnaB@legacywealth.com
Steve Holdsworth	11	SteveH@legacywealth.com
Cathy Ingram	12	CathyI@legacywealth.com
Administrative	13	HallieP@legacywealth.com

ADVISORS AND STAFF:

For your convenience, we have enclosed a Staff Reference List as a supplement to this letter. This listing provides background information as well as each individual's function within the organization.

ADV PART II FORMS AVAILABLE FOR CLIENTS:

Our ADV Form Part II is available. This is our official disclosure document and is updated at least annually. To request one, please call our office.

We hope you find this information helpful. If at any time you have a question, please call us. We are here to serve you. Thank you once again for choosing Legacy Wealth Management.

Sincerely,

Financial Planner

During the Relationship

ACTION PLANS

I think the action plan is the most critical paper you produce. It certainly lets the client in on the game plan, but it is so much more. Particularly now, when many advisers are scrambling to figure out their added value in the adviser-client relationship, having an action plan that spans a year or two helps the client understand the process of planning. Many consumers are still under the impression that a financial plan is a product; we only reinforce that thinking when we provide a big book with all their issues addressed. It seems to me that the use of action plans makes a better statement.

It is vitally important to document ongoing activities with clients. We tend to outline our recommended actions in a letter to the client as opposed to having a formal document for this. The following is an example of an action letter that we sent to a client.

Dear CLIENT:

Harold and I enjoyed meeting with you yesterday and are pleased to welcome you as a client. As we discussed in our meeting, you are particularly concerned with decisions regarding your estate planning, in light of your new windfall. We have prioritized your concerns and agreed on the following course of action:

1) We will have both the NIM-CRUT and Irrevocable Life Insurance Trust (ILIT) reviewed by our consultants at KPMG. Any changes to the NIM-CRUT should be addressed prior to its funding with the shares of XX stock.

2) Additionally, as Harold mentioned, we will review the strategy of utilizing an Irrevocable Life Insurance Trust.

3) We recommend that you immediately review your property and casualty liability coverage with your agent and consider, at a minimum, raising your umbrella liability limits to $5 million of coverage from the $1 million of current protection.

4) We recommend that you speak with Joe Lawyer about the preparation of a living trust. We do not recommend consideration of the trust as either a probate avoidance tool or for privacy reasons but rather to facilitate management of your assets in the event of your incapacity. In addition, we recommend that at a minimum you have prepared and execute durable powers of attorney, living wills and health care powers for both of you. Once the trust is created, you will need to re-title your non-tax-sheltered assets into trust name. This will not prevent you from funding the NIM-CRUT once our analysis is complete and will not create an additional tax liability. Ultimately, the trust will hold title to those assets not transferred to the NIM-CRUT. We'll be pleased to assist in this matter.

5) I have also enclosed a number of forms for your execution along with a return envelope. These include:

- Limited Power of Attorney forms granting us specific authorizations over XX existing Fidelity accounts.
- A Fidelity account application for the NIM-CRUT. Once the charitable trust has been funded and the initial sale of the XX shares complete, we will provide you with wiring instructions in order to fund this new account.
- A Fidelity account application for your IRA and a transfer form for

bringing over your current balance from Vanguard funds.

- A Fidelity account application to open a personal account in the name of XX. This account will hold the assets not transferred into the NIM-CRUT and will be re-titled in the name of your living trust upon its completion.

- Two copies of our basic advisory agreement. One is for your records and a second to be returned to us.

- A client information sheet required by the SEC to be filled out in its entirety.

- A copy of our ADV Part II.

We'll be in touch with you soon to follow up on our review of the NIM-CRUT and ILIT. Please call should you have any questions in the interim.

Cordially yours,

Financial Planner

ACTION PLAN AND AGENDA

Ross Levin of Accredited Investors, Inc. in Edina, Minnesota, has developed action plan formats from his Access program so that each issue that requires action will continue to be listed on the client's internal review document until it is marked "complete."[1] The actions are assigned to Ross, staff, or the client at the time they are created and are tied to an annual goal that Ross and the client have forged together at the beginning of the year. Ross covers how this works in his book, *The Wealth Management Index* (McGraw Hill Professional Publishing, 1997).

Ross sends an agenda to each client before his review meeting. The action tasks that have not been completed are listed on this letter, so the client knows what topics will be discussed. He finds that this method helps to manage their expectations and demonstrates the value of their periodic meetings together.

CLIENT DIARIES

If you are not keeping copious notes on your interactions with clients, I believe you should re-think your procedures. Obviously keeping good records is a prudent move for liability reasons, but we have found over the years that the more we chronicle interactions with our clients, the better we can control the relationship with them. For example, we list family members, important dates, travel experiences, and other nonfinancial information so that we can make our contact with the client more personal. We also have used our client diaries to spot trends in client behavior that we need to address. If a client is constantly going over the same ground, we know that we have been unsuccessful in communicating with him. If a client continually expresses fear about the markets, the economy, or his portfolio, we set up a special risk coaching appointment because this behavior may be an indication that we need to reinforce some old concepts.

CLIENT LETTERS ON TOUGH SUBJECTS

The good people at Kochis Fitz Tracy Fitzhugh & Scott write some of the best client letters I have ever read and on some of the toughest topics. This retainer letter that Tim Kochis shared with us is an effort to explain and justify a change in fees. The letter is well prepared and reflects much thought and care. It might prove helpful to you in your practice.

Dear CLIENT,

Over the years, our business has grown substantially ... in terms of the number of clients we serve, the volume and intensity of services we offer, and in the size of our staff. We are making every attempt to ensure that, as we grow, we continue to provide *all* of our clients with the quality of service they have a right to expect.

Today, all of our new clients engage us to provide both initial and ongoing comprehensive personal financial planning services and discretionary management of their investment portfolios. The planning services are paid for by fees calculated by the hour of professional service and the portfolio management services are compensated by a small annual percentage of the assets under management. Ongoing updating and refinement of the non-portfolio aspects of the client's financial plan are now usually paid for by an annual "retainer," billed at the start of the year.

This overall formulation has evolved for our clients because it provides many substantial benefits for them:

- The overall plan is *regularly* reviewed and updated because a very key component—the investment portfolio—gets regular and intense attention.

- The investment plan—usually the centerpiece and engine of the overall financial plan—is implemented, monitored, and refined as appropriate in a timely, cost-efficient, and dispassionate fashion.

- As the discretionary manager of the portfolio, we are able to access "institutional" mutual funds that, in several cases, are less costly and/or better performers than those available for us to merely recommend to non-discretionary management clients.

- The annual updating retainer both provides for our continuous attention to the client's overall planning situation and removes any fee sensitivity to the client's calling us whenever questions arise or a new planning issue requires attention. We are "on call"; the fee for the year has already been paid.

Because this has worked so well for other clients, we urge you to adopt this program as well. In recognition of our existing relationship, we are prepared to offer a substantial discount from the normal "minimums" that would apply to new clients. While we will want to discuss the specifics of your ongoing planning needs to arrive at a firm number for your circumstances, we may be able to settle on an annual retainer as low as $1,500. Similarly, where we now normally require at least a $X million investment portfolio for new clients, we will be happy, in your case, to accept discretionary management responsibility for a portfolio at a $$$ threshold. Our fees would be ##% per year for the first $1 million and, then, #% per year for amounts above that level.

We realize that even these discounted terms may amount to your incurring costs greater than you have in the past. We believe, strongly, that the much-enhanced package of services will be well worth the greater expense.

FEATURE	COMPREHENSIVE "NEW" SERVICE PROGRAM	CURRENT PROGRAM (TO BE DISCONTINUED NO LATER THAN 12/31/XXXX)
Investment Services	Discretionary management by Kochis Fitz	Kochis Fitz recommends portfolio construction
	Best available, institutional quality mutual funds, at institutional pricing	Best available retail funds
	Ongoing portfolio monitoring and adjustment, initiated by Kochis Fitz (includes capture of available tax losses and timing of capital gains)	N/A
	Periodic performance monitoring against relevant benchmarks, using industry standards for performance calculations	N/A
Comprehensive Personal Financial Planning Services	Pre-paid, "on call" status for all personal financial issues	N/A
	Quarterly letters commenting on your portfolio's investment performance and prompting a meeting to review your overall financial plan	N/A
	At least one pre-paid face-to-face meeting per year to thoroughly review all relevant financial issues, initiated by Kochis Fitz	Meetings *when* and *if* you call; at incremental fee cost

(continued on the following page)

FEATURE	COMPREHENSIVE "NEW" SERVICE PROGRAM	CURRENT PROGRAM (TO BE DISCONTINUED NO LATER THAN 12/31/XXXX)
	Annual summary of all major financial decisions and status report of all pending issues	N/A
Background, Reference, and Educational Materials	Updated editions of *Concepts*	Same
	Periodic tax planning "Alerts"	Same
	Investment Commentary ... quarterly	Year-end issue only

In summary, we are convinced that these new arrangements will better meet your *ongoing* needs and will keep your financial plan and its most important implementation up-to-date.

We understand that you may have a number of questions about this new program and that it may require some time for you to decide to go forward on these terms. Consequently, we've postponed the deadline for these new arrangements until January 1st of next year. In the meantime, if you would like us to do work for you under existing arrangements, we are very happy to do so. If you ultimately decide not to adopt the new program, we will, with regret, provide you with a list of alternative planners whom we believe are in a good position to help you.

Please call with any questions. We're eager to get you underway in this new service program as soon as you're ready.

Sincerely,

Financial Planner

Tim graciously shared another letter on a topic other advisers have had some trouble addressing, the issue of raising minimums. This letter carefully outlines the need to change the minimums, then uses the opportunity to explain the concept of a "team" approach to client relationships. It ends by mentioning the fact that they have expanded their professional staff, and introduces the new members on a second page. Tim told me that this letter was sent to their referral sources as well as to existing clients to be certain that everyone who might refer a client will know to send someone who meets their new criteria.

Dear Clients and Friends:

We're writing to inform you of our decision to raise the minimum financial advisory fees and the minimum investment management portfolio size for new clients of the firm. In order to ensure that all of our clients receive the quality of attention they have a right to expect of us, effective July 1, XXXX, we can no longer accept new client engagements where the initial financial consulting fees would be less than $X,000 or the size of the portfolio to be managed would be less than $X million.

In order to ensure that we're appropriately allocating our key resources, we can only offer the direct involvement of one of our principals, as the primary client contact, in cases where the engagement includes the management of investment portfolios of at least $2.5 million, in the case of Linda and Tom, and $4 million in the case of Tim.

These new thresholds do not apply in the case of corporate-sponsored financial planning engagements. There, we have no specific expectation of managing a client's investment portfolio, and economies of scale and of delivery method permit considerable customization in pricing.

Further, these new portfolio size thresholds for Linda, Tom, and Tim do not change our vitally important rule that all clients "belong" to the firm as a whole. In all cases, all of our clients—current and new—have the benefit of the insight and experience of our entire team.

While each of you has probably come to regard some one person in our firm as your primary contact and we have come to view that same person as the one primarily responsible for responding to your needs, each of you has a claim on the entire reservoir of our combined professional talents and, at all times, the work that we do for you is the result of the collaborative effort of at least two of our people. All investment management decisions, for example, are the result of collegial input and seasoned judgment from the entire professional staff. We're convinced that this whole is much better than any one of its parts. Nevertheless, the principals of K&F exercise, again in all cases, final authority to execute those decisions.

As you know from earlier communications, we have substantially expanded our professional staff within the past several months. The enclosed summary displays the credentials of this enhanced team. That expansion and this increase in our new client thresholds are two parts of a deliberate effort to make sure that the quality and timely responsiveness of our services to all clients do not suffer. As business people, we are of course interested in new clients, but not at the expense of continuing to provide highest quality service to the clients who have already given us their loyalty and support. Our first responsibility is to you.

Thank you,

Financial Planner

A BIG CHANGE IS COMING LETTER

Over the years I think we all have discovered that some clients can get very disturbed over change. I was speaking with an adviser not long ago about staff changes. "We take a picture of our staff every year for our holiday card. I've looked over them for the past several years," he said. "The same old partners are in the front, and the sea of faces changes constantly in the back." I know that when we have had staff changes, clients have been practically disoriented. But, what if you change your business structure? What if you change partners? David Drucker and Mary Malgoire amicably separated their practices a few years ago. David decided to move his practice to Albuquerque, New Mexico, so he needed to tell his clients about the split and the move. I liked David's letter and thought you might find it useful one day.

Dear CLIENT:

As we've discussed recently in person and by mail, Malgoire Drucker Inc. has "subdivided" into two new firms—The Family Firm,

Inc., which will represent all of Mary Malgoire's clients, and Sunset Financial Management, Inc. ("Sunset"), which will represent all of my clients. The purpose of this letter is to forward to you the first of two sets of forms that need to be signed to make this change, and to tell you a little about Sunset.

The enclosed forms are a new Letter of Understanding and a letter of termination to Malgoire Drucker Inc. The signing of these documents is merely a formality—there are no substantive differences between the enclosed Letter of Understanding and your existing Letter of Understanding other than a name change and, in some cases, an increased level of service (with no fee increase) designed to create greater uniformity among all of my client contracts. If you see any changes that concern you, please call me to discuss them.

The termination letter simply fulfills your duty under your existing Letter of Understanding to give notice of your desire to terminate that contractual arrangement. It also signifies your understanding of the "dual management" that will exist in the future. This refers to the arrangement Sunset will have with Charles Schwab whereby the MDI staff, who have served you in the past by providing investment support services to me, can continue to do so. To make this possible, both Sunset and The Family Firm will have a Limited Power of Attorney (called "dual management") under a joint master account with Schwab.

The second set of forms you will receive in a week or two will be primarily related to your accounts at Charles Schwab and moving them to the new Sunset master account mentioned above.

As you can imagine, this restructuring is a complicated matter, since we need to coordinate a number of regulatory and investment account changes. *It will be very helpful if you will return these forms in the envelope provided as soon as possible.* Mary and I appreciate your prompt attention to this.

As you know, I will be working in my customary locations until my family and I occupy our Albuquerque, NM home in July of 1998. The staff you've come to know at Malgoire Drucker Inc—Lisa St. Claire,

Lexy Burke, Steve Thalheimer, Doris Lerman and our new office manager, Wanda Mumford—will all join me in continuing to serve you both before and after my move.

OUR MISSION STATEMENT

You may or may not recall MDI's mission statement which has been posted in our reception area for many years, and which we include in the letters we write to you each year when we tell you what's new with our firm and its services. That mission statement is ...

"Providing individuals and families with a trusted and enduring advisory relationship so that they may not only achieve long-term financial well-being but also realize personal aspirations."

Note that this mission statement is not just about money. We might have said, "Our mission is to maximize your wealth," but we all know that that is not enough. We must be able to use our money to make our dreams come true. If we don't figure out a way to make the two come together, then increasing our financial wealth—by itself—is an empty achievement.

As a wise person once said, "When we lie dying one day, will we wish that we'd spent more hours at our jobs?" To the contrary, our regrets will probably be about wanting more connectedness with our loved ones and friends, and having a greater quality of life together. For my wife and me, this move to the Southwest is a small step in the direction of making this mission statement real for us. It is going from a familiar and "safe" place that has simply become too fast-paced for us, to a more relaxed place of many unknowns but great promise—a place we believe will be ideal for raising our daughter. (And don't worry, "more relaxed" doesn't mean inattentive to *your* needs!)

In any job like mine, where teaching and guidance are involved, it is important to practice what one preaches. I've always done that with my personal investing. I use the exact same models, research, procedures, and investment vehicles in my personal investment program that I recommend for each of my clients. But, with this move, I would like to think I am modeling much more than reasoned investing habits—I'm hopefully modeling the mission statement that Mary and I have professed for many years. I believe we must all strive to make financial security a foundation for a more meaningful life.

ACCESSIBILITY

The most important service you receive from me is my advice to you. Of course, to advise you, I must be accessible to you. It has always been my goal to make it easy for you to reach me (one phone number that finds me wherever I am) and to reply promptly. This must never change because it is essential to our relationship. In that regard, beginning next July, I will have an "800" number at which you will find me always.

SERVICES

You may wonder how my move is going to affect you, in spite of assurances I've given you in the past that my service to you will be unchanged. The services you receive will not be unchanged but, rather, improved.

As effective as Mary's and my partnership has been over the years, and as highly as we have regarded each other to this day, it is a partnership, and you must expect a slower pace to needed change and innovation than in a firm with one "CEO" acting on his or her vision, alone, as to how things should work. Thus, my corporate changes will benefit you as I move forward, just as I think Mary's clients will benefit from the same freedom of innovation that she will enjoy, e.g., without the need for my constant "OK."

My first *new* service, of which most clients are already aware, is my site on the World Wide Web (www.sunset-finmgt.com). This will not benefit *all* of my clients because not all use computers or "surf" the Internet but, for those who do, they will get the same information I will provide to everyone—just a little bit faster.

My most beneficial services to you will always be to help you make important decisions and thereby free you up to use your time more productively or in a more satisfying way. Almost everything of value to us in our fast-paced existence meets one of these objectives. To this end, I am continuing to make contacts in a variety of other personal service businesses that can benefit you in ways described above. I will make available to you referrals to these persons or business, as those relationships solidify, in areas such as

- bill-paying services;
- personal computer setup and consultation;
- elder care social workers and related services;
- medical claims processing;
- and a growing list of other personal service providers.

If this reminds you of services you have been seeking that are not on this list, please let me know so that I can add them, and help you find the expertise you need.

More frequent contact is on my list of operational items on which to expand. In surveys I have conducted with all of my clients over the last several years, the one need that arises most often is more frequent contact. It will be a primary goal to achieve this, using a variety of mechanisms, including direct contact by phone and meetings (when in town each quarter), more mailings, more e-mail bulletins to those clients using e-mail (in addition to my Web page), and more mailings of articles of interest to you, and other means of contact.

As always, feel free to tell me what you want my service to be for you, and what you value the most. I welcome such feedback at all times. And before I conclude this letter, I want to thank you again for your patronage, support, and for giving me the opportunity to serve you.

Sincerely,

Financial Planner

Dear Financial Planner:

I have been advised that Malgoire Drucker Inc. has "subdivided" into two new firms—The Family Firm, Inc., which will represent all of Mary Malgoire's clients, and Sunset Financial Management, Inc., which will represent all of David Drucker's clients. I further understand that Ms. Malgoire and Mr. Drucker have amicably and, by design, effected this subdivision and that each desires that his or her clients affiliate themselves with their respective firms.

Accordingly, in order to continue my relationship with David J. Drucker as a client of Sunset Financial Management, Inc., I hereby give notice to Malgoire Drucker Inc. (now The Family Firm, Inc.) that I am terminating my relationship as a client of that firm. Also, I understand that my investments at Charles Schwab & Co. will be dually managed, with Sunset Financial Management, Inc. being primary, and The Family Firm, Inc. being secondary, solely for the purpose of enabling the staff of Malgoire Drucker Inc. (now the staff of The Family Firm, Inc.) to continue to provide the same investment support services to Sunset that I enjoyed prior to the subdivision of the two firms.

Sincerely,

{Client Name}

NERVOUS NELLIE LETTERS

Occasionally events happen in the world that directly affect our clients' lives. We feel it is especially important to respond to these as quickly as possible. If we believe the event will disturb clients, we immediately write a letter, then send it by snail mail, flash fax, or e-mail, however the client prefers to get his information. We figure that our clients will be getting many opinions about the event and want to be seen as proactive. We want to let them know we're aware of current events and are actively considering how these events might affect their lives. We also want to help them formulate their own opinions. Here are a couple of letters that my partner Harold created in response to specific events.

Dear CLIENT:

It would be hard not to be concerned about the impact on the markets of our government's machinations over its debt management. We thought you would like to know our thoughts.

- This isn't a first. A similar crisis occurred twice during the Reagan administration and once under Bush.
- The probability of an actual default on capital market obligations is very slim. There are numerous sources of emergency reserves that would allow the government to limp along for a while.

- The potential upside is that this posturing will lead to a meaningful deficit reduction package, one that balances the budget by 2002. If so, that will be good news for both the bond and stock markets.

There are a few possible downside scenarios:

- Even without an actual default, the current crisis will result in the markets demanding a risk premium on government paper driving up treasury rates. As U.S. government bonds tend to set the base for all bonds, it would result in a general increase for all bonds and ultimately a push upwards for inflation.

- There is no significant budget reduction. That would result in a negative for the bond and stock markets.

- There is a real default. The consequences of this scenario are unknown, but the market disruptions could be significant.

We have spoken to most of our managers and, across the board, they agree with us that no significant action is appropriate at this time. The markets in general, obviously, agree based on their actions for the last few days.

Most important, keep in mind the EB&K mantra—FIVE YEARS, FIVE YEARS, FIVE YEARS—and rest assured, we'll continue to monitor the markets, our managers, and your portfolios.

Please give us a call if you have any questions or concerns or would just like to chat.

Cordially yours,

Financial Planner

Dear CLIENT:

The recent market volatility is certainly not a secret. Unfortunately it's such a "good story" that the media, as expected, seem to be doing everything in their power to panic the world. While we could be on the verge of a bear market, we want to assure you that you're well positioned as a long term investor with a diversified portfolio, invested in hundreds of high investment grade bonds and thousands of good companies throughout the world. Your portfolio is prepared to weather any storm or to take advantage of any sudden surge to the upside.

Still, we recognize that everyone prefers markets that trend steadily upwards. Although we may not be able to do anything about the market direction (at least in the short term), we want you to know that, as always, we are carefully monitoring all of your investments closely. In addition, during periods of particularly volatile markets such as the last week, we initiate a special program of increased performance monitoring and benchmarking of our managers and attribution analysis of our clients' portfolios.

Most important, we wanted to remind you what we've told you all. "We don't make our clients rich but we don't make them poor. We help them sleep well at night and go about enjoying their life without worrying about their investments." We consider it our primary responsibility to help you "sleep well" during poor markets. Towards that end, please call us to chat or stop in if the recent or future market volatility causes you any concern. In fact, call to say hi or stop in even if it doesn't.

Cordially yours,

Financial Planner

YOU WON'T TAKE MY ADVICE?

Lou Stanasolovich has a solution for people who do not want to follow his advice. He sends them a "no action" letter. I tend to think more along the lines of my good friend Lynn Hopewell who usually tells someone who refuses to take his advice: "You don't need me. It's obvious you know more than I do." Personally, I don't think I'd keep someone as a client who hired me for my advice then refused to take it, but I think Lou's letter is a good one. I just hope I never have to use it.

Dear CLIENT:

Everyone's financial circumstances involve a balance between risk and reward, opportunity and protection.

You have two items to be protected: the present assets you have acquired and the future income you will receive. Opportunities which are lost may not come again, or if they do, the remaining time for growth has been foreshortened.

The job of a financial planner is to measure these risks and communicate them effectively to you. We try to help you form a balance between the risk exposure and the expense of insurance or the inconvenience of risk avoidance.

You have indicated your desire not to take action at this time on a recommendation we consider critical to your future. Naturally, this is your prerogative. Please give this matter further thought and if you continue to feel the same way, please contact me.

Cordially,

Financial Planner

In the End

A NEW ADVISER STOPPED ME AT A CONFERENCE not long ago and asked me where we find the time to send so many letters to our clients about events and circumstances. "I'm too busy trying to manage other things for them. I don't have time to communicate with them," he told me. I resisted the urge to invite this guy to seek out another profession. What we do is communicate with them—all the time and in many different ways. Once we stop that free flow of interaction, they might as well be getting advice off the Internet.

GREENBAUM AND ORECCHIO, INC.
Wealth Management Services

4 96 Kinderkamack Road • Oradell, NJ 07649-1523
(201) 261-1900 • Fax (201) 261-9365
Info@InvestmentCounsel.com

Agreement for Wealth Management Services

A. **PARTIES** This Agreement is made between Tom Smith ("Client") whose principal residence is at 123 Main Street Old Tappan, NJ 07675, and Greenbaum and Orecchio, Inc., whose principal office is located at 496 Kinderkamack Road, Oradell, New Jersey 07649-1523.

B. **INTENT** Client agrees to hire Greenbaum and Orecchio, Inc. to provide Client with wealth management services. Greenbaum and Orecchio, Inc. agrees to perform these services for Client. Both parties intend to be legally bound by this Agreement.

C. **TERM** This Agreement shall remain in force as long as mutually agreed to by Client and by Greenbaum and Orecchio, Inc. This Agreement may be terminated at any time, by either Client or by Greenbaum and Orecchio, Inc., for any reason, upon 30 days written notice to the other party. Upon termination, Greenbaum and Orecchio, Inc. agrees to refund to Client that portion of Client's prepaid fee for which no services have been provided.

Client may terminate this Agreement and receive a full refund of all fees paid to Greenbaum and Orecchio, Inc. by giving written notice within five days after the date of this Agreement.

D. **CONFIDENTIALITY** All information furnished by Client to Greenbaum and Orecchio, Inc., including Client's identity, shall be treated as confidential. Greenbaum and Orecchio, Inc. agrees not to voluntarily disclose confidential information without Client's prior consent (unless required by law, court order or agency directive, or unless Greenbaum and Orecchio, Inc. expects, in its reasonable opinion, that it will be compelled by a court or government agency, or unless such information becomes publicly available or known other than as a result of actions of Greenbaum and Orecchio, Inc.). In the event Greenbaum and Orecchio, Inc. is compelled to disclose confidential information by legal process, Greenbaum and Orecchio, Inc. will attempt to give prior written notice to Client. Client authorizes Greenbaum and Orecchio, Inc. to disclose Client's confidential information to:

_____
_____
_____
_____

E. **FEE-ONLY GUARANTY** Greenbaum and Orecchio, Inc. agrees to restrict its compensation solely and exclusively to the professional fees it receives directly from its clients for professional services rendered to its clients. Whenever Greenbaum and Orecchio, Inc. recommends that Client own a specific financial product, or utilize the services of a specific custodian, Greenbaum and Orecchio, Inc. and its employees will not accept any sales commissions, prizes, vacation trips, gifts or meals valued in excess of $100 from those specific financial product vendors or custodians.

F. **FIDUCIARY OATH** Greenbaum and Orecchio, Inc. shall exercise its best efforts to act in good faith and in the best interests of Client. Greenbaum and Orecchio, Inc. shall provide written disclosure to Client prior to the engagement of Greenbaum and Orecchio, Inc. and thereafter throughout the term of the engagement, of any conflicts of interest which will or reasonably may compromise the impartiality or independence of Greenbaum and Orecchio, Inc.

Greenbaum and Orecchio, Inc., or any party in which Greenbaum and Orecchio, Inc. has a financial interest, does not receive any compensation or other remuneration that is contingent on any Client purchase or sale of a financial product. Greenbaum and Orecchio, Inc. does not receive a fee or other compensation from another party based on referral of Client or Client's business.

EVENSKY, BROWN & KATZ
INVESTMENT POLICY AGREEMENT

1.   Nature of Agreement

This agreement is for the development of an investment policy and is entered into between the undersigned and Evensky, Brown & Katz.

Evensky, Brown & Katz is a registered investment advisor under the Investment Advisors Act of 1940, and provides the investment planning services provided in this agreement.

This agreement is intended to outline the responsibilities of the respective parties with regard to the investment planning services to be provided to you by Evensky, Brown & Katz.

2.   Purpose

You are desirous of having an investment policy prepared to assist you in attaining your financial goals, and hereby retain Evensky, Brown & Katz to assist in the preparation of such a policy. We agree to prepare a professional policy statement which will reflect your specific goals, risk tolerance and investment constraints.

3.   Confidentiality

We agree to keep confidential all information received from you and your advisors pertaining to your financial affairs except as otherwise required by law. The firm, as part of its services, may consult with attorneys or other professionals regarding the client's financial affairs. You agree to the disclosure of any information which Evensky, Brown & Katz deems appropriate for carrying out the objectives of the advisory agreement.

4.   What Evensky, Brown & Katz Will Do

Based upon the data supplied by you, we will review and evaluate your stated investment situation. We will prepare a written investment policy which both summarizes our findings and presents recommendations which we believe will assist you in attaining your stated goals.

Based upon stated goals and objectives provided to us by you and upon our analysis of the information supplied, we will make specific recommendations concerning generic products, services, and/or strategies which we believe will best assist you in attaining your goals and objectives.

EVENSKY, BROWN & KATZ
INVESTMENT ADVISORY AGREEMENT

THIS INVESTMENT ADVISORY AGREEMENT is between **EVENSKY, BROWN & KATZ (we or us)** and **(you) and is dated as of the date executed by Evensky, Brown & Katz.** Evensky, Brown & Katz is registered with the Securities and Exchange Commission under the Investment Advisors Act of 1940 and you wish to retain us to act as your investment advisor for various accounts in accordance with the terms and conditions of this Agreement.

This Agreement sets forth responsibilities of the parties with regard to the investment management services to be provided by Evensky, Brown & Katz.

(1) We will give you the benefit of our continuing study of economic conditions, security markets, and other investment issues. On the basis of these studies, we shall provide advice from time to time regarding the allocation and investments of your assets including money market accounts, CDs, municipal and government securities, unit investment trusts, REITs, mutual funds, annuities, limited partnerships, insurance investments and other investments introduced in the future. Generally, advice on specific stocks will not be given.

(2) We will, after consulting with you, recommend that you maintain and/or establish, in your name, accounts into which you shall deposit funds and/or securities, which shall be referred to as "managed assets."

(3) You may at any time increase or decrease your managed assets. Your managed assets will, at all times, be held solely in your name and will require your authorization for withdrawal.

(4) We will periodically provide you with a statement setting forth the funds and securities, which constitute your managed assets at the end of each period. You shall in addition receive directly from all corresponding brokers, banks, mutual funds, partnership sponsors and/or insurance companies which hold your investments, a statement reflecting your investment(s) in their custody.

(5) In accordance with the documents executed at Charles Schwab & Co., you will grant to us the limited discretionary power, authority to make exchanges and transfers of your managed assets, and authority to bill our fee to your account.

(6) You shall pay Evensky, Brown & Katz for its services a quarterly fee based upon the market value of your managed assets, in accordance with Evensky, Brown & Katz current fee schedule (attached). Fees are due in advance, and billing will commence with the beginning of the quarter of the contract date. Fees may be subject to a minimum in accordance with the schedule. You may arrange to have the fees deducted from an appropriate account.

CHAPTER 9

CLIENT MANAGEMENT ISSUES

*The best argument is that which seems
merely an explanation.*

— DALE CARNEGIE

I used to work for a realty group in Chicago that syndicated commercial residential properties in the Chicago area. We also managed the properties after they were syndicated. Each quarter we provided reviews on the properties' performance to our investors. Along with our review letter we included a partnership income check. Nothing much changed from quarter to quarter, so it was difficult to find new information to impart each time. My boss was fairly creative, but after some time even he got stymied. We finally bet each other that if we sent the same letter again and again, nobody would even notice. After four quarters, there were no comments from our investors. In the fifth quarter we had to change the letter because we were also sending a K1 along with it. Still no comments. Finally, we withheld a check because we were having some problems with our new computer system. We still sent the letter. Boy, did we get calls. The moral of the story? If you're sending money, nobody cares what you have to say.

Client Reviews

UNFORTUNATELY, OUR REVIEWS TODAY DO NOT INCLUDE a check, but we have noticed that when the portfolios are up, no matter how little, there are no comments. As soon as the returns head into negative territory, people start squawking.

I firmly believe that if you focus on portfolio performance in your reviews, your clients will also focus on them. That's why our quarterly reviews include a plethora of information unrelated to market performance. Further, we believe that the reviews we provide should reflect the clients' choice of information. We have standard forms, but the client is also offered the opportunity to pick and choose what will appear in his review package from these forms.

REVIEW NOTIFICATION

Many advisers simply send out their reviews when they are completed. Many insist that the client come in for a review meeting to discuss the material. We've done both. Now we ask the client if they want to meet, by sending them a card about two weeks in advance of the completion of the reviews, so that they can decide if they want to call a meeting. Of course, we don't use these if we want to call a meeting (see illustration at right).

THE REVIEW COVER LETTER—SETTING THE STAGE

Our review letters function as a cover letter for the review package we provide clients. Our partner Peter usually writes whatever is on his mind each month when reviews are being prepared. As a result, these review letters often seem like an informal conversation with a sage investor who has experience and perspective. Many times it is a comment on markets, like the highlights letter below. Sometimes it is a talk about financial planning issues or world events.

Highlights Letter

Dear CLIENT:

Ten years ago Cisco Systems, a technology firm founded at Stanford University in 1984, went public. In March, for a brief period,

---

E̲K̲
B̲

Dear: _____   Date: _____

We are preparing your current review.

If you would like to visit our office and have us review it with you
or if you would like to schedule a phone review, please call us at
(305) 448-8882.

Should you prefer to see the review and call with any questions
you might have, we will mail the review on its completion.

EVENSKY, BROWN & KATZ

---

the company passed Microsoft (another relative newcomer) for the title
of the world's most valuable enterprise in terms of stock market value.
While this accomplishment is laudable, what really impresses is the
contribution Cisco and similar companies have made to the quality of
our lives. Cellular phones and the Internet are just two innovations that
have radically altered our lifestyles and will continue to improve the way
we do business and communicate. Biotech companies are cataloging
information about our genetic code, which should ultimately lead to the
discovery of cures for diseases that today are considered untreatable.
The potential of these technological advances has not been lost on the
investing public during the last few years.

Lately, however, we have been witnessing some wild gyrations in
the market prices of these technology stocks. At some point the true
value of these high fliers should become evident. Companies that have
something meaningful to offer us will become the General Electrics of
tomorrow, and those that don't, probably won't survive. Benjamin

Graham, the father of fundamental investment analysis, summed it up best when he stated that "in the short run the stock market is a voting machine and in the long run, a weighing machine." This is a major reason we believe that a thoughtfully constructed, diversified portfolio will provide returns that should enable you to achieve your long-term goals.

Cordially,

Financial Planner

Our reviews also include a one-page epistle from Peter, who puts the economy in perspective. We call it "Highlights of the Economy and the Markets." We find this to be a helpful commentary, particularly when clients are trying to "measure" their portfolios against what's happening in the rest of the economy. If their portfolio is off, it helps them to understand what sectors of the economy contributed to the decline. I've reproduced a sample for you below.

Highlights of the Economy and the Markets

We must admit that the first five months of the year 2000 were a bit more interesting than your average period of late. The U.S. economy continued to power ahead, generating substantial growth in output, income, and employment. Meanwhile, the financial markets went through some wild gyrations—some good, some bad. There was even a hint in the air that the long-dormant value style of investing might be supplanting growth as the wave of the future. Surely, this was just another one of those recurring dreams that turn out not to be true when morning arrives.

Those hot technology stocks began the year just as they finished the last; roaring ahead like the party would never end. For this group the term "price/earnings ratio" disappeared from the lexicon and was replaced by "price/sales ratio." After a while, even this measure of a company's worth started to appear a bit scary. Then as the first quarter wound down, some air pockets developed and a number of the highest flying Internet and biotech stocks started plunging—the losses in many cases approaching 70 percent from peak values. For the first five months of the year virtually every major domestic index was down.

More specifically, the S&P 500 lost 2.8 percent; the small-cap Russell 2000, 5.2 percent, and the Nasdaq, 16.4 percent.

World markets didn't fare much better than those in the United States. The MSCI indices of developed markets and emerging markets fell 7.7 percent and 11.1 percent, respectively, in the first five months of 2000. Rather than focusing on particular countries, global investors seemed to pay more attention to specific industry segments. As in the United States, the most popular sectors were technology, telecommunications, and media, both on the upside and the downside.

The major driving force behind the early year's domestic bond market performance was the Treasury's repurchase of some longer maturity issues. For the first time in many years the government found itself with more money than it knew what to do with—thus the buy-back program. The result of this initiative was an inverted yield curve, with the 10-year Treasury yielding 6.28 percent and the 30-year, 6.01 percent at the end of May.

Once again, with a few cracks starting to show in the domestic markets, are we approaching a "dip-buying" environment or beginning the long-expected correction? At this juncture, it doesn't seem like much assistance will come from the Fed, who after raising the discount rate 50 basis points in May is threatening to boost interest rates once again this summer. If those rates get much higher, some of those investor dollars may exit stocks and find their way into the bond market.

Spraker, Fitzgerald & Tamayo put their quarterly review commentary in the form of a newsletter. Ron Tamayo tells me they include a market report, and an economic report, along with an editorial corner and company news. This gives their clients more material to read about than just portfolio performance. I have included it on the CD-ROM as FORM 9-01 (see FORM 9-01 on page 222).

POLICY REVIEW

We provide an asset allocation pie chart as part of the review to show the client where his portfolio is currently against his target portfolio allocation. This helps us focus more on allocation than performance. On the CD-ROM you'll find FORM 9-02, a policy analysis program in Excel that allows you to input the client dollars for different asset classes. It will then show you percentages for that class. The report also includes two pie charts, one for the target allocation, and one that is the current position, based upon the numbers you input. Some portfolio management software has this built in now. However, if you don't have that available, this is an easy way to show clients their allocation and focus on that, rather than portfolio performance (see FORM 9-02 on page 223).

MANAGER REVIEWS

We also include manager review pages as part of our review documents (see FORM 9-03 on page 224 and on the CD-ROM). We prepare a one-page document for each manager and include a narrative that discusses, among other things, the manager's style and buy-and-sell discipline. The page also includes a sector breakdown in a colorful pie chart and a list of the top ten holdings within the portfolio. We have found this very useful, particularly when a client wants to buy a hot stock. We can show them that they probably own it already within a professionally managed portfolio.

Occasionally, one of our advisers prepares a "Manager Spotlight," a more in-depth view of one of our approved managers (see FORM 9-04 on page 225 and on the CD-ROM). Again, including material on the managers and their styles helps take the focus off a client's portfolio performance.

Rebalancing

WE DON'T BELIEVE IN MICRO-MANAGING INVESTMENTS, which is why we are slow to make changes within a portfolio. We do set rebalancing parameters when we create an investment policy, and our clients' portfolios are reviewed on a quarterly cycle. We don't, however, put all of our clients on a calendar quarter. Each client is assigned a quarterly

ALLOCATION VARIANCE

ASSET CLASS	STYLE	SUBCLASS	MAJOR CLASS
Fixed Income			+ 7%
Equity			+ 7
U.S Large Cap		+ 5%	
U.S. Large Cap Growth	+ 3%		
U.S. Large Cap Value	+ 3		
U.S. Small Cap		+ 5	
U.S. Small Cap Growth	+ 3		
U.S. Small Cap Value	+ 3		
International		+ 5	
Emerging Market		+ 3	
Real Estate	+ 2		
Alternative	+ 2		

review schedule depending on the month he begins his relationship with us. As a result, approximately one-third of our clients are reviewed each month. It's during this review that we determine if the portfolio allocation has exceeded its rebalancing parameters. We divide the asset classes into major and sub classes, so we are not making minute changes too frequently. The illustration above is an example of an allocation variance taken from an investment policy statement.

You will note that the portfolio must be over- or under-weighted by 7 percent in debt to equity and/or by 2 percent, 3 percent, or 5 percent in subclasses for us to consider rebalancing. We then factor in the impact of trading costs, including transaction fees, spreads, and taxes, before we initiate any trades.

Another Excel spreadsheet that we think is pretty nifty is our strategy analysis sheet. I referred to this briefly in Chapter 7, but since we also use this form as a trading ticket and as a rebalancing tool, I thought I would mention it again. The spreadsheet appears on page 171 and is on the CD-ROM as FORM 7-02. This is actually the strategy page we put in our investment policies, except now we open up the hidden columns to allow us to use it for rebalancing and trading.

You will notice that now we can view the owners and the ticker symbols for the assets. There is also a total column for the current dollars, and one for the proposed allocation. Off to the right are columns that allow you to break out the assets by ownership. Our current portfolio software is linked to this Excel sheet so that our client's holdings are dropped into the template. Then, we can use this page as a rebalancing page.

Unfortunately, it's all too easy to accidentally rebalance multiple accounts by using the funds in an IRA to fill the need in a personal account. To avoid this error, each account is totaled at the bottom of the page to ensure that you have not mixed dollars from accounts with different ownership. Once we are happy with the results, we simply turn it over to our trading department which closes up some of the columns and uses it as a trading document.

Transfer and Termination

IT'S NEVER EASY TO LOSE A CLIENT. It's not even easy if you are the one who is terminating the relationship. I have found, though, that if you are honest and straightforward, you have no regrets later. I have included some sample termination letters in this chapter that I thought might be useful to you at some point in your career.

TERMINATION LETTER

Whenever a client has terminated us, we immediately send a letter to the custodian of his account resigning our discretionary authority over the account. At the same time, we also offer to help facilitate our client's move to a new firm and/or his new adviser to ensure that the transfer runs as smoothly as possible. We are in a small community and we do not want to leave any relationship on a sour note. I will say that once in a while it's hard to hide the excitement and celebration dance we do when losing a client relationship that we have not enjoyed. This hasn't happened to us very often, but when it does, writing that termination letter is cathartic. Here is an example of a letter we write when the client calls us or, if by chance, the custodian informs us that the client has requested that our name be removed from the account as adviser.

Dear CLIENT,

It is my understanding that you have terminated your relationship with Evensky, Brown & Katz, effective DATE.

In order to facilitate the preparation of your future income tax returns, I am enclosing realized gain and loss reports for the current year. In addition, I am including unrealized gain and loss reports, which provide the cost basis for your current holdings.

Please acknowledge your receipt of this letter by signing below and returning it in the enclosed envelope. Upon receiving your signed letter, any prepaid fees, as of the termination date stated above, will be returned.

In the meantime, if there is anything further we can do to ease your transition, please feel free to contact us. PARTNER, ADVISER, and our staff at Evensky, Brown & Katz were pleased to serve as your financial advisers and wish you the best in your future endeavors.

Cordially,
Financial Planner

LETTER RELEASING ACCOUNT TO CLIENT

Lou Stanasolovich has a specific letter for a terminating client who does not communicate directly with his adviser, but instead just asks that the account be released to the client exclusively. I have always felt uncomfortable on the rare occasions on which someone has done this. It just affirms that we did not have good communication from the beginning.

Dear CLIENT:

Waterhouse informed me that you were transferring your accounts from Waterhouse, which means you are terminating your contract with Legend. Therefore, I am enclosing an invoice for the unpaid portion of your asset management fee (the fee calculation is enclosed). The fee will be billed from your Waterhouse Institutional Services account as it has been in the past.

For your convenience, we have included all cost basis information that originated from your managed accounts.

We would also like to remind you that we will no longer be responsible for providing distributions from your Waterhouse Institutional Services accounts. You will have to initiate those yourself.

For your convenience, we will keep all your accounts as adviser accounts until (Month Day, Year). They will then be switched over to retail accounts (trading fees are more expensive and we will not receive copies of statements).

We at Legend wish you nothing but the best of luck. Please let us know if there is anything we can do for you in the future.

Cordially,

Financial Planner

FEE REFUNDS

When a client terminates, there is generally a question of whether rebated fees are due to him. We bill ahead, so this is usually the case, as in this letter that Lou Stanasolovich provides:

Dear CLIENT:

(As you requested), I am enclosing a check for the unearned portion of your asset management fee (the fee calculation is enclosed). (We did not charge you any financial planning fees; therefore, there is not a refund for this service.) (Also enclosed is a check for the unearned portion of your financial planning fee. The fee calculation is enclosed.)

For your convenience, we have included all cost basis information that originated from your managed accounts. We have also enclosed cost basis information as best we have it for those securities which you had purchased outside of Legend.

(We would also like to remind you that we will no longer be responsible for providing distributions from your Waterhouse Institutional

Services accounts. You will have to initiate those yourself. Nor will we be responsible for calculating or initiating IRA distributions from your IRA accounts.) You will also need to contact Vanguard yourselves when you require anything other than the normal check-writing privileges or to make deposits.

For your convenience, we will keep all your accounts as adviser accounts until _____. They will then be switched over to retail accounts (trading fees are more expensive and we will not receive copies of statements).

We, at Legend, wish you nothing but the best of luck. Please let us know if there is anything we can do for you in the future.

Cordially,

Financial Planner

UNPAID FEES

If you bill in arrears, often when a client terminates, fees will be due to you. Lou prefers to handle this by asking the client for a check, rather than by making a final billing to the account. Here is a sample of how he handles that.

Dear CLIENT:

(As you requested), I am enclosing an invoice for the unpaid portion of your asset management fee (the fee calculation is enclosed). The fee will be billed from your Waterhouse Institutional Services account as it has been n the past. (Please send us a check for the amount due in the enclosed postage-paid return envelope. We will not bill this amount from your account.)

For your convenience, we have included all cost basis information that originated from your managed accounts. We have also enclosed cost basis information as best we have it for those securities which you had purchased outside of Legend.

(We would also like to remind you that we will no longer be responsible for providing distributions from your Waterhouse Institutional Services accounts. You will have to initiate those yourself. Nor will we be responsible for calculating or initiating IRA distributions from your IRA accounts.) You will also need to contact Vanguard yourselves when you require anything other than the normal check-writing privileges or to make deposits.

For your convenience, we will keep all your accounts as adviser accounts until _____. They will then be switched over to retail accounts (trading fees are more expensive and we will not receive copies of statements).

We at Legend wish you nothing but the best of luck. Please let us know if there is anything we can do for you in the future.

Cordially,

Financial Planner

ONE LETTER YOU'D LIKE TO WRITE

I have been talking about how gracious you should be when a client is terminating. One year, *for venting purposes only*, I wrote the following letter to a departing client. Of course we never sent it, but it sure made me feel good.

Dear CLIENT:

I was ecstatic to hear that you removed our name as adviser from your account. Since we have been working together I have been frustrated, grumpy, and have put on ten pounds. In reviewing our client diary I note that you called twelve times, challenging our use of value funds. Finally, you called Schwab and traded these funds yourself, buying your own stock picks. I was happy to hear that you bought Home Depot at its all-time high. I figure you've lost about $320,000 by now.

Just for the record, I did not enjoy helping your daughter, a selfish, spoiled, and thoroughly unpleasant teenager, invest her bat mitzvah money in your cousin's new Internet IPO. I got a little tired of explaining to her why the price went way, way, down after the initial offering.

As for working with your anal-retentive wife, I can only blame myself for continuing to accept her calls after she wanted us to find the $1.22 error in her money market, calling us inaccurate and unprofessional. I resisted the temptation to point out that she has overdrawn this same money market account five times in the past year.

My staff and I wish you the success in the market that you so richly deserve.

With great relief,

Financial Planner

Remember, this was strictly a venting letter. I did not send it and the client *never* saw it. Sometimes, you just gotta get it out! I think I've gotten better at managing the relationships and client expectations through reviews and other periodic communications with clients. I also think that over the years I have gotten better at recognizing the signals of relationships that aren't going to work.

Managing the Relationship

IN YEARS PAST, MANY ADVISERS PUT GREAT EMPHASIS on the almighty review process. I think today we feel that periodic reviews are essential for managing the client's expectations, but they do not have to focus heavily on performance. They're much better used to educate and reinforce other aspects of your relationship with the client.

Finally, I know I've learned an important lesson over the years about relationships with clients. If it isn't working, gracefully let it go, move on, and *try* not to take it too personally.

Spraker, Fitzgerald & Tamayo – 1st Quarter 2000 Newsletter
Page 1

INTRODUCTION

Nature can be a powerful and strangely efficient force. Forest fires provide a perfect example. Despite the most advanced technologies, techniques and strategies humans can offer, given the wrong conditions forest fires can rage uncontrolled for days or weeks. But, eventually, the forces of nature inevitably shift and the fire runs its course. The effects can be double edged. While acres may be damaged, the positive underlying effect is that it clears the way for new growth that over time can be a source of renewal and opportunity.

The same is true for the stock market. We've had a forest fire this year. While stock prices and portfolio values were damaged, it created an opportunity to buy good quality companies and benefit from new growth. We believe the current market correction will enable a clearer distinction between market leaders and laggards and may have broken the back of reckless speculation.

MARKET REPORT

What caused the latest correction? We believe there was no single event or news that triggered the sell-off. Instead, it was the culmination of several destabilizing factors ending with the March Consumer Price Index (CPI) report. With the core CPI rate rising 0.4%, the largest gain in more than five years, visions of a more aggressive Fed flooded the press. This touched off a wave of selling, which was greatly exaggerated by margin calls, as individual investors and day-traders panicked. It was exacerbated by investor liquidations to pay taxes on tremendous capital gains from 1999.

The following are some highlights and comments about the market this year and what to expect for the remainder.

▲ The NASDAQ closed at a record high 5048 on March 10th, Dow Jones Industrial Average closed at a record high 11722 on January 14th.
▲ The Standard & Poor's 500 index closed at a record high of 1527 on March 23rd.
▲ The NASDAQ, DJIA and S&P 500 all suffered market corrections of 37%, 16% and 12% respectively in the first quarter.
▲ We continue to believe the NASDAQ will again lead the DJIA and the S&P 500 indices this year.
▲ We also believe the Federal Reserve is likely to raise rates again in May. However, we see inflation concerns moderating in the second half of this year.
▲ We continue to remain very optimistic about long-term market prospects. The economic backdrop remains very favorable for the bull market to continue.

ASSET CLASS RETURNS PERIOD ENDED 03/31/00

Asset Class	Index	1Q00 (%)	1 Year (%)	3 Year (%)	5 Year (%)
Large Company Stocks	Dow Jones Industrial Average	-5.0	11.6	18.4	21.3
	S&P 500 Index	2.0	16.5	25.6	24.5
	NASDAQ Composite	12.4	85.7	55.8	41.7
Small Company Stocks	Russell 2000 Index	7.1	37.3	17.8	17.2
Foreign Stocks	Morgan Stanley EAFE Equity	-0.1	25.4	16.6	12.7
Domestic Bonds	Lehman Govt/Corp Bond Index	2.7	1.7	6.8	7.1
	INFLATION (CPI)	1.1	3.1	2.1	2.4

Source: Weisenberger

3
pages
on CD-ROM

CLIENT NAME
POLICY ANALYSIS
DATE

	DESCRIPTION	POLICY ALLOCATION	CURRENT $ HIDE COL BEFORE PRINTING	CURRENT ALLOCATION
FIXED	MONEY MARKET	3 %	$21,782	3 %
	U.S. FIXED INCOME	31 %	$189,721	26 %
	INTERNATIONAL	5 %	$37,791	5 %
	TOTAL FIXED	**39 %**		**34 %**
EQUITY	US LARGE CAP	26 %	$244,965	33 %
	US SMALL CAP	9 %	$96,854	13 %
	INTERNATIONAL	19 %	$107,788	15 %
	REAL ESTATE	7 %	$40,166	5 %
	TOTAL EQUITY	**61 %**		**66 %**
	TOTAL PORTFOLIO	**100 %**	**$739,067**	**100 %**

POLICY ALLOCATION

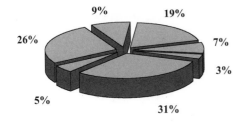

CURRENT ALLOCATION

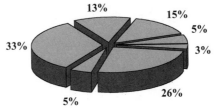

*Numbers may not add to 100% due to rounding error

1
page
on CD-ROM

SEI International Equity Fund

International Developed

This fund's portfolio is derived from the Wilshire 5000 Index; an index consisting of all publicly traded common stocks in the United States. The managers first divide that universe into those of the 750 companies with largest capitalizations, generally between $1.8 billion and $213 billion. This group constitutes approximately 82% of the total market value of the stocks included in the Wilshire 5000 Index. Wilshire analyzes each company based on fundamental factors such as price to earnings ratios, earnings growth, dividend payout ratios, return on equity, and the company's beta. Companies that have above average earnings or sales growth and retention of earnings and command higher price to earnings ratios fit the managers' concept of growth. From this group of securities consisting of between 150 and 500 names, the fund portfolio is constructed.

Top Ten Holdings:

Top Ten Holdings:	% of Net Assets:
Vodafone Airtouch	5.1%
Erricsson (B)	5.1%
Nippon Tel & Tel	4.9%
Nokia Oyj /Nok1V.He	4.9%
Total Fina Elf	3.8%
Deutsche Bank	3.6%
Ntt Docomo	2.9%
Eni Spa	2.6%
Novartis, Registered	2.5%
Glaxo Wellcome	2.4%
Total	17.6%

Data as of 6/30/2000

Sector Weightings:

- ☐ Utilities
- ■ Energy
- ⊠ Financials
- ▨ Industrial Cyclicals
- ■ Consumer Durables
- ▨ Consumer Staples
- ◈ Services
- ▦ Retail
- ⊞ Health
- ☐ Technology

21
pages
on CD-ROM

Accessor Small –Mid Cap Fund   October 2000

Management:	Symphony Asset Management
	San Francisco, CA
	Praveen Gottipalli, Dir. Of Investments
	David Wang, Portfolio Manager
Asset Class:	Small Cap Core
Benchmark:	Wilshire 4500
Total Assets:	$375M

Evensky Brown & Katz hired Symphony Asset Management in February 1999 to actively manage a core small cap strategy. This strategy was intended to provide our clients with an exposure to the universe of domestic stocks characterized by the Wilshire 4500 index. This universe is considered the total U.S. investable market minus the S&P 500 Index (Wilshire 5000 – S&P 500 = Wilshire 4500). Previously, all U.S. small company exposure in our clients' portfolios was provided via style specific management, either a growth style or a value style. As markets swing between favored styles, we at EBK felt it important to add a core small-cap component to steady the performance deviations in your portfolio. Symphony's portfolio seeks to add value above the index, but maintains strict alignment with the index's sector and sub-sector weightings to control the portfolio's risk parameters. This is an element monitored closely by EBK and the fund's management company, Seattle-based Accessor Capital.

Accessor Capital also tracks the portfolio's performance relative to the benchmark to determine Symphony's management fee. Symphony is compensated on a performance–fee basis, earning the maximum fee only when exceeding the benchmark (W4500) by 9% over a three-year period. This is a strong incentive for Symphony's management to stay consistent with their philosophy and not engage in speculative positions that might result in increased risk and/or style drift. As of August 31, 2000 the

2 pages on CD-ROM

TAKE CARE O' YOU

A NEW BUILDING IS GOING UP a few streets away from my office. I can see it clearly from my office window. A huge tower crane sits on top of the construction shell and every day I watch the crane pull heavy equipment and supplies to the top. In what seems like no time, another floor has been added. One day, they'll take the crane away and I'll be staring at a new edifice, changing the landscape in our town permanently.

Putting new programs, forms, or practices into place can involve painstaking development, particularly if you are creating it all at once. Take a clue from the construction business.

The chapters in Section 5 are materials delivered to you by the Katz tower crane, facilitating the creation of one more story on your business. Chapter 10 includes ideas and forms for client-related activities, as well as for your business, your staff, and you. Chapter 11 is a collection of interesting ideas, thoughts, and insights that I've collected over the years.

10

BUSINESS- AND CLIENT-RELATED TIPS AND TOOLS

Good sense about trivialities is better than
nonsense about things that matter.

—MAX BEERBOHM

This chapter is a potpourri of neat stuff you can use to improve yourself, your staff, and your practice. You might use these tips and tools in conjunction with a company retreat, which is an excellent time for team-building and visioning. Be sure you have the retreats away from the office, and use a facilitator if possible. We will be adding more materials like these to our Web site, www.evensky.com, so stay in touch.

Coaching

LAST YEAR I ATTENDED A SESSION with a Certified Personal Professional Coach, Will Mattox of Cheshire, Oregon (Will@financial-coaching .net). I liked Will immediately when he announced to the group, "I help people make change and move forward." "Hey," we all said, "That's what we do." "Ah, but," Will countered, "how many of you do it for yourselves?" He had us there. Will walked us through five basic coaching activities that we can use for ourselves and with our clients.

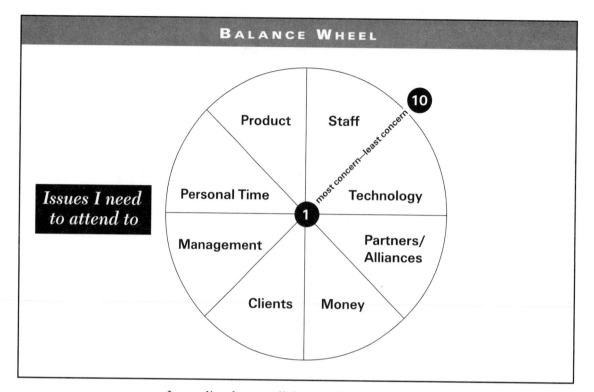

Immediately, we all found them useful in dealing with problems, but more importantly, in helping formulate effective solutions. I thought I'd share them with you.

BALANCE WHEEL

This activity helps you to quantify the things that are distressing you or preventing you from moving forward. Draw a circle, then divide it into eight parts. Fill each section with those things that are of concern to you. Here is the one I did (see illustration above). Next you'll want to rank these items according to your level of concern and mark the segment on the pie accordingly (see illustration *Balance Wheel Rankings* at right). The center represents zero (most concern). The outer edge represents a ten, or least concern.

Now you can address the items that you feel need work. On this chart, staff is about a four. Using the concern about staff as an example, let's break down these issues and prepare a "Staff Concern" wheel (see illustration *Balance Wheel Breakdown* at right).

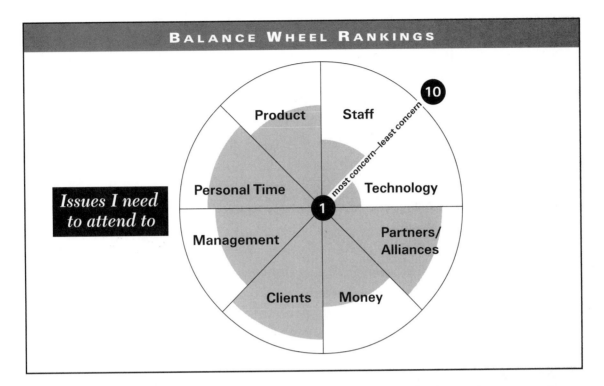

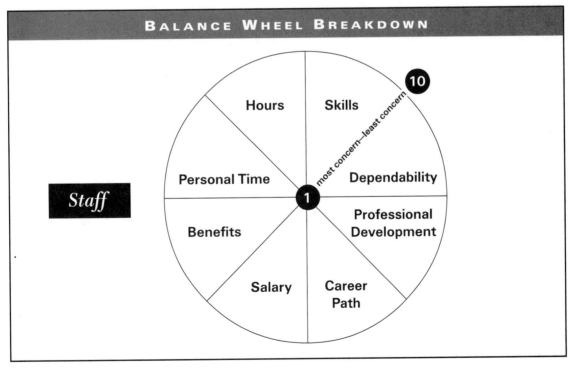

Using this method, you can narrow the focus on issues in your practice that require some strategic thinking.

CREATE SMART GOALS

We planners may not have invented the acronym, but creating goals is what we planners do every day. Goals should be:

Specific

Measurable

Achievable

Realistic

Timely

Will recommends that you create three-month, one-year, and five-year goals using this method.

ASK POWERFUL QUESTIONS

These are questions that begin with "What" or "How." Some of the more obvious ones are,

What do you want?

What are your first steps?

What do you expect?

How will you get there?

BREAK DOWN YOUR TASKS INTO SINGLE DAILY ACTIONS (SDA)

For example, one adviser in our group said technology (or lack thereof) was plaguing him. He had settled on some new software, but he was waiting until he knew it was compatible with the software that he was currently using. He thought he was "on hold" until he realized that he could be performing SDAs to get him a bit further every day. After some thinking, he decided to read about his targeted portfolio software for fifteen minutes every morning.

KEEP AN ACCOUNTABILITY LOG

Will maintains that change comes from two sources. The first of these would be an event with strong emotional impact. For example, last year I was involved in an auto accident when some idiot plowed into me at an intersection. Now, each time I come to an intersection, not just the one where I was hit, I move slower and look longer than I did before the accident. Secondly, change happens through repetition. It's estimated that it takes about twenty-one days to break an old habit or to create a new, more productive habit in its place. If you are not accountable for taking the new actions, you will seldom acquire the new habit. By keeping an accountability log, you are consciously tracking the positive changes that will take you to the goal. The repetitive action ensures success.

SHIFT INVENTORY

I attended the FPA Oregon Regional Retreat last year and spoke with many advisers about their practices. Most expressed concern about managing changes within their organizations, and in particular, about how to delegate and become more efficient. Advisers in general often register the same concerns, so I called Dick Zalack, President of Focus Four, who is one of our profession's best-known practice management consultants. Based in Cleveland, Dick helps sole practitioners become better small-business owners and entrepreneurs. In fact, you might want to get Dick's book, *Are You Doing Business or Building One?* (Praxis Press, 2000). You can get Dick's book by contacting him at 330-225-0707. I discussed our dilemma with Dick, who told me about Shift Inventory. I then asked him if he would contribute his concept to this book. He said yes, and here it is. FORM 10-01 on the CD-ROM is provided as a worksheet to help you with this concept (see FORM 10-01 on page 250).

> One of Parkinson's Laws says, "Work tends to expand to fill the time available." Zalack's Corollary says, "The harder you work at reducing the length of your to-do list, the longer it becomes." Or, "The more successful you are, the more work you generate." As the head of your own financial planning business, you are more than familiar with those facets of being in business for yourself.

The question is not, "How can I work harder and longer?" but "What can I do to get back to doing what I do best?"

When you started the business, you were able to spend almost all of your available working hours using your unique talents, whatever they were—creating great financial plans, finding highly profitable investments, signing up new clients, creating new leads. As you became more successful, you had to start doing more of the things at which you were merely excellent—sales, sales calls, sales training. Your further success then required you to spend more of your time on those things at which you were only competent—meetings, reports, etc. And finally, you discovered you needed to spend your valuable time, energy, and creativity on those things at which you were incompetent!

For me, that included filling out forms, spelling, and anything that had to do with graphic design. The problem we have in this downward progression is that our unique skill gets lost in what I like to call adminitrivia—the details of running a business. And it was that unique skill that allowed us to start our business and be successful in the first place.

What needs to be done, then, is to get back to using our core skills and spend more time doing what makes us who we are. The goal of programs like Focus Four is to help the entrepreneur build a structure around himself which insulates him from the "stuff" of business and allows him as much time as possible to use his time, energy, and creativity (unique talents) to build the business. After all, the sole responsibility of the business owner is to ensure the future viability of the business. That is our ultimate job. No matter how successful we are at generating revenue, if we do not spend time, energy, and creativity in planning for the growth and future of the company, there will come a time when the business will stagnate and perhaps even cease to exist.

When you are insulated from adminitrivia and free to use your unique talents, you will be able to ensure your company's future success. And you do that with something I call The Shift Inventory. The Shift Inventory allows you to look at all the myriad details of your everyday activities and shift as many as possible to someone else's to-do list.

Let's be honest here. All those details, the ones at which you are incompetent to excellent at, need to be addressed and then acted upon. They just don't need to be done by you! So the first thing you must do is discover what all is included in the list of things you no longer need, should, or want to do.

The first step in the Shift Inventory is the inventory. Begin by reviewing your to-do lists for the last month. Look at everything you "had to" do. Write down each activity and then follow that with the answer to this question, "Should we (the company) be doing this?" If the answer is "No," stop doing it. If the answer is "Yes," write down why it needs to be done. Be brutally honest. Don't rationalize.

Then comes a harder set of questions and answers: "Should I be doing it?" If you think the answer is "yes," then write down why you should be the one to do it. If your answer is "no," then write down who should be doing it and "when." If you have the person in place, then shift the activity to him or her. If you don't have someone, then you need to get someone. You can either hire (look for someone with values and attitude that match yours and then train them to be competent in this area) or bring in experts.

In my case, I do both. I bring in advertising and public relations people to plan campaigns, graphic designers to create the material, writers to create the words, and marketing experts for our direct mail campaigns. I create a virtual company using outside experts to help me be successful in areas in which I am only excellent, competent, or incompetent.

The most important person I have, however, is someone I hired, my administrative assistant. This person helps me coordinate all my activities, keeps my calendar straight, sets up my paydays, focuses my foundation days, and performs the two most important functions someone can do for a business owner—keeping me free from admini-trivia and giving me as much time free as possible to use my unique talents. In addition, my administrative assistant holds me accountable for doing what I say I will do. I now have the time I need to do what only I can do—think strategically and create plans to achieve the goals of the company.

As your business progresses, you will see a major change occur. Most of us started our businesses because we were the chief gun-slinger in producing revenue. We could generate income like no one else. We were the main producer. But as time goes on and the business grows, what becomes apparent is that we can hire people to produce revenue. Maybe not up to our individual gun-slinging capacity, so we hire two or three producers, but what we discover is that what we can't do is hire anyone to create the vision for the company. From the very beginning, we were the only person who knew where the business was ultimately going. What we need to do now is spend more time in thinking about the future and creating plans to achieve our goals. We are the only ones who can do that. We just need more time in our schedule. That's the function of the Shift Inventory and the administrative assistant.

If it's been a while since you've thought about the future of your business, now would be a good time to be crystal clear about what kind of business you want to create and what the model will be. What volume of sales do you want? What size staff? What kind of market will you go after? What kind of products will you carry? What will be your image in the community? What kind of customer service will you have? What kind of staff training? And so on.

Once you have the model clearly identified and written down, you should invest your time, energy, and creativity in creating processes and systems that will help achieve your goals. The infrastructure you create to protect you and ensure the success of the business will have two goals of its own:

- To ensure a consistent and repeated stream of income-generating opportunities; and
- To retain those clients who came to you as a result of these systems and processes.

As you shift from primary producer to leader, you will need to invest more of your time, energy, and creativity in steering your business instead of rowing it. You will hire more producers and train them well. And you will spend more of your time coaching them and developing your staff. And you will discover that when your business is working the best, you are spending more of your time supporting your staff and helping them to work and less and less time doing the actual producing.

You can achieve success like this by using the Shift Inventory to eliminate those things from your daily schedule that can be done by others and to free up your time so that you can create the vision and develop the plan necessary to steer your business to your preferred future.

Business Analyses

MY FRIEND MARK RALPHS of Financial Planning Corporation in Southport, United Kingdom has created an unusual way of managing the revenues from his client base. I thought it might stimulate you to a new and perhaps more profitable practice.

YIELD MANAGEMENT IN AN IFA PRACTICE

Have you ever wondered why when flying with some of the more successful airlines, few of the passengers have paid the same fare? Yet on some less successful airlines (often national and subsidized) most of the passengers are on a flat discount ticket. The answer is Yield Management. Where capacity is restricted, it is good practice to manage the supply of your service to those customers who can and will pay premium prices for your service.

My business partner Moira O'Shaughnessy piloted such an exercise for our firm and whilst we intuitively knew that we always had to be rigorous in our dealings with clients, the results genuinely took us aback.

Often quoted is Wilfredo Pareto's principle of the top 20% of your customers producing 80% of your income. Which is broadly correct. What it does not show is from where the top 20% of your profit comes. Here you need to differentiate between different classes of clients and apply a measure of A-R-G-E—Asset Revenue Generating Efficiency.[1]

We have developed a weighted model for our own purposes, but in its simplest form consider the following information:

REVENUE RANK	CLIENT	REVENUE	INPUT	AVERAGE	UNIT VALUE RANK	ARGE	ARGE RANK
5	Able	$12,000	8	$1,500	3	8	3
7	Brinson	$7,000	12	$583	9	16	-7
11	Crown	$4,250	10	$425	11	22	9
1	Davies	$25,000	40	$625	8	9	4
8	Erikson	$7,000	20	$350	12	20	8
3	Fawcett	$18,000	10	$1,800	2	5	-1
12	Garrett	$1,500	8	$188	13	25	11
13	Hughes	$1,200	9	$133	14	27	12
2	Ibbotson	$22,000	25	$880	5	7	2
4	Jennings	$17,500	5	$3,500	1	5	-1
6	Kray	$9,500	12	$792	6	12	5
9	Lewis	$6,000	9	$667	7	16	-7
10	MacKay	$4,500	4	$1,125	4	14	6
14	Nimmo	$1,000	2	$500	10	24	10

Whether you are fee based, commission based, or charge on the basis of assets managed, you should be able to have a standard measure of input. It may be the number of appointments or hours allotted to a client. The above shows that the highest revenue earner was client Davies with $25,000 but he required more effort to service than some others, so he only averaged $625 per unit putting him in eighth ranking for unit value.

Simply ranking revenue or unit value does not tell the whole story, and that is why Pareto alone is misleading. A simple "A-R-G-E" can be calculated by adding together the ranking of revenue and the ranking of unit value, and then ranking the score in ascending order. This shows what you would expect: that Fawcett, Davies, and Jennings are all worthwhile clients. It has been said that what you do not know can hurt you the most. The clients like Brinson who have a high revenue figure can be expensive clients to have.

In our own investigations we discovered what we would expect from the top two quartiles. Intuitively we knew to spend more than 50% of our time with these clients, and the results of those efforts accounted for more than 85% of our revenues. What shocked us was the bottom quartile. It still consumed 18% of our effort, reflecting our subconscious belief that we should not spend too much time with these clients. However their contribution to revenue was only 2%.

Our response was to ignore the bottom quartile entirely. Unless they contacted us we made no contact. The third quartile was evaluated, and if they had referred us to first- or second-quartile clients, they remained; otherwise they were introduced to a new pricing policy that ensured that they at least matched the unit values of the bottom members of the second quartile. If this was not met they were tactfully "graduated."

We are now five years on from the initial program and we still find the necessity to purge from time to time. This focuses our minds when recruiting new clients, to ensure that they are of "investment grade."

Mark offers another bit of perspective, this time on targeting business performance using moving averages.

MOVING AVERAGES

Not everyone has the luxury of a constant predictable stream of income. Some may rely upon project-based fees or commissions. The traditional planning tools sold or distributed by the sales support industry usually have annual targets, and each week or month the calculation is made as to whether or not the individual being assessed is ahead or behind their target.

There are many problems with this method of measurement. If the individual is ahead of "Target" they may become complacent. Likewise if they are behind, it can become overwhelmingly difficult to meet what once seemed like reasonable annual targets.

For many years we have done two specific things that allow us to move ahead. The first is to have quarterly targets. These are set each quarter, and if they are achieved, all is well and good. If they are not, we draw a line under the failure and move on to a nice fresh quarter. Ninety days is long enough to plan and execute and not so long that you can't just draw a veil over it if the success was not apparent.

The second key stage is our monitoring of performance (see illus-

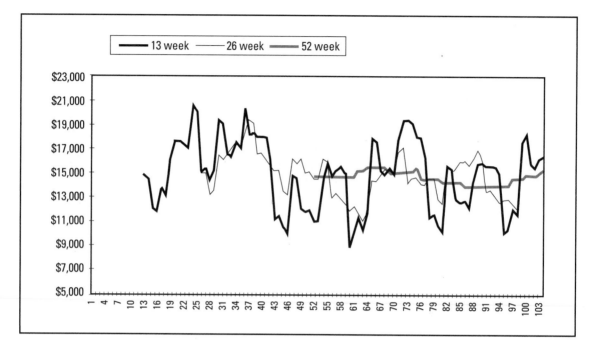

tration above). For this we do not use cumulative figures or year-to-date but a series of moving averages. We measure all activity on a weekly basis and review the moving average over 13 weeks, 26 weeks, 52 weeks, and a trend line.

From this chart of moving averages we can deduce a number of things; there are a number of seasonal shifts in production and by the second year (beyond week 53) we can see that both the 13 week and 26 week averages are well down. This means that production is low. However by week 70 things have improved. We've found that if the 13 and 26 week lines are above the 52 week line, things are likely to improve over the longer term.

WHAT SORTS OF THINGS CAN ALTER THE CHARTS?

The 13 and 26 week line can drop quite dramatically when a particularly high production week falls out of the frame. This is most apparent when the 13 week line is going up yet the 26 week line takes a sudden drop.

By feeding in past sales data or banking data it is possible to use a simple Excel program to draw these charts and even to do regression analysis. If performance is not as good as you wish, it is an indication that analysis of marketing position and technical competence, or maybe an organizational rebalancing, is required, but it also serves to remind us that this is a marathon and not a sprint and we need to keep the bigger picture in view.

A word of caution. Whilst these charts are helpful in seeing the bigger picture, they are no replacement for the conventional cash flow analysis and profit and loss accounting. They just provide another dimension.

Compliance and Back-Office Forms

BECAUSE OUR INDUSTRY IS SO HIGHLY regulated, there are certain completed forms that you must have in order to comply with SEC regulations (check out www.sec.gov/rules/extra/iarules.htm for more information). We've developed a few forms over time that may make it easier for you to develop your own compliance and procedure manual. Here are a few I like.

INSIDER TRADING

This simple trade request form was designed in order to track employee trades according to the Securities Act of 1934 on insider trading (see FORM 10-02 on page 251). Each time an employee makes a trade, a form must be completed and signed by a principal. We also require that all employees sign an acknowledgement of this policy (see FORM 10-03 on page 252). We print the pertinent portion of the act and present it, along with a copy of our Insider Trading Policy, to every staff member. Both forms are on the CD-ROM.

PRIVACY LETTER

As I write this, the SEC has made a new ruling regarding client privacy. No formal recommendations have yet to come from the SEC, but here is a privacy notice distributed by Metropolitan Insurance Company that I really like.

**THIS NOTICE IS FOR YOUR INFORMATION.
NO RESPONSE IS REQUIRED**

Privacy Notice To Our Customers   MetLife@ and Affiliates

Metropolitan Life Insurance Company ("MetLife") and each member of the MetLife family of companies (an "Affiliate") strongly believe in protecting the confidentiality and security of information we collect about you. This notice refers separately to MetLife and each of the Affiliates listed below by using the terms "us," "we," or "our." This notice describes our privacy policy and describes how we treat the information we receive ("Information") about you.

Why We Collect and How We Use Information: We collect and use Information for business purposes with respect to our insurance and other business relationships involving you. These business purposes include evaluating a request for our insurance or other products or services, evaluating benefit claims, administering our products or services, and processing transactions requested by you. We may also use Information to offer you other product or services we provide.

How We Collect Information: We get most Information directly from you. The Information that you give us when applying for our products or services generally provides the Information we need. If we need to verify Information or need additional Information, we may obtain Information from third parties such as adult family members, employers, other insurers, consumer reporting agencies, physicians, hospitals and other medical personnel. Information collected may relate to your finances, employment, health, avocations or other personal characteristics as well as transactions with us or with others, including our Affiliates.

How We Protect Information: We treat Information in a confidential manner. Our employees are required to protect the confidentiality of Information. Employees may access Information only when there is an appropriate reason to do so, such as to administer or offer our products or services. We also maintain physical, electronic, and procedural safeguards to protect Information; these safeguards comply with all applicable laws. Employees are required to comply with our established policies.

Information Disclosure: We may disclose any Information when we believe it necessary for the conduct of our business, or where disclosure is required by law. For example, Information may be disclosed to others to enable them to provide business services for us, such as helping us to evaluate requests for insurance or benefits, performing general administrative activities for us, and assisting us in processing a transaction requested by you. Information may also be disclosed for audit or research purposes; or to law enforcement and regulatory agencies. For example, to help us prevent fraud. Information may be disclosed to Affiliates as well as to others that are outside of the MetLife family of companies, such as companies that process data for us, companies that provide general administrative services for us, other insurers, and consumer reporting agencies. Our affiliates include financial services companies such as life and property and casualty insurers, securities flrms, broker dealers and financial advisors and may also include companies that are not financial services companies. We may make other disclosures of Information as permitted by law.

Information may also be shared with our Affiliates so that they may offer you products or services from the MetLife family of companies. We may also provide Information: (i) to others outside of the MetLife family of companies, such as marketing companies, to assist us in offering our products and services to you, and (ii) to financial services companies outside of the MetLife family of companies with which we have a joint marketing agreement. For example, an agreement with another insurer to enable us to offer you certain of that insurer's products. We do not make any other disclosures of Information to other companies who may want to sell their products or services to you. For example, we will not sell your name to a catalog company. We may disclose any Information, other than a consumer report or health information, for the purposes described in this paragraph.

Access to and Correction of Information: Generally, upon your written request, we will make available Information for your review. Information collected in connection with, or in anticipation of, any claim or legal proceeding will not be made available. If you notify us that the Information is incorrect, we will review it. If we agree, we will correct our records. If we do not agree, you may submit a short statement of dispute, which we will include in any future disclosure of Information.

Further Information: In addition to any other privacy notice we may provide, a recently enacted federal law established new privacy standards and requires us to provide this summary of our privacy policy once each year. You may have additional rights under other applicable laws.

For additional information regarding our privacy policy, please contact us at our website, www.metlife.com, or write to us at

MetLife, PO Box 318,

Warwick, R.I.   02887-9954.

Metropolitan Life Insurance Company, NY, NY

Metropolitan Insurance and Annuity Company, NY, NY

Metropolitan Tower Life Insurance Company, NY, NY

A Stranger at the Door

NOT LONG AGO, I WAS SITTING AT MY DESK quietly attending to my daily work when our new receptionist ran excitedly into my office. "There's a guy here who says he's from the S-E-C. I don't know what that is, but he looks important and intimidating." The best preparation for a surprise SEC audit is to have your documentation in apple pie order. Our comptroller, Mena Bielow, suggests that you prepare a compliance book that has copies of the forms that an SEC auditor would want to see during a surprise audit. Mena, in fact, keeps a document checklist in the book, indicating what is needed when the auditor drops in the door, and where these files and information are kept. This book is so thorough that if she were on vacation, we would easily be able to locate everything and complete the audit without her. (Not that we'd want to.) Here is a copy of Mena's Compliance Book Index:

➲ **List of All Clients by Adviser**

➲ **List of All Clients in Alphabetical Order**

➲ **List of New Client Investment Advisory Agreements**

➲ **Client Confidentiality Policy**

➲ **Personal Securities Transactions Policy**

➲ **Insider Trading Policy**

➲ **Privacy Policy**

➲ **Attestation**

➲ **EBK Rules and Schedule of Designated Responsibilities**

➲ **Lists of Accounts Closed**

➲ **List of Accounts by State**

➲ **EBK Organizational Chart**

Smooth Operations

JOHN CAREY, WHO RUNS THE OPERATIONS DEPARTMENT for RW Rogé & Company, Inc. in Bohemia, New York, offered this bit of operations advice. At the end of each day, all the operations work, including any loose papers, goes into a big envelope marked "DAY'S WORK ENVELOPE." They simply file this envelope away for thirty days. If there has been a trading error or a problem with a transfer, they refer to that day's activities in the envelope.

John offered two other tips for back offices that I couldn't omit.

➲ **Institute a document routine** to write down names of people you speak with and the times you speak with them. When there is a problem, you'll have an audit trail to help solve it.

➲ **Prepare everything expecting the worst outcome,** so you have a plan of action in case there is a problem.

Another important document you should have your staff sign is the client confidentiality agreement (see FORM 10-04 on page 253 and on the CD-ROM). I believe it is vital to have these agreements with your staff. Even more importantly, I believe you need to tell your clients that you have these in place. There is nothing they like better than to know that you are obsessively concerned about their confidential information.

Manager Due Diligence

A FEW YEARS AGO AT ONE OF OUR Alpha Group study meetings, Lou Stanasolovich presented questionnaires for us to use to evaluate fund managers. Lou has refined his documents through the years, so that by now they are the most comprehensive questionnaires I've seen. Lou sends them to every fund manager that he is screening for possible use. I don't know how you currently complete your due diligence of fund managers, but these kinds of questions can help you glean important information before you invest your client's money. The questionnaire is on page 254 as FORM 10-05 in a condensed space-saving version. The longer version with lines to write on appears on the CD-ROM.

Once you've hired the manager, it's important to keep tabs on their activities. We devised two Excel charts to track our managers' performance over time. These are strictly in-house reports that we update each week. The first one (see FORM 10-06 on page 259 and on the CD-ROM) lists our managers, broken down by asset class on one page. We color code it to list those managers that are approved, those that are on the watch list, and those that we are prepared to fire. The list we've provided here is an example only and is not color-coded.

The second chart (see FORM 10-07 on page 260 and on the CD-ROM) is a weekly performance chart of all managers in our universe, color-coded as approved, on the watch list, or ready to be fired. We keep this as a running performance list that we can go back to weeks, months, and years later.

Client-Related Forms

CHECKLISTS, FORMS, AND STANDARDIZED documents can ensure that the work gets done in a consistent manner and makes it easy to track usual activities. Using Excel and Word you can customize these activity sheets, making them both functional and attractive. Here are some of my favorites because over the years they have saved us time and money.

TASK MANAGER FORM

We've used this one (see FORM 10-08 on page 261 and on the CD-ROM) for years to help us track our contact with our clients. We believe that the more contact, the easier it is to manage expectations and the better chance you have of keeping the client. Nowadays it is a part of our relationship manager software, but I have included it on the CD-ROM in a Word document. In my book *Deena Katz on Practice Management*, I explain how we code clients according to the revenue they represent. A "gold" client, for example, means the client has $1 million to $3 million in income and they receive additional concierge services. On this Task Manager, we refer to this as "level." In this example we show a gold level client.

CLIENT PROGRESS SHEET

Our staff has found FORM 10-09 invaluable (see FORM 10-09 on page 262 and on the CD-ROM). We list all the possible activities that we must complete for a new client. This form follows the client progress from the first phone call through termination (if that happens). There is accountability because someone has to initial and date that each task has been completed. Particularly with new clients, there are so many activities that need tracking. This is a good way to see that there is follow-through.

FEE CALCULATION FORM

Charlie Haines of Charles D. Haines, Inc. in Birmingham, Alabama, shared a handy Excel fee calculation program. You'll find it as FORM 10-10 on the CD-ROM and on page 263. The fees shown in the program are for illustrative purposes only, but you can put your own schedule in easily. When you put the total amount of the portfolio in the bottom portion (on the line for "Total Assets Less Alt. Inv." for each client), the fee automatically calculates according to your schedule. It is also attractive, so you can send it directly to the client.

NON-MANAGED ACCOUNTS

Often we have clients who want their own trading accounts. We offer to track them simply because we believe (and we have not been wrong so far) that we can do a better job with asset allocation than they can, picking the hot stock of the last ten minutes. We do have them sign a "Non-Managed" account form (see FORM 10-11 on page 264 and on the CD-ROM).

VALUE ADDED

David Norton of Norton Partners, in Bristol, U.K., devised this Excel form (see FORM 10-12 on page 265 and on the CD-ROM) to help clients understand the adviser's value. David tries to quantify the relationship. David fills this out with the client after the first year of the engagement. He then adds the tangible value (e.g., "tax savings") with the intangible ("Having a trusted adviser") to direct the client's focus to the added value that his adviser provides. David puts his fees on the line "Fixed Price Investment for the Year."

CLIENT SURVEYS

The best way to find out whether your clients are happy with your relationship and service is to ask them. I think surveys are the best way to do this, although I am not certain whether sending them yourself is the best strategy. When we did it, all our clients responded that we were wonderful. I believe they were too intimidated to respond honestly, knowing that the forms come back directly to us. We then sent a survey they could respond to anonymously through a service that tallied the results and summarized the responses. I think we got a much clearer picture of how our clients feel than when we did it ourselves.

Kirk Hulett, Vice President of Human Resources and Practice Management at Securities America Financial Corporation, believes that surveys are one of the best ways to get a large amount of data about your clients in a small amount of time. You can find out about the satisfaction with your services or whether you should be adding new ones. You can also ask about their buying or saving habits, educational background, or other personal information that you may not have already addressed with them. Most advisers use surveys to find out about client's perception about the firm's services, custodian services, and to determine new services to add, or services to discard. The following are a few useful examples. Kirk has provided us with sample surveys (see FORM 10-13 on pages 266–267), templates of letters (see FORM 10-14 on page 268) you can use for this purpose, and a sample agenda (see FORM 10-15 on page 269) for a client advisory group. These forms are also on the CD-ROM.

Fidelity Investments Institutional Brokerage Group provides a Client Satisfaction form as part of their PracticeMark marketing site. They have allowed me to reproduce it for you (see FORM 10-16 on page 270 and on the CD-ROM). Our survey is provided as FORM 10-17 (see FORM 10-17 on the CD-ROM and on page 271). Both ask about relationship and services, although Fidelity's works great for 401(k) clients because it asks about plan administrators.

Doing Better Business

WHEN I WAS A TEACHER JUST OUT OF COLLEGE, I found that the more time and thought I put into my lesson plans, the better the experience was for the kids, and for me. One year I had so many kids in my classroom that I went home exhausted every evening. Consequently, I didn't have time to plan, prepare, and reflect. It showed up in the interactions I had with my students, other teachers, and the administration. I learned that running to keep up isn't good for anyone. I hope some of these business- and client-related tips and tools will help you and your staff take a breather and figure out where you are going next. I expect the effort will result in a better experience for everyone, especially your clients.

RESULTS PLUS

Shift Inventory

Task	Should we be doing? Yes/No	If yes, Why?	Should I? Yes/No	If yes, Why?	If no, Why?	When?

EVENSKY, BROWN & KATZ
Trade Request Form for Principals and Employees of EBK

Trade Date:_____

Account #: _____   Name:_____

	Quantity	Description	Total Amount
BUY	_____	_____	_____
BUY	_____	_____	_____
BUY	_____	_____	_____
BUY	_____	_____	_____
BUY	_____	_____	_____
BUY	_____	_____	_____
BUY	_____	_____	_____
BUY	_____	_____	_____
SELL	_____	_____	_____
SELL	_____	_____	_____
SELL	_____	_____	_____
SELL	_____	_____	_____
SELL	_____	_____	_____
SELL	_____	_____	_____
SELL	_____	_____	_____
SELL	_____	_____	_____

This Form has to be approved by the President of EBK prior to placing an order in your account. Please use one form per account.

Approved by:_____   Date: _____

FEDERAL ACTS

SECURITIES ACT OF 1934

Trading on Non-Public Information

"127. If a person buys or sells a security, including an option contract, while in possession of material non-public information, the individual will be held liable to any buyer or seller of the security."

"131. If the SEC concludes that an individual has violated the 1934 Act by buying or selling securities while in possession of "material non-public information," or has communicated "material non-public information" to another individual, the SEC may bring an action in a federal court. Any penalty for insider trading (i.e., trading on material non-public information) will be determined by the court based on the facts and circumstances of the particular case. The penalty may be up to three times the profit gained or loss avoided in the illegal transaction. If an employee engages in insider trading, the employer or persons in authority to direct the employee's actions will also be subject to penalties as controlling persons. Civil penalties against controlling persons may be up to $1 million or three times the amount of profit gained (or loss avoided) on the transaction, whichever is larger. Controlling persons will be liable for these penalties only where they knowingly or recklessly failed to enforce procedures and policies to prevent insider trading."

Evensky, Brown & Katz
Insider Trading Policy

A. Insider trading is prohibited for all officers, shareholders, directors, associated persons, clerical personnel and customers.

B. All officers, shareholders, directors, associated persons and clerical personnel will be required to sign an attestation of knowledge and understanding of Federal and State law requirements regarding insider trading.

ATTESTATION

I hereby acknowledge that I am aware of Federal and State law requirements and Evensky, Brown & Katz policy and procedures relating to the use of material, non-public information in the trading of securities.

Therefore, I shall not engage either for a client or on my own behalf in a securities transaction that would be promulgated by having material, non-public information. I understand that if I have been discovered in such practice, I shall be subject to immediate dismissal and the relevant trading information shall be disclosed to the State of Florida and the SEC.

EMPLOYEE   DATE

Client Confidentiality Policy

Client confidentiality is of paramount importance in the financial service industry. All client information shall be considered confidential in accordance with the provisions of the "Code of Ethics and Professional Responsibility" for CFP licenses.

All information about XXX Financial and its clients are considered to be confidential. Employees shall not disclose any confidential information at any time during <u>or after</u> employment with the firm.

Company files are available to employees in the course of their normal work on a "need to know" basis only. No employee shall permit any person whomever to examine or make copies of any reports or any other documents prepared by XXX Financial, its clients, or documents which come into an employee's possession by reason of employment with this firm. In the event of questions regarding the use of information, any person associated with XXX Financial, who has a question regarding the propriety of using client information in any manner, other than for the benefit of the client, shall ask the Compliance Officer of XXX Financial for a determination of propriety.

Unauthorized use of client lists, client names, addresses, and/or phone numbers, both during employment and after termination of employment, is a potential criminal violation of the laws of the state of XX. The Company will prosecute any violations to the fullest extent of the law.

Upon termination of employment, an employee shall turn over to the President all documents, papers, memoranda, electronic media, and other matter in his or her possession or under his or her control, which may have, in any way, to do with the above-described confidential information.

My signature below indicates that I have read, understand and agree to comply with the terms and conditions set forth in this policy.

_____   Date

Employee's Signature

_____

Employee's Name Print

QUESTIONNAIRE FOR
DOMESTIC EQUITY INVESTMENT MANAGERS
(CONDENSED VERSION)

THE BASICS

1. What is the objective of the fund?
2. What is your investment philosophy?
3. (a) Is your investment style more value, growth, or growth-at-a-price oriented? Please explain.
   (b) How has your investment style changed over the last five years? Is it likely to change in the future? If your investment style goes out of favor, what action will you take?
4. What percentage of your investment selection process is top down (macroeconomic analysis) versus bottom up (company analysis)? Please explain in detail.
5. What is the Price-to-Cash Flow ratio of the fund? (As of _____)
6. What is the Price-to-Book ratio of the fund? (As of _____)
7. What is the Price-Earnings ratio of the fund? (As of _____)
8. What is the Earnings Growth Rate of the underlying companies of the fund on a weighted average basis? (As of _____)
9. What has been the portfolio turnover and where is it going to be trending over the next three years?

TAX ISSUES

10. (a) How tax efficient is your fund?
    (b) Do tax implications affect your investment decisions?
    (c) What is the fund s effective tax turnover?
11. What form of tax accounting do you use? Average, FIFO, HIFO, or other?

EXPENSES AND FEES

12. (a) What are the current expenses of the fund and how will they be dropping over what period of years, and at what asset levels?
    (b) Please break down the components of your expense ratio.
13. What is your fee schedule for the mutual fund? List the breakpoints.
14. For the mutual fund, what is your average trading cost? What are the effective annual costs? How do you control the spread?
15. Do you intend at any point to offer Institutional shares for the mutual fund?
16. If applicable, will you offer a separate share class without 12(b)1 charges? If so, when?
17. What is your fee schedule for separate accounts? What is the minimum size for separate accounts?
18. When are dividend and capital gain distributions made?
19. What states is the fund not registered in?

ASSETS

20. What is your total asset base under management that is managed similarly to the mutual fund? Please break it out by type of account. (Examples: Mutual Funds, Private Accounts, Variable Annuity, Separate Accounts)

21. How much money are you comfortable managing in the fund? What is the overall total you are comfortable managing in all similarly managed accounts including the mutual fund? Does the portfolio manager of this fund also manage any hedge funds?

22. If the assets exceed that amount, what will you do? Circle one and explain.
    - Buy larger stocks
    - Buy more stocks
    - Close the fund
    - Add to cash reserves
    - Buy foreign stocks

23. How many stocks are currently in the portfolio? (As of _____)

24. How many stocks were there two years ago?

25. Do you expect this number to materially change from today's total in the next five years?

CAPITALIZATION

26. List the range of market capitalizations that you normally buy? Do you consider this cap size to be small, medium, or large? Why?

27. (a) What is the median capitalization size of the stocks that are in the mutual fund?
        (As of _____)
    (b) What is the weighted average capitalization size of the stocks that are in the mutual fund?
        (As of _____)
    (c) What is the average cap size of the stocks that are in the mutual fund?
        (As of _____)

28. If a stock in the fund enters a different level of market capitalization than would normally be in the fund, what is your sell discipline?

FOREIGN COMPONENTS

29. What percentage of net assets do you usually invest in foreign companies, if any?

30. If applicable, what kinds of guidelines have been established that govern the type of foreign companies the fund invests in?

31. If applicable, what is your exposure to Emerging Markets?

INTERNAL ASPECTS

32. If you close the fund, what type of access to the fund will you provide for us on an ongoing basis? Will we as a firm be treated as a client and allowed to add additional monies to the fund regardless of which investors actually own the fund? Please explain your firm's policy.

33. Provide a copy of your internal trading procedure that prevents conflicts of interest. For example, are any of your professionals allowed to invest in individual securities for their own account? What about your policy on front running?

34. Are your employees required to invest in your fund? What about your retirement plans? Please provide a copy of policies or procedures that address this issue.

35. Please provide us with a copy of any public disclosure that lists professionals of the fund and their ownership positions in it.

21
pages
on CD-ROM

DECISION-MAKING PROCESS

36. What is your investment decision-making process?
37. How is your investment decision making process organized?
38. Who is involved in your investment decision-making process?
39. Is your investment decision-making process team-based (who are the players) or does one individual make final decisions?
40. If one individual makes all final decisions, how would the fund function if something were to happen to that person such as death, retirement, or resignation?
41. How long have the current decision-makers been in place at the fund?
42. Has there been any professional turnover on the fund over the past five (5) years? Please list all individuals who left and why.
43. Are the buy/sell decision-makers on the fund responsible for other accounts or funds? Please explain who is responsible for what and in what capacity.

INVESTING STRATEGIES

44. How is your strategy developed and implemented?
45. Please explain your stock selection process.
46. What parameters are used in selecting issues for investing? Specifically, what are you looking for? Please make it clear which criteria are most important.
47. Please describe your sell discipline.
48. Do you have an investment time horizon or expected holding period during which an investment should reach your targets?
49. During the current manager's tenure, have there been any decisions (sector, themes, individual positions) that have had a significant impact on performance (either positive or negative)? Please elaborate.
50. How do you control risk?
51. (a) To what extent do you use cash? What is the minimum amount of cash you would hold?
    (b) If you are not always fully invested, what factors would lead you to hold cash? Is there a maximum amount of cash you would be likely to hold?
52. To what extent do you purchase bonds, convertible securities, and/or preferred stocks, etc.?
53. Do you sell short? If so, please explain your investment process and up to what percentage of the fund will you short securities?
54. (a) Is there a policy regarding industry diversification? To what extent might you have large concentrations in specific industries? Currently, what is the industry diversification of your holdings? Please give the percentage makeup of the portfolio of each industry. Attach a separate list. (As of _____)
    (b) How has this changed in the last year?
55. Do you select stocks by sectors (industries)? If so, how do you pick them?
56. Does the fund use leverage? If so, to what extent?

SOFT DOLLARS, CREDIT AND LEVERAGING

57. Do you use soft dollars? For what purposes? To what extent? What is the estimated value of this annually for the current year? Is this expected to change materially?
58. Does the fund have a line of credit established to meet redemptions, leverage the funds, etc.? If so, how large is it? Also, please explain how it will be utilized and under what circumstances.
59. Do you have a policy regarding investments from market timers? How is this enforced?

60. Does the fund borrow from other mutual funds within your mutual fund family? If so what borrowing capacity is there and at what interest rate? If not do you intend to do so and/or are you in the process of applying to the SEC for permission to do so?
61. Does the fund purchase derivative securities? If so, to what extent and what types?

RESEARCH

62. (a) How do you obtain your research, both internal and external? To what extent are economic forecasts relied on?
    (b) How many companies/management do you and/or your professional staff actually visit each year?
    (c) How much of your research is internal versus external?
       Internal % _____   External % _____
    (d) How big is your research staff and what specific role does it play in the research process?
63. In what types of markets will the fund outperform and underperform?
64. (a) How do you add value?
    (b) Against which style-based index do you measure your performance? Why?
    (c) In terms of basis points, how much do you expect to outperform the S&P 500 or the style-based index you answered in part (b), whichever is more relevant?

ADVISER SERVICES

65. (a) What type of services will you provide to investment advisers and is the portfolio manager willing to meet with us? Who should we contact to arrange such a meeting?
    (b) Is it possible to arrange for short phone interviews with the fund's portfolio manager once or twice a year? If so, who should we contact to arrange the call?
66. What percentage of the fund's assets are attributable to retail investors versus institutional investors?
67. Is the fund available to the retail market, to the institutional market or both? On what supermarket platforms are your funds available? (Please be specific and state how it is available, i.e., Schwab Institutional OneSource (NTF).) What additional charge does the fund incur to be in the NTF programs? Are there any platforms you have chosen not to work with?
68. Please list your five largest institutional investors in the fund, and the percentage of fund assets they account for. What percentage of the fund's assets overall are invested from RIAs?

FIRM VITALS

69. What is different or unique about your firm or fund?
70. What is the ownership structure of the firm? How will we be notified of major changes in ownership?
71. What is the interaction between the portfolio manager and the fund's independent board of directors?
72. When was the management firm founded? If you have any general information or a brochure on the management firm, we would appreciate it being enclosed with your answers. Please enclose both Part I and II of your ADV form.
73. Who are the key people in your firm and/or associated with your fund? Please list the names, ages, previous experience and their current roles of all investment managers, chief investment officer, chief executive officer, president, etc. and the analysts who work on the fund. Attach additional information separately if necessary.
74. Where are the people doing the investment analysis and making the investment decisions located?
75. How do we contact them?

PROFESSIONAL DUTIES AND COMPENSATION

76. How is the compensation of the portfolio manager, as well as other key individuals structured? Please explain all forms of compensation including how bonus systems work and an employee's ability to buy into the firm as a shareholder or partner.

77. How is your research staff compensated?

78. (a) What percentage of the portfolio manager's work time do non-portfolio responsibilities require? Break out marketing separately.
    (b) How large of a distraction are these responsibilities from their focus on the fund?

79. If applicable, explain your or your firm's contract with the fund as a sub adviser in terms of its length, and under what conditions it can be terminated prior to the end of the contract date?

80. If the portfolio manager(s) of the fund is not a shareholder or partner of the firm, how long (until what date) are they contractually obligated to remain with the firm and fund? Under what circumstances can they leave or be terminated prior to the end of their contract?

81. If the fund is less than ten years old, or if the manager has changed within the last ten years, does the current portfolio manager have a quarterly return track record, on individual accounts, covering the period prior to the fund's formation and which is based on an investment approach identical to that of the fund? Are these returns audited? Please enclose this information (gross of fees) along with any relevant explanations.

BENCHMARKS

82. Please attach quarterly total returns for the fund going back to 1980 or the fund's inception, whichever is later. Include only data for the period during which the current manager has been in charge of the fund.

83. What have been the key factors in building the fund's performance? What have been the biggest mistakes?

84. Please indicate who you believe are your two best fund manager competitors, and why?

85. What do you do differently than your closest competitors in an attempt to add value and produce superior returns?

86. Are there any unique resources available to the firm or the fund which you feel gives you any sort of advantage or would be of interest to perspective investors?

Please add us to your mailing list so that we can automatically receive the periodic reports on your fund. Also, please send a current prospectus, statement of additional information, most recent report, and proxy statement. Please also send annual and semi-annual reports going back five years or to the starting date of the current portfolio manager (whichever is latest).

7/28/00

FIDELITY PORTFOLIO

Oppenheimer Real Asset	21.80%
Barr Rosenberg Int'l Small Cap	7.60%
DFA 6-10 Value	4.10%
Matthews Pacific Tiger	0.00%
Undiscovered Behavioral Growth	-1.20%
S&P 500 *	-2.61%
DFA Int'l Value	-2.70%
Deutsche Index 500	-2.90%
Wilshire Target LC Growth	-3.00%
DFA US Large Cap Value	-4.30%
Vanguard Extended Market	-4.30%
Accessor Small Cap	-7.40%
SSgA Emerging Mkt	-11.70%
Montgomery Emer Mkt	-13.10%
Montgomery Int'l Inst.	-13.90%

OPPORTUNITY PORTFOLIO -11.86%

Monument Internet A (40%)	-28.10%
Guinness Flight Wired Index (25%)	4.40%
Nasdaq 100 Index (35%)	-4.93%

SEI PORTFOLIO

SEI Small Cap Value	6.60%
SEI Large Cap Growth	0.60%
SEI Small Cap Growth	-0.50%
S&P 500 *	-2.61%
SEI S&P 500 Index Class A	-3.00%
SEI Large Cap Value	-5.70%
SEI International Equity	-9.50%
SEI Emerging Markets	-15.10%

ALL MANAGERS

Oppenheimer Real Asset	21.80%
Barr Rosenberg Int'l Small Cap	7.60%
SEI Small Cap Value	6.60%
DFA 6-10 Value	4.10%
SEI Large Cap Growth	0.60%
Matthews Pacific Tiger	0.00%
SEI Small Cap Growth	-0.50%
Undiscovered Behavioral Growth	-1.20%
S&P 500 *	-2.61%
DFA Int'l Value	-2.70%
Deutsche Index 500	-2.90%
SEI S&P 500 Index Class A	-3.00%
Wilshire Target LC Growth	-3.00%
DFA US Large Cap Value	-4.30%
Vanguard Extended Market	-4.30%
SEI Large Cap Value	-5.70%
Accessor Small Cap	-7.40%
SEI International Equity	-9.50%
SSgA Emerging Mkt	-11.70%
Opportunity Fund	-11.86%
Montgomery Emer Mkt	-13.10%
Montgomery Int'l Inst.	-13.90%
SEI Emerging Markets	-15.10%

SOURCE: EVENSKY, BROWN & KATZ

9 pages on CD-ROM

EBK for Internal Use Only

WEEK ENDING	1997	1998	1999	Month of January	Month of February	Month of March	1st Quarter	Month of April	Month of May	Month of June	2nd Quarter	7/7/00	7/14/00	7/21/00	Past Week 7/28/00	YTD 7/28/00
S&P 500 *	33.35%	28.58%	21.04%	-5.02%	-1.89%	9.78%	2.29%	-3.01%	-2.05%	2.47%	-2.66%	0.02%	2.11%	-2.04%	0.73%	-2.61%
Russell 1000 Index	32.85%	27.02%	20.91%	-4.09%	-0.27%	9.11%	4.36%	-3.33%	-2.59%	2.55%	-3.44%	1.73%	2.51%	-2.06%	-4.83%	-1.87%
Deutsche Index 500	33.24%	28.75%	20.75%	-5.03%	-1.89%	9.73%	2.23%	-3.00%	-2.10%	2.45%	-2.72%	0.20%	2.00%	-1.90%	-4.00%	-2.90%
SEI S&P 500 Index Class A	32.82%	28.18%	20.60%	-5.04%	-1.93%	9.79%	2.25%	-3.05%	-2.11%	2.41%	-2.81%	0.20%	2.10%	-2.00%	-4.10%	-3.00%
Russell 1000 Value	35.18%	15.63%	7.35%	-3.26%	-7.43%	12.20%	0.48%	-1.16%	1.05%	-4.57%	-4.69%	2.68%	1.02%	-1.26%	-1.69%	-3.48%
DFA US Large Cap Value	28.12%	11.98%	4.80%	-7.05%	-8.98%	14.14%	-3.43%	2.99%	-0.22%	-6.96%	-4.39%	3.20%	2.80%	-3.10%	-0.60%	-4.30%
SEI Large Cap Value	36.74%	11.35%	4.90%	-6.37%	-7.94%	12.75%	-2.81%	-0.44%	1.10%	-5.61%	-4.99%	2.30%	1.80%	-1.40%	-1.90%	-5.70%
Russell 1000 Growth	30.49%	38.71%	33.16%	-4.69%	4.89%	7.16%	7.13%	-4.76%	-5.04%	7.58%	-2.70%	0.82%	3.87%	-2.78%	-7.72%	-1.58%
Wilshire Target LC Growth	32.44%	40.04%	34.30%	-6.79%	3.51%	8.22%	4.41%	-4.62%	-5.64%	7.93%	-2.87%	-0.80%	2.60%	-2.10%	-5.80%	-3.00%
SEI Large Cap Growth	34.76%	38.80%	34.20%	-4.69%	5.56%	8.53%	9.19%	-5.29%	-5.70%	7.31%	-4.17%	0.40%	3.20%	-2.10%	-7.00%	0.60%
Russell 2000 Index	22.37%	-2.55%	21.26%	-1.61%	16.51%	-6.59%	7.08%	-6.02%	-5.83%	8.72%	-3.78%	2.12%	2.90%	-3.96%	-6.45%	-2.35%
Russell 2000 Value	31.78%	-6.45%	-1.49%	-2.62%	6.11%	0.47%	3.83%	0.59%	-1.53%	2.92%	1.95%	3.45%	2.01%	-1.80%	-2.24%	7.27%
DFA 6-10 Value	30.75%	-7.30%	13.00%	-0.75%	9.28%	0.30%	8.87%	-3.51%	-4.16%	4.98%	-2.92%	0.30%	3.10%	-1.50%	-3.80%	4.10%
SEI Small Cap Value	35.11%	-2.84%	-7.00%	-4.54%	-0.52%	6.94%	1.56%	1.98%	-0.62%	2.14%	3.52%	1.60%	2.40%	-1.60%	-1.40%	6.60%
Russell 2000 Growth	12.95%	1.23%	43.09%	-0.93%	23.27%	-10.51%	9.29%	-10.10%	-8.76%	12.92%	-7.37%	1.08%	3.61%	-5.67%	-9.75%	-9.50%
Wilshire 4500	25.69%	8.63%	35.49%	-1.17%	15.55%	-3.70%	9.94%	-12.13%	-7.56%	11.18%	-9.41%	1.81%	5.12%	-3.08%	-7.85%	-4.40%
Vanguard Extended Market	26.74%	8.32%	36.40%	-1.48%	15.66%	-3.76%	9.66%	-11.87%	-7.38%	11.87%	-8.66%	0.70%	5.10%	-2.90%	-8.20%	-4.30%
Accessor Small Cap	36.15%	15.34%	27.30%	-4.49%	13.99%	-2.45%	6.21%	-10.00%	-7.95%	10.78%	-8.22%	0.50%	5.30%	-3.40%	-7.90%	-7.40%
Undiscovered Behavioral Growth		33.20%	65.70%	1.44%	17.82%	-3.13%	15.79%	-5.02%	-10.03%	7.05%	-8.52%	0.50%	5.60%	-6.70%	-8.00%	-1.20%
SEI Small Cap Growth	8.38%	5.59%	75.20%	-1.44%	28.71%	-8.03%	16.67%	-14.11%	-8.35%	20.86%	-4.86%	-2.10%	5.50%	-5.70%	-9.70%	-0.50%
MSCI EAFE	1.78%	20.00%	25.27%	0.40%	1.29%	4.48%	2.24%	-9.62%	-2.39%	1.27%	-2.53%	0.14%	-0.41%	-2.15%	-6.31%	-8.72%
SCHWAB INT'L INDEX SEL		15.96%	33.80%	-7.85%	1.39%	5.81%	-1.14%	-5.44%	-2.80%	3.75%	-4.65%	0.30%	-0.30%	-2.30%	-3.10%	-10.00%
Montgomery Int'l Inst.	10.15%	28.69%	26.80%	-5.24%	5.53%	2.06%	2.06%	-8.86%	-6.57%	4.11%	-11.35%	0.20%	1.50%	-1.60%	-6.20%	-13.90%
DFA Int'l Value	-3.14%	14.87%	16.30%	-7.72%	-2.49%	5.48%	-5.08%	-2.58%	1.85%	6.99%	6.16%	0.00%	-0.10%	-1.60%	-1.70%	-2.70%
Barr Rosenberg Int'l Small Cap	-11.89%	4.12%	24.70%	-2.21%	8.84%	2.07%	8.65%	-4.83%	0.09%	6.67%	1.61%	0.50%	-0.20%	-0.90%	-2.10%	7.60%
SEI International Equity	-1.86%	19.29%	39.60%	-5.73%	5.26%	1.27%	0.49%	-6.26%	-3.41%	3.92%	-5.91%	1.00%	0.30%	-1.90%	-4.60%	-9.50%
MSCI Emerging Mkts Free	-13.41%	-27.52%	63.70%	-2.28%	-5.37%	0.33%	-3.38%	-8.26%	-8.26%	4.52%	-12.03%	1.40%	0.70%	-2.60%	-4.80%	-11.70%
SSgA Emerging Mkt	-8.80%	-15.94%	64.80%	-0.79%	-0.24%	2.39%	1.34%	-10.05%	-2.60%	4.89%	-8.10%	0.90%	1.20%	-3.30%	-5.50%	-13.10%
Montgomery Emer Mkt	-3.14%	-38.28%	63.20%	-0.08%	2.77%	-0.07%	2.61%	-10.10%	-3.41%	3.79%	-9.88%	1.60%	1.80%	-0.80%	-6.10%	0.00%
Matthews Pacific Tiger	-40.89%	-2.86%	83.00%	1.14%	1.69%	8.37%	11.44%	-10.56%	-6.03%	10.57%	-7.06%	1.10%	0.60%	-3.20%	-5.50%	-15.10%
SEI Emerging Markets	-9.12%	-31.95%	70.30%	-1.09%	6.24%	-2.07%	2.92%	-10.71%	-5.81%	4.92%	-11.76%					
Montgomery Focus Emer Mkts				0.24%	0.76%	6.29%	7.35%	-10.03%	-5.36%	6.63%	-9.21%					
Oppenheimer Real Asset	N/A	-44.85%	36.80%	7.10%	6.16%	-1.39%	12.11%	-2.23%	10.96%	6.90%	15.97%	-6.20%	1.50%	-3.20%	-0.70%	21.80%
Opportunity Fund						-3.38%	10.39%	-14.78%	-11.92%	10.73%	-13.34%	-6.14%	-4.98%	0.36%	-2.21%	-11.86%
Monument Internet A						-14.32%	0.18%	-21.55%	-13.81%	15.85%	-21.67%	-0.20%	8.80%	-2.40%	-12.90%	-28.10%
Guinness Flight Wired Index				-0.30%	17.27%	6.93%	13.51%	-5.77%	-7.27%	7.83%	-5.78%	0.90%	2.80%	-1.40%	-5.40%	4.40%
Nasdaq 100 Index				-2.00%	8.33%	1.75%	19.84%	-13.47%	-13.07%	6.94%	-9.23%	2.68%	4.89%	-3.60%	-10.44%	-4.93%
Mathews Asia Technology				-0.05%	19.02%	-9.85%		-20.84%		6.09%	-18.61%	-2.35%	0.72%	-4.17%	-8.09%	-38.83%
DFA 1 Year	6.00%	5.70%	4.60%	0.20%	0.63%	0.50%	1.34%	0.36%	0.40%	0.72%	1.48%	0.10%	0.20%	0.10%	0.20%	3.50%
PIMCO Low Duration	8.24%	7.16%	3.00%	-0.12%	0.73%	0.74%	1.35%	0.22%	0.31%	1.21%	1.75%	0.10%	0.00%	0.30%	0.00%	3.70%
SEI Short Duration Gov't	6.94%	7.08%	2.70%	-0.05%	0.55%	0.66%	1.16%	0.35%	0.39%	1.11%	1.86%	0.10%	-0.10%	0.20%	0.20%	3.60%
Blackrock Core Fixed	9.02%	8.16%	-0.60%	-0.34%	1.31%	1.52%	2.34%	-0.12%	-0.34%	2.19%	1.72%	0.20%	-0.20%	0.50%	0.00%	5.20%
PIMCO Total	10.16%	9.77%	-0.30%	-0.51%	1.23%	1.48%	2.21%	-0.28%	-0.02%	2.12%	1.82%	-0.10%	-0.10%	0.40%	0.00%	4.90%
SEI Interm-Duration Gov't	8.18%	8.47%	0.00%	-0.35%	0.77%	1.21%	1.64%	-0.04%	0.28%	1.72%	1.96%	0.20%	-0.30%	0.50%	0.00%	4.20%
Vanguard Short Muni	4.07%	4.32%	2.60%	-0.12%	0.37%	0.34%	0.91%	0.21%	0.23%	0.73%	1.17%	0.00%	0.10%	0.10%	0.10%	2.50%
Thornburg LTD Muni	7.20%	5.18%	0.80%	-0.13%	0.48%	0.79%	1.14%	-0.13%	-0.13%	1.57%	1.31%	0.10%	0.40%	0.00%	0.20%	3.50%
SEI Interm-Term Muni	7.76%	5.59%	-0.80%	-0.21%	0.54%	1.41%	1.75%	-0.40%	-0.39%	2.08%	1.28%	0.30%	0.40%	0.10%	0.20%	4.20%
Deutsche Muni Bond	8.15%	5.43%	-1.20%	-0.49%	0.99%	1.48%	1.98%	-0.24%	-0.32%	1.86%	1.29%	0.20%	0.40%	0.10%	0.20%	4.40%

* S&P 500 weekly numbers do not reflect the inclusion of dividends. Monthly and quarterly numbers do.

SCHWAB MONEY MARKET FUNDS - 7 DAY COMP. YIELD - 7/28/00

Reg. MM 7-day yield	6.10%
Value Advantage	6.47%
Tax-free Value Advantage	3.81%

SOURCE: EVENSKY, BROWN & KATZ

Task Manager 20xx-20xx

Client Name:_____   **Client Level:**_____

Personal interests/Possible reason for call

_____

_____

_____

_____

Client Contact	Jan	Feb	Mar	Apr	May	Jun	Jul
Care call from Partner							
Care call from Advisor							
Flash report							
Article of Interest							
Review Cycle - Ptnr/Adv							
Estate Planning Review							
Special Event							
Birthdays							

Client Contact	Aug	Sep	Oct	Nov	Dec	Jan	Feb
Care call from Partner							
Care call from Advisor							
Flash report							
Article of Interest							
Review Cycle - Ptnr/Adv							
Estate Planning Review							
Special Event							
Birthdays							

Goals: 1._____

2._____

3._____

Client: _____   Spouse / Partner: _____

Schwab/SEI: _____   BDPB CLIENT? _____

Approx. Initial Investment: $ _____

Policy Type: FIXED INCOME _____ (Taxable/Sheltered)

Paperwork requirements:	Intials	Date	Notes:
Brochure mailed (Puff Package)			
Data Gathering Guide returned			
Client information sheet (Completed entirely)			
Risk Tolerance			
Policy Agreement			
Advisory Agreement w/Fee Schedule			
ADV given to client			
Investment Policy Delivered			
Policy Type Summary Page Signed			
➤ Duplicate statements to RKG?			
Other			

Supporting Documents	Client	Date	Spouse	Date
Brokerage/Fund/Pension Statements Received				
Trust Documents				
Will				
Living Will				
POA-Durable Powers				
Health Care Powers				
Insurance Documents				
Other				

Billing & Review:	Initials	Date	Notes
Date invested:			
Individual vs. portfolio			
Gross or net of fees			

Data entered into CP and/or BAM.	CENTERPIECE		BAM	
	Initials	Date	Initials	Date
Account information				
Policy information				
Client Information Sheet				
Review schedule				
Staff notified of New Client				
Birthday List				
Marked for Gift Level (always 5 for holiday card)				
(Also coded Diamond/Platinum, Gold, Silver, Copper)				
Marked as Client?				

Files and Folders:	Initials	Date
Blue folder created		
Leather binder created and sent		
Other		

No Longer a Client/Deceased	CENTERPIECE		BAM	
	Initials	Date	Initials	Date
Exit Letter				
Remove Client Status				
Change to Former/Deceased				
Remove Level Status				
Remove from Birthday List				
Remove from Insites				
Remove Advisor/Partner				
Remove from Billing Schedule				
Remove from Review schedule				
Remove Keywords or Classifications				
Other				

Charles D. Haines, Inc.
YOUR FEE CALCULATION
Client Name
Date

ANNUAL FEE SCHEDULE

Portfolio Size	For illustrative purposes ONLY % of Portfolio	Maximum Fee
$0 to $500,000	1.50%	$7,500
$500,001 to $750,000	1.25%	$10,625
$750,001 to $1,000,000	0.95%	$13,000
$1,000,001 to $2,500,000	0.80%	$25,000
$2,500,001 to $4,500,000	0.65%	$38,000
$4,500,001 to $7,000,000	0.45%	$49,250
$7,000,001 to $10,000,000	0.30%	$58,250
over $10,000,000	0.15%	
		mm/dd/yy

FEE CALCULATION BY PORTFOLIO

Your Assets	Amount	Client #1	Client #2	Alternative Inv.
Total Assets Less Alt. Inv.	$5,000,000	$5,000,000	$0	$0
Fee Percent for Alt. Inv.				1.0%
% of Total Portfolio	100.0%			$0.00
Billing Periods Per Year	4			4
Period Fee Calculation	**$10,062.50**			**$0.00**
Net Period Fee	**$10,062.50**	**$10,062.50**	**$0.00**	**$0.00**

NON-MANAGED ACCOUNT

CLIENT NAME _____

DATE _____

ACCOUNT #

_____

I acknowledge that the above account number _____ is a **COURTESY** account with XXXXXX Institutional under the aegis of Evensky, Brown & Katz. I understand that EB&K will maintain my account under the XXXX umbrella.

Evensky, Brown & Katz is taking no formal responsibility for the management of this account.

Signed _____

Date _____

Advisor _____

Client Name			

Value Pricing - Value Added Services in year ended		mm/dd/yy	

Value of portfolio (one year ago) $1,000,000

1. Financial Returns

	Value Added $
Investment return (note ** below)	0
Pension investment return (note ** below)	0
Tax efficient investment	0
Tax savings - income tax	0
Tax savings - capital gains tax	0
Tax savings - inheritance tax	0
Tax benefits of pension contributions	0
Reinvested commission savings	0
Discounts obtained	0
Charges saved	0
Commissions received and offset	0
Other financial returns (specify)	0
	0

** Note that short term investment returns are not within our control and so a long term view (five years cumulatively) needs to be taken of these areas.

2. Other Valued Benefits

Valued benefits of knowing that your tax affairs are being dealt with efficiently and effectively		0
Valued benefits of not having to deal with the IRS		0
Valued benefits of unlimited access to our time and expertise	0.0%	0
Valued benefits of having financial matters dealt with straightforwardly and without jargon	0.0%	0
Valued benefits of knowing that there are no unexpected fee charges from us	0.0%	0
Valued benefits of knowing you are on course to achieve your objectives	0.0%	0
Valued benefits of knowing how much income you will need in retirement	0.0%	0
Valued benefits of knowing whether or not you can afford a particular course of action	0.0%	0
Valued benefits of knowing that the market is researched thoroughly and well on your behalf	0.0%	0
Valued benefits of knowing whether you can afford to finance your desired lifestyle	0.0%	0
Valued benefits of knowing that you can relax and not have to read the weekend financial press	0.0%	0
Valued benefits of impartial, non-product driven advice	0.0%	0
Valued benefits of having a trusted adviser	0.0%	0
Valued benefits of our role as facilitator	0.0%	0
Valued benefits of time saving from outsourced chores compared with cost of own time	0.0%	0
Valued benefits of extra leisure time achieved	0.0%	0
Valued benefits of peace of mind	0.0%	0
Valued benefits of security from proper insurance cover	0.0%	0
Valued benefits to business owner (value of business, peace of mind, leisure)	0.0%	0
Valued benefits - other (describe)	0.0%	0

Total Value Added	$

Fixed Price Investment for the Year	

Net Value Added	$

1 page on CD-ROM

SECURITIES
AMERICA

PRACTICE
MANAGEMENT

Sample Surveys

1)   Sample Surveys

Five sample surveys. Each survey uses a different type of rating
scale. You can adapt these survey forms to the goals of your survey.
You can add and delete the questions and the question formats.

*Client surveys should be approved by a registered principal before
distribution to clients.

2)   More Survey Questions

A list of additional possible survey questions. These questions can be
adapted for different types of rating scales.

1

Example #1

Client Satisfaction Survey

Thank you for taking the opportunity to complete this client satisfaction survey. This is an opportunity for me (your registered representative) to find out how I can better fulfill your needs. Please answer the following questions about how I have performed as your registered representative. All responses will remain confidential (surveys will be returned to my accountant and then analyzed), so feel free to honestly evaluate my performance.

Instructions:
Please read each item carefully. Circle the number that best corresponds to your degree of satisfaction with your registered representative in the given areas. Circle only one response per item using the following scale.

> 1 = Extremely Dissatisfied (ED)
> 2 = Dissatisfied (D)
> 3 = Neither Dissatisfied nor Satisfied (N)
> 4 = Satisfied (S)
> 5 = Extremely Satisfied (ES)

When you have completed the survey please place it in the enclosed envelope and return the survey as soon as possible.

	ED	D	N	S	ES
1. Performance of my investments	1	2	3	4	5
2. Timeliness of follow-up calls	1	2	3	4	5
3. Accuracy with which my account is handled	1	2	3	4	5
4. Rep's knowledge of products	1	2	3	4	5
5. Rep values my business whether large or small	1	2	3	4	5
6. The advice the rep provides me about investment opportunities	1	2	3	4	5

SOURCE: SECURITIES AMERICA, INC.

9
pages
on CD-ROM

SECURITIES
AMERICA

PRACTICE
MANAGEMENT

Sample Letters
Letters to accompany your survey and to remind clients to return your survey.
**These letters should be pre-approved by a registered principal
before distribution to clients.**

[DATE]

Mrs. Any Client
1220 Any Street
Any Town, Any State

Dear Ms. Client:

I'm writing today to ask you a favor.

In approximately one week, you will be receiving a survey from me to find out how satisfied you are with my services. My number one priority is to serve the needs of my clients.

To help me do this, I am asking all of my clients to please fill out a survey about how I'm doing right now, and how I could serve you better. It should take about 10 minutes to complete.

A stamped envelope is also enclosed. Please return the completed survey in this envelope.

Thank you in advance for your assistance with the survey. I will be circulating a summary of the results to you and to other clients later this year. Please call me if you have any questions.

Best regards,

Roberta Representative
Registered Principal

4
pages
on CD-ROM

SECURITIES
AMERICA

PRACTICE
MANAGEMENT

Sample Agenda for Client Advisory Group Meeting

Moneypenny Retirement Planning
Client Advisory Group
September 8, 2001
Oak Hills Country Club

Purpose Statement*: The Client Advisory Board provides advice, opinions, and ideas to MoneyPenny Advisory Group on client service, marketing, and all aspects of the client-adviser relationship.*

Agenda

5:30   Cocktails and Appetizers

6:00   Welcome and Introductions

6:30   Dinner

7:30   Marketing
    ❖ Review Marketing Plan
    ❖ Review New Brochure

8:00   Client Service
    ❖ Describe positive and negative client service experiences
    ❖ Review format of quarterly performance reports

8:20   Open Discussion

8:30   Conclude

1
page
on CD-ROM

CLIENT SATISFACTION WORKSHEET

client **satisfaction**

PLEASE FILL IN (YOU CAN TYPE RIGHT ON THE LINE)

Your current clients are your most valuable assets. Have you checked with your clients lately to determine if their satisfaction level is where it should be? Use the following questions to help you understand where your clients' perspective is, and what you can do to make your relationship as strong as possible. This worksheet can be an effective tool to help you learn what attributes of your practice your best clients appreciate — which can provide you with a powerful sales message to target future prospects.

HOW WOULD YOU RATE YOUR RELATIONSHIP WITH US?

☐ Excellent ☐ Very Good ☐ Average ☐ Below Average ☐ Poor

Comments: _____

_____

_____

HOW SATISFIED ARE YOU WITH OUR CUSTOMER SERVICE?

☐ Very Satisfied ☐ Somewhat Satisfied ☐ Satisfied ☐ Slightly Less than Satisfied ☐ Unsatisfied

Comments: _____

_____

_____

HOW WOULD YOU RATE THE FOLLOWING STATEMENTS:

1=Strongly Disagree, 2=Somewhat Disagree, 3=Neither Disagree nor Agree, 4=Agree, 5=Somewhat Agree, 6=Strongly Agree

- I am satisfied with the level of client service my financial advisor provides   _____
- I would like to hear from my financial advisor more often   _____
- In the past 6 months, I have considered consolidating the management of my assets   _____
- I am satisfied with the performance of my portfolio   _____
- My financial advisor's personnel handle my affairs with professionalism and intelligence   _____
- I would recommend associates or family members to my advisor   _____
- My financial advisor is able to meet all of my financial planning needs   _____

Comments: _____

_____

_____

OVERALL, HOW WOULD YOU RATE US?

☐ Exceed expectations ☐ Meet expectations ☐ Do not meet expectations

Comments: _____

_____

_____

1
page
on CD-ROM

Evensky, Brown & Katz Client Survey

PLEASE RATE YOUR TEAM'S PERFORMANCE IN THE FOLLOWING AREAS:

	VERY SATISFIED	SATISFIED	NEUTRAL	DISSATISFIED	VERY DISSATISFIED	NOT APPLICABLE
1. Overall staff rating	_____	_____	_____	_____	_____	_____

PERSONNEL

2. Courtesy of staff	_____	_____	_____	_____	_____	_____
3. Knowledge of staff members	_____	_____	_____	_____	_____	_____
4. Promptness answering phones	_____	_____	_____	_____	_____	_____
5. Timeliness of follow-up calls	_____	_____	_____	_____	_____	_____

TIMELINESS

6. Setting up new accounts	_____	_____	_____	_____	_____	_____
7. Follow up on account transfers	_____	_____	_____	_____	_____	_____
8. Processing disbursements	_____	_____	_____	_____	_____	_____

ACCURACY

9. Setting up account transfers	_____	_____	_____	_____	_____	_____
10. Processing disbursements	_____	_____	_____	_____	_____	_____

Do you have any suggestions to improve our service to you?_____

_____

_____

_____

What is your opinion of how Schwab is handling your account (e.g., statements, accuracy and timeliness)?

_____

_____

_____

_____

1
page
on CD-ROM

CHAPTER

11

LAGNIAPPE—IDEAS TO USE
AND EXPAND

Ideas are a dime a dozen.
People who put them into action are priceless.

— UNKNOWN

When I was a kid, we always had roast beef on Sundays. Every Sunday. I think it was because my folks were ministers and my mom could prepare it, shove it in the oven, and have it ready by the time we got home from church. One year, when my sister was about ten, she asked our mom to teach her to cook the roast. Mom set all the ingredients on the kitchen counter. She trimmed the roast, seasoned it, and at the very end of the process, cut both ends off. "Why do you cut off the ends?" asked my sister, Sharon. "My mom always does it that way," Mom replied. Unsatisfied with the answer, my sister called Grandma for an explanation. "My mom always does it that way," answered Grandma. By then my sister, frustrated, called Great Grandma. "Why do you cut the ends of the roast?" Sharon asks. "Why," explained Great Grandma, "my pan was too small."

We're fortunate to be in a profession in which practitioners share so openly with each other. I've certainly been lucky in my professional life to have so many advisers share their creative projects with me. I am certain it has given me an advantage with my staff and with my clients. That's why I'm particularly pleased to be able to pass some of the things I learned along to you. No question, it's much more efficient to "honestly steal" good ideas than to try to invent all these things yourself. More importantly, you can adapt ideas and concepts that others have taken time, effort, and considerable thought to develop. You don't have to cut off the ends of the roast without an explanation of why.

One good thing about writing a book is that you get to include materials in it that you appreciate. If you've chosen well, others will find them useful, too. They might even enjoy them. In the previous chapters I grouped together numerous ideas under themes. Not surprisingly, many of the most interesting ideas don't fit so neatly into specific categories. In this last chapter I want to share some of the more eclectic thoughts, insights, and reflections that I have collected over the years, in listening to speakers, reading articles, and networking with friends. In New Orleans they'd call this "lagniappe," just a little bit extra, the thirteenth doughnut in the baker's dozen. Maybe you'll find something in here that will speak volumes to you.

Concepts to Own

- ➲ Question basic assumptions
- ➲ Question certainties
- ➲ Become better informed with less certainty
- ➲ Honor the beginner's mind
- ➲ Ask me anything
- ➲ Question anything
- ➲ Allow mistakes

On Planning

TWO GEMS FROM MARK TIBERGIEN, Moss Adams Advisory, Seattle, Washington: "Don't begin your planning when you're three cars behind the flowers." "Life Cycle of a planning firm—Wonder, Blunder, Thunder, Plunder."

NUMBER OF YEARS MONEY WILL LAST

NUMBER OF YEARS MONEY WILL LAST - 3% INFLATION

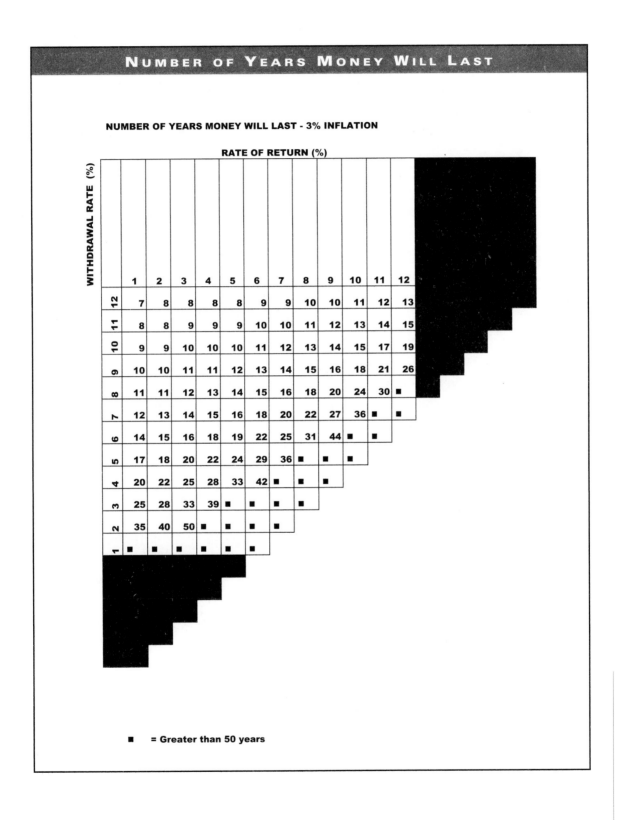

RATE OF RETURN (%)

WITHDRAWAL RATE (%)	1	2	3	4	5	6	7	8	9	10	11	12
12	7	8	8	8	8	9	9	10	10	11	12	13
11	8	8	9	9	9	10	10	11	12	13	14	15
10	9	9	10	10	10	11	12	13	14	15	17	19
9	10	10	11	11	12	13	14	15	16	18	21	26
8	11	11	12	13	14	15	16	18	20	24	30	■
7	12	13	14	15	16	18	20	22	27	36	■	■
6	14	15	16	18	19	22	25	31	44	■	■	
5	17	18	20	22	24	29	36	■	■	■		
4	20	22	25	28	33	42	■	■	■			
3	25	28	33	39	■	■	■	■				
2	35	40	50	■	■	■	■					
1	■	■	■	■	■	■						

■ = Greater than 50 years

On the Value of Advice on the Internet

"THE IRONY OF THE INFORMATION AGE is that it has given new respectability to uninformed opinion." (Veteran reporter John Lawton, sixty-eight, speaking to the American Association of Broadcast Journalists in 1995).

How Long Will Your Money Last?

ADMITTEDLY THE MINI-PRESENTATION on the preceding page is a little self-serving, inasmuch, I'm stealing it from a book I did on retirement planning.[1] Still, I think it's really cool and I've found it to be very helpful demonstrating to some clients the multiple impact of inflation and the need for real cash flow.

The table on the previous page gives you a quick way to estimate how long your assets will last, depending upon what they are earning and how much you withdraw annually. You may have seen something like this in the past, but this one is different because it is indexed for an annual inflation rate of 3 percent. The column at the top lists rates of return from 1 percent to 12 percent. The rows on the left list withdrawal rates, from a high of 12 percent of principal a year at the top to a 1 percent of principal at the bottom.

Opportunity Costs

MY PARTNER HAROLD WROTE A SMALL BOOK for Y2K to help our clients deal with their concerns about the unknown impact it might have on the market. Although Y2K is long gone (and with not even a ripple), one of the tools he developed for the book has proved useful in helping some clients deal with their asset allocation decision. The tool provides a simple calculation that gives the client an idea of how much potential return (opportunity cost) he will be giving up should he increase his allocation from stocks to bonds. Because the table in Harold's system is based on specific market expectations, I'm providing it to you as an idea, not a solution. If you find the idea useful, it will be easy to redesign the table to meet your market expectations.

MARKET EXPECTATIONS ASSET CLASS	AVERAGE	GOOD
Bonds	5%	7%
Stock	11%	23%

OPPORTUNITY COST FACTORS

PORTFOLIO ALLOCATION	AVERAGE RESULTS	GOOD RESULTS
All Bonds	1.05	1.07
90% Cash/10% Stocks	1.06	1.09
80% Cash/20% Stocks	1.06	1.10
70% Cash/30% Stocks	1.07	1.12
60% Cash/40% Stocks	1.07	1.13
50% Cash/50% Stocks	1.08	1.15
40% Cash/60% Stocks	1.09	1.17
30% Cash/70% Stocks	1.09	1.18
20% Cash/80% Stocks	1.10	1.20
10% Cash/90% Stocks	1.10	1.21
All Stock	1.11	1.23

To use this table a client would determine the amount of his portfolio and his current allocation. For example, assume $100,000 is invested 40 percent in bonds and 60 percent in stocks. He would then determine how big a shift he was considering. For example, he might contemplate a shift from the 40/60 allocation to a 60/40 allocation. Using the factors in the table, he would then determine the projected guesstimate for the future value of each portfolio by multiplying the appropriate factor times the portfolio value.

Current Portfolio Value	= $100,000		
40/60 Average Result Factor	= 1.09	40/60 Good Result Factor	= 1.17
60/40 Average Result Factor	= 1.07	60/40 Good Result Factor	= 1.13

OPPORTUNITY COST CALCULATION

	CURRENT PORTFOLIO	PROPOSED PORTFOLIO	OPPORTUNITY COST
Average Market Results	$109,000	$107,000	$2,000
Good Market Results	$117,000	$113,000	$4,000

Been There, Done That, Got the T-Shirt— A New Era

WE HAVE BEEN TALKING ABOUT THE "NEW ERA" for the past two years. I don't know, as you read this book, what phase of the "New Era" you think we will be in, but I thought I would like to share a few observations on the subject that I've recently read:

FROM *HOW TO SECURE CONTINUOUS PROFITS IN MODERN MARKETS,* BY JOHN DURAND:

.... we live in a "new era," says Dr. Anderson, in which the laws of economics are suspended, in which all financial records are broken, and in which an indefinite continuance of the breaking of financial records may be confidently looked forward to, is believed by a good many people.

FROM *BUSINESS WEEK*

For five years, at least, American business has been in the grip of an apocalyptic, holy-rolling exaltation over the unparalleled prosperity of the "new era," upon which we, or it, or somebody has entered. Discussions of economic conditions in the press, on the platform, and by public officials have carried us into a cloudland of fantasy where all appraisal of present and future accomplishment is suffused with the vague implication that a North American millennium is imminent. Clear, critical, realistic and rational recognition of current problems and perplexities is rare.

It's sobering to reflect that both of these observations were published in September 1929.

Food for Thought

PEOPLE WHO KNOW ME WOULD BELIEVE it unlikely for me to write a book without some reference to food. You might think about this idea for clients, for staff, or even for your building manager. We keep a crystal dish of candy on our receptionist's desk. Daily, the building engineer visits to pick up his sugar fix. As a result, he always knows if a light is out or the sink is stopped up. Guess who gets great service? The Federal Express, UPS, and mail carriers appreciate treats too. They stop in, even if they don't have a package for us and don't mind taking something as an unscheduled pickup.

Cookie Man

JERRY FRIDAY, SALES DIRECTOR for ACT Learning Centers in Duluth, Minnesota, takes cookies with him to meet with prospective clients. It's been a great success and clients call him "the cookie man." Instead of asking prospective clients if they would like something ten minutes into the meeting (don't wait too long or it might break the meeting mood), our receptionist waltzes in with a tray of cookies or pastries. She then asks if anyone would like a drink to go with it. Call Mrs. Fields.

Moving Up the Food Chain

LEW WALLENSKY, A CERTIFIED FINANCIAL PLANNER with Lewis Wallensky & Associates in Los Angeles, California, shared this idea with me. As I read it, I wondered, "Do they serve better food at the tables with people who've been around longer?" (Just kidding, Lew.)

> Two years ago, we had a 30th anniversary party for our clients. There were over 200 in attendance. This in itself is not unusual. Many planners have client appreciation nights. But what we have done is seat clients at tables according to how many years they have been clients. Over 75 percent of the people there were at tables of 15 years or longer. We are proud of that record. Thus people sat at 30, 25, 20, 15, 10, or 5 year tables. We had two full tables of clients who have been with us 25–30 years. We even had two tables where we sat three generations of the same family. Prior to the 30th anniversary, we had the 25th, 20th, 15th. As each five years passed, clients wanted to move up

BEVERAGE MENU

BEVERAGES

Coffees Regular

Green Mountain Blend *smooth, aromatic, mild*

Colombian Supremo *hearty, bright, flavorful*

Nantucket Blend *buttery, nutty, rich*

French Roast *dark roast*

Rain Forest Nut *vanilla, caramel, cashew*

Coffees Decaffeinated

Vermont Country Blend *mellow, smooth*

Hazelnut *buttery, nutty, rich*

Hot Teas

Plantation Mint	**Darjeeling**
Vanilla Maple	**Perfect Peach** *decaffeinated*
Raspberry Zinger *decaffeinated*	**Green Tea** *decaffeinated*

Soft Drinks

Sprite

Coca-Cola

Diet Coke

Water

to the next level. This has been a wonderful experience and tradition. This year we are planning to do the 33rd (note it is not a multiple of 5) which is of course a third of a century.

Coffee Anyone?

WHEN ANYONE WALKS INTO OUR OFFICE, they are handed our beverage menu (see illustration at left). If it's a client, our receptionist already knows what drinks he or she prefers (we keep that information in our database), but we always give guests a chance to change their minds. We find that when a client looks at the menu, he often makes a suggestion for additions. For example, because of an idea from a caffeine-free client, we now have several flavors of decaffeinated green tea for our health enthusiasts.

Lastly, on the subject of food, remember—never underestimate the value of edible perks.

Branding

HERE'S AN OVERUSED BUT IMPORTANT WORD for your repertoire: branding. The more competition we have, the more important "branding" becomes. I read this great book, *22 Immutable Laws of Branding: How to Build a Product or Service into a World-Class Brand,* by Al Ries and Laura Ries (HarperCollins, 1998). They use an analogy to describe the concept, "... branding in the marketplace is very similar to branding on a ranch. A branding program should be designed to differentiate your cow from all the other cattle on the range. Even if all the cattle on the range look pretty much alike."[2] The idea is to get people to think of your "cow" when they think of a good planning firm. Some product companies have been very successful at this. Xerox is so well known that the word has become a replacement for the generic term "photocopy." Band-Aid should really be "adhesive bandages." White-Out is any liquid stuff you can use to cover your paper errors. I don't know about you, but I wouldn't mind if the world described what we do as getting a "Katz-Plan." Spend some time thinking about how you can position yourself and your business to build your brand and grow your business.

On the Future

MORE PEARLS FROM MARK TIBERGIEN: "When you want to buy a red car, all you see are red cars. Are you going to recognize an opportunity when you see it?"

Mark, commenting on the future of the small practitioner in this highly competitive marketplace: "Sole practitioners will always make a living, they just won't make an impact."

A Final Word

I TALKED ABOUT THE UNDISCOVERED MANAGERS' white papers earlier in this book. While I believe that Mark Hurley and the gang there have made some good observations about the future of this industry, there is one which I fervently hope they got absolutely wrong: the closing of our open environment of sharing advice, information, and expertise that we have enjoyed all these years. I would never have survived in this industry if it had not been for all the mentors who talked me through the good, the bad, and the bizarre of my practice; all the friends who've shared their failures so I could avoid their mistakes; and all the industry leaders whose vision extended far beyond my own.

Look at where you are today in your practice. If you're a silver-haired (or in my case, silver-haired masquerading as a redhead) planner, remember that someone was there years ago to help you get where you are. Return the favor. If you're just starting out, find a mentor and as you gain knowledge and expertise, continue to share what you know with others. You'll benefit and certainly the profession will benefit.

NOTES

INTRODUCTION

1. Take a look at Mark Hurley's white papers on their Web site at www.undiscoveredmanagers.com. "The Future of the Financial Advisory Business and the Delivery of Advice to the Semi-Affluent Investor," *Undiscovered Managers* (September 1999) and "The Future of the Financial Advisory Business Part II: Strategies for Small Businesses," *Undiscovered Managers* (September 2000).

2. *The Final Frontier: The Opportunities and Challenges of Internet Delivery* (Corporate Executive Board: Washington, D.C., 1999), 92.

3. My mother-in-law also reports that Dr. Tichenor's is great for cleaning the carburetor of her car. Its extraordinary broad range of uses might have something to do with the fact that it's 70 percent alcohol.

4. Sorry, I've included a CD-ROM but you'll have to supply the alcohol.

CHAPTER ONE

1. Mark Hurley, "The Future of the Financial Advisory Business and the Delivery of Advice to the Semi-Affluent Investor," *Undiscovered Managers* (September 1999). This can be read on their Web site at www.undiscovered managers.com.

2. RIA Group Boston, "Achieving Higher Visibility," *Financial Advisory Practice* (October, 1998): 7-11.

CHAPTER TWO

1. VIP Forum, "The Final Frontier: The Opportunities and Challenges of Internet Delivery," *Corporate Executive Board* (1999): 5.

2. "The Industry Standard," Jupiter Communications (May 1999): 17–24.

CHAPTER FOUR

1. Client Fit Ratio℠ is a trademark of Polstra & Pardaman, LLC. If you choose to adapt their form to create a fitness test for your firm, Polstra & Dardaman, LLC requests that you credit them when sharing your system with others.

CHAPTER SIX

1. *20th Index of Investor Optimism* (1999 Gallup Poll in cooperation with Paine Webber).

2. Roger C. Gibson, *Asset Allocation: Balancing Financial Risk* (New York: McGraw-Hill, 2000). Roger C. Gibson, et al, *Simple Asset Allocation Strategies* (New York: Marketplace Books/Traders Library, 2000).

3. My partner, Harold Evensky, covers our cash-flow reserve account strategy in detail in his book *Wealth Management* (New York: Irwin Professional Publishing, 1996).

4. Caveat—Although the most current Web version was used for the preparation of this book, don't be surprised if the version you see at the link is slightly different. PIE Technologies is constantly improving their products.

5. In case you're wondering, the choice of 1,000 games was arbitrary. We could have selected 10,000 games but the results would have been so similar, the extra running time would not have been worth the effort.

6. Remember, the selections were random, so the series of all positive returns was random. Still, this isn't too surprising as this allocation only had five negative years during the past thirty.

7. A term used in William P. Bengen's excellent articles on this subject. "Determining Withdrawal Rates Using Historical Data," *Journal of Financial Planning* (October 1994); "Asset Allocation for a Lifetime," *Journal of Financial Planning* (August 1996); and "Conserving Client Portfolios During Retirement, Part III," *Journal of Financial Planning* (December 1997).

8. You'll note that the Monte Carlo failure rate result for the 40/60 portfolio in the illustration "Monte Carlo Simulation for Game Two" on page 149 is slightly different from that in the illustration "Monte Carlo Simulation for Game Three" on page 150 (100 percent vs. 99 percent). This is a result of having run *only* 1,000 games.

CHAPTER SEVEN

1. The following are a few books that discuss the IPS detail. Harold Evensky, *Wealth Management* (New York: Irwin Professional Publishing, 1996); Don Trone, William Albright, and Philip R.Tayler, *The Management of Investment Decisions* (New York: Irwin Professional Publishing, 1996); and Norman Boone and Linda Lubitz, *The Investment Policy Statement Guidebook* (available from Ibbotson Associates through their Web site at www.ibbotson.com).

CHAPTER EIGHT

1. This is described in his excellent book. Buy it. Ross Levin, *The Wealth Management Index* (New York: McGraw Hill, 1997).

CHAPTER TEN

1. For a full explanation of A-R-G-E, see C. H. Lovelock, *Managing Services—Marketing, Operations and Human Resources* (New York: Prentice Hall, 1992).

CHAPTER ELEVEN

1. Deena Katz, *Taking Charge of Your Retirement* (New York: Lee Simmons Associates, 1997).

2. Al Reis and Laura Reis, *22 Immutable Laws of Branding* (New York: Harper-Collins, 1998), 7.

INDEX

ABOUT BLOOMBERG

BLOOMBERG L.P., founded in 1981, is a global information services, news, and media company. Headquartered in New York, the company has nine sales offices, two data centers, and 85 news bureaus worldwide.

Bloomberg, serving customers in 126 countries around the world, holds a unique position within the financial services industry by providing an unparalleled range of features in a single package known as the BLOOMBERG PROFESSIONAL™ service. By addressing the demand for investment performance and efficiency through an exceptional combination of information, analytic, electronic trading, and Straight Through Processing tools, Bloomberg has built a worldwide customer base of corporations, issuers, financial intermediaries, and institutional investors.

BLOOMBERG NEWS℠, founded in 1990, provides stories and columns on business, general news, politics, and sports to leading newspapers and magazines throughout the world. BLOOMBERG TELEVISION®, a 24-hour business and financial news network, is produced and distributed globally in seven different languages. BLOOMBERG RADIO™ is an international radio network anchored by flagship station BLOOMBERG® WBBR 1130 in New York.

In addition to the BLOOMBERG PRESS® line of books, Bloomberg publishes *BLOOMBERG® MARKETS*, *BLOOMBERG PERSONAL FINANCE™*, and *BLOOMBERG® WEALTH MANAGER*. To learn more about Bloomberg, call a sales representative at:

Frankfurt:	49-69-92041-200	São Paulo:	5511-3048-4530
Hong Kong:	85-2-2977-6600	Singapore:	65-212-1200
London:	44-20-7330-7500	Sydney:	61-2-9777-8601
New York:	1-212-318-2200	Tokyo:	81-3-3201-8950
San Francisco:	1-415-912-2980		

FOR IN-DEPTH MARKET INFORMATION and news, visit the Bloomberg Web site at **www.bloomberg.com,** which draws from the news and power of the BLOOMBERG PROFESSIONAL™ service and Bloomberg's host of media products to provide high-quality news and information in multiple languages on stocks, bonds, currencies, and commodities.

ABOUT THE AUTHOR

DEENA B. KATZ, CFP, has shared her expertise on *Good Morning America* and *CBS This Morning* and was the authority selected by *Consumer Reports* to evaluate the work of other planners. She is the editor-in-chief of the *Journal of Retirement Planning* and has published extensively for other magazines such as *Financial Planning* and *Financial Advisor*. In the January 2001 issue of *Financial Planning*, she was named by her peers as one of the five most influential people in the planning profession. She was among the top 250 planners selected by *Worth* magazine in September 2001 and was listed in the top 100 by *Mutual Funds* magazine. Ms. Katz is an internationally sought-after speaker for national and international legal, accounting, and financial organizations and the author of the acclaimed book *Deena Katz on Practice Management*.

FOR MORE INFORMATION go to www.evensky.com or contact the author directly at DeenaKatz@evensky.com with questions or comments.